ONE HOLY PASSION

Catherine Martin

Exodus 19:4

" YE HAVE SEEN WHAT I DID UNTO THE
Egyptians, AND HOW I BARE YOU ON
EAGLE'S WINGS & BROUGHT YOU UNTO MYSELF."

CATHERINE MARTIN

ONE HOLY PASSION

QuietTime
MINISTRIES

PALM DESERT, CALIFORNIA

Cover by Quiet Time Ministries.
Cover photo by Catherine Martin—myPhotoWalk.com

Interior photos by Catherine Martin available at MYPHOTOWALK.COM—CATHERINEMARTIN.SMUGMUG.COM

One Holy Passion—A Sacred Journey In Exodus To God's Amazing Love
Copyright © 2017 by Catherine Martin
Published by Quiet Time Ministries
Palm Desert, California 92255
www.quiettime.org

ISBN-13: 978-0-9979327-5-1

Printed in the United States of America
17 18 19 20 21 22 23 24 25/ ACS / 10 9 8 7 6 5 4 3 2 1

Dedicated to …
the One who is the lover of my soul,
the Lord Jesus Christ.

Dedicated to my husband
David G. Martin,
who has been my beloved companion
for thirty-five years
on this journey of faith.

Dedicated to
all those hearts who have said yes to Jesus
in every generation.
Thank you for being my example
of how to love the Lord
and live by His Word.

May we answer God's invitation
respond to His One Holy Passion,
and love Him with all our heart, soul, mind, strength…
one holy passion.

You yourselves have seen what I did to the Egyptians,
and how I bore you on eagles' wings, and brought you to Myself.

EXODUS 19:4

The proof of God's amazing love is this:
that it was while we were sinners
that Christ died for us.

ROMANS 5:8 PHILLIPS

For you are a holy people to the LORD your God;
the LORD your God has chosen you to be a people for His own possession
out of all the peoples who are on the face of the earth.
The LORD did not set His love on you nor choose you because you were more
in number than any of the peoples, for you were the fewest of all peoples,
but because the LORD loved you…

DEUTERONOMY 7:6-8

He rescued us from the domain of darkness,
and transferred us to the kingdom of His Beloved Son.

COLOSSIANS 1:13

CONTENTS

Have you come to the Red Sea place in your life,
Where, in spite of all you can do,
There is no way out, there is no back,
There is no other way but—through?
Then wait on the Lord with a trust serene
Till the night of your fear is gone;
He will send the wind, He will heap the floods,
When He says to your soul, "Go on."

And His hand will lead you through—clear through—
Ere the watery walls roll down,
No foe can reach you, no wave can touch,
No mightiest sea can drown;
The tossing billows may rear their crests,
Their foam at your feet may break,
But over their bed you shall walk dry shod
In the path that your Lord will make.

In the morning watch, 'neath the lifted cloud,
You shall see but the Lord alone,
When He leads you on from the place of the sea
To land that you have not known;
And your fears shall pass as your foes have passed,
You shall be no more afraid;
You shall sing His praise in a better place,
A place that His hand has made.

ANNIE JOHNSON FLINT

❧ Introduction ❧

Have you come to the Red Sea place in your life? Do you have the peace of God that surpasses all understanding? Do you have the assurance of God's amazing love?

She looked in the mirror and saw an unexpected reflection. Where was the sparkle in the eyes? Where was the constant smile? She had walked through a valley of loss that was more heart-wrenching than she had ever known. She had watched many of her dearest friends and most of her family including her mother and father, one by one, become ill and go home to be with the Lord. Alone in her loss, broken and wounded, she could see no easy way out. No hope. It had been a season of loss that impacted every aspect of her life. Her heart seemed filled with devastation and disappointment without and within from many different directions. Only God knew the depth of her experience. She called it the valley of the shadow, her dark night of the soul. Would she be able to survive it all? Only God knew.

I confess. That woman was me just two years ago. And in my dark night, I held on to God only by a thread, trusting only what He said in His Word in Isaiah 41:10. "Do not fear, for I am with you; Do not anxiously look about you, for I am your God. I will strengthen you, surely I will help you. Surely I will uphold you with my righteous right hand." He was with me. He would help me. And I need not fear. But yet I was afraid. There it was. Afraid of how I would survive. Afraid of how I could heal from so much hurt and pain. Afraid of how we would make it personally, financially, and emotionally. Searching deep down within myself at that time, my faith struggling with despair, and I felt as though I had no answers.

In my dark valley, some lines of poetry by Annie Johnson Flint came to my mind. It was something I had memorized without even trying because it was so utterly profound. The opening stanza played on my mind, line by line:

"Have you come to the Red Sea place in your life,

Where in spite of all you can do,

There is no way out, there is no way back,

There is no other way but through?"

I thought, "This is exactly where I am—the Red Sea place. And I see no way out, no way back, only through." So where is the Red Sea place described in the Bible? Exodus. It did not take long before I became convinced by the Holy Spirit that the Lord wanted me to study Exodus—that God had something life-changing to teach me in Exodus. Throughout my life and my ministry, I have always trusted in God to lead me into the passages in His Word where He wants me to live. And once again, in my dark valley, He was faithful to reach through heaven into my heart and guide me with His Word.

In the days ahead, I was drawn like a magnet to Exodus; I simply could not resist. I grabbed my favorite Bible and began doing what I know to do in studying God's Word—observation, interpretation, and application. Praise God I have Kay Arthur and my seminary professors to thank for teaching me inductive Bible Study so many years ago. So I started marking key words, recording observations, looking up words in my Hebrew and Greek word study tools, using commentaries in my Logos Bible Study Software, and writing out in The Quiet Time Journal what God was teaching me.

What I saw in Exodus began a journey of healing and heart transformation. I experienced many *Aha!* moments as I lived in Exodus. I have many more truths to learn from this amazing book of the Bible. I am still on this adventure with the Lord. But one truth has stood out to me above all others—God's passionate, unfailing love for me, His child. I saw the truth of His words in Jeremiah 31:3, "I have loved you with an everlasting love." I realized that the greatest truth that stands out in the Bible, from Genesis to Revelation, is God's passion for His people—His extravagant, immeasurable, unconditional, amazing love. His love is so great that He goes to any length to save them, rescue them, deliver them, provide for them, sustain them, and protect them.

He is adamant and resolute in His love and has a definite plan and purpose in mind. Those truths will literally change your life. Paul discovered the reality of God's love for him in one of his dark moments, "At my first defense, no one came to my support, but everyone deserted me. May it not be held against them. But the Lord stood at my side and gave me strength" (2 Timothy 4:16-17). When you see the greatness of God's love, you realize that even if everyone else forsakes you, God will never forsake you.

It is one thing for me to talk about the greatness of God's love, but quite another for you to believe it, and to ultimately experience His love firsthand in your own life. And that is what spending quality quiet time in Exodus is going to do for you. As you take time alone with God in His Word, He is going to transform you by changing the way you think (Romans 12:1-2 NLT). That's what He has done for me as I have lived, day by day, with God in His Word. Through my own journey in Exodus, I experienced a divine rescue and found the way through and the way out. It has been a sacred journey, one that I will never forget. God showed me that He rescues us so that we can know, love, and serve Him. Losses become gains. God causes all things to work together for good when we surrender them into the hands of the One who loves us and lives with us moment by moment from now until we enjoy our life with Him in heaven. That is the truth from God's Word. And Jesus promises that when you know the truth, "the truth will make you free" (John 8:32). Oh yes, dear friend. God is greater than anything that you are experiencing right now. He loves you with passion, power and purpose. And He wants you to walk in freedom.

I think of you, the one who is beginning this quiet time study. You have walked a unique path and you have experienced God's love and leading to this point in many ways, though you may not realize it right now. And it may be that you have also endured a degree of suffering. Perhaps you have known rejection, loss of a job, the death of loved ones, financial hardship, or illness. Perhaps you have been ridiculed by others directly or behind your back, feeling like an outcast on the outside looking in, by people you called friends, by your family, by your church. And you may be feeling devastated and disillusioned wondering how you will make it through. You are in need of knowing the way out—in need of a rescue. If this is you, my friend, then perhaps you are at your Red Sea place in life. Whatever your dark night or life journey, you are in need of a deeper relationship with your Lord, a more intimate walk with Him, a greater trust in God's Word, and a more intimate knowledge of His love and care for you.

I want to invite you to take this sacred journey with me through Exodus to see God's great love for you. It is one holy passion—His passion for you. And the result will be a holy passion building in you to love and serve Him all your days. Take to your heart, dear friend, the words of God in Isaiah 43:18-19—"Forget the former things; do not dwell on the past. See, I am doing a new thing! Now it springs up; do you not perceive it? I am making a way in the wilderness and streams in the wasteland." This is a new day for you that will take you to a new place in your walk with the Lord.

One Holy Passion is going to take you on a sacred journey with the people of Israel from Egypt to the Red Sea place, through the desolate wilderness into the glorious Promised Land. You might think of the theme of this book as *the way out*. It is all about freedom and the experience of God's amazing love. The journey will be a pilgrimage of the heart where you will learn to fly into the very arms of God as you grow in trusting Him. God describes your flight in Exodus 19:4—"You yourselves have seen what I did to the Egyptians, and how I bore you on eagles' wings, and brought you to Myself." We will spend most of our time in the first sixteen chapters of Exodus, but we will also focus on powerful themes throughout the book that show us more about God's passion for us and our growing passion for Him. Oh, how He loves us and oh, how we grow in our love for Him.

But there is more to this story. The journey seen in Exodus is a picture of your life. And you are going to see that you are meant for more than you can even imagine right now. "No eye has seen, no ear has heard, and no mind has imagined what God has prepared for those who love Him" (1 Corinthians 2:9 NLT). Paul tells us that the things we read about in the Old Testament with the people of Israel happened as examples for us (1 Corinthians 10:11). What a radical truth for us to understand. What we read in Exodus about the people of Israel that occurred thousands of years ago teaches us things that will transform our life now.

We cannot read the Old Testament without the New Testament. Augustine, an early Christian theologian and philosopher, has said, "The new is in the old concealed; the old is in the new revealed." Author and theologian R.C. Sproul writes of the interrelationship of the two testaments of the Bible: "The key to understanding the New Testament in its fullest is to see in it the fulfillment of those things that were revealed in the background of the Old Testament. The Old Testament points forward in time, preparing God's people for the work of Christ in the New Testament." Selah! [Pause, and calmly think of that!]

One Holy Passion will take you from Exodus into the powerful New Testament truths of the Lord Jesus Christ and your intimate relationship with Him. And you will see that it is not merely a story. It is reality for you and for me. The reality of Christ—His finished work on the cross and His ongoing work in and through you — is a journey of spiritual growth until you step into heaven and stand face to face with Him. The truth is that there are many Red Sea places in life and more than one wilderness experience. I have written this book that you may experience intimacy with God no matter where you are in your journey.

Something God has used over the years to help me know and love Him more is myPhotowalk Devotional Photography. As I have walked out in His magnificent creation with my Nikon and Sony cameras and His Word, looking through the lens has slowed me down to see His intricate design. I have watched Him paint beauty and color into the landscape at sunrise and sunset, and I have realized how He can paint that same kind of beauty and color into the landscape of my life. Nothing is impossible with God. *One Holy Passion* includes many of the images I have photographed in one of my very favorite places in the world—the beautiful red rock country of Sedona and Oak Creek Canyon. I grew up in Arizona and have made more than one significant commitment to the Lord during time spent alone with Him sitting by the creek or high on a mountain. Each day of study includes a fine art black and white image from my Sedona, Arizona photography portfolio. All images are processed with Nik Silver Efex Pro and Adobe Photoshop for you to use as meditation and study to see the great power of the Master Designer who created the universe. myPhotoWalk and Quiet Time Ministries proudly offer custom color prints of our devotional photography exclusively through SmugMug at catherinemartin.smugmug.com.

Together we will embark on this journey through Scripture in the form of quiet times alone with the Lord. Each quiet time is organized according to the PRAYER™ Quiet Time Plan™:

Prepare Your Heart

Read and Study God's Word

Adore God in Prayer

Yield Yourself to God

Enjoy His Presence

Rest in His Love

Each week consists of five days of quiet times, photo selections from my devotional photography, and then a devotional reading on Days 6-7. Each quiet time includes devotional reading, devotional Bible study, journaling, prayer, worship, hymns, and application of God's Word. Journal Pages and Prayer Pages (adapted from *The Quiet Time Notebook*) to record your thoughts and prayers are in the Appendix of this book. With *One Holy Passion* and your Bible you have everything you need for rich quiet times with the Lord. Because schedules vary, you can be flexible and you may choose to take more than one day for each quiet time. You may complete each quiet time at your own pace, taking as little or as much time as you can give to spend alone with the Lord. If you desire to learn more about how to have a quiet time, I encourage you to get my book *Six Secrets to a Powerful Quiet Time*. To learn more about different kinds of devotional Bible studies for your quiet time, I encourage you to read my book *Knowing and Loving the Bible*.

VIEWER GUIDES

At the end of each week you will find your Viewer Guide to take notes from the video message. In each message, Catherine teaches from God's Word, and challenges you to draw near to the Lord. These inspirational and instructional messages are especially designed to accompany your studies each week. These messages are available on the companion *One Holy Passion* DVDs, downloadable Digital M4V Video, downloadable Digital MP3 Audio, as well as HD 1080p Digital M4V of the HD Leader's Kits for a professional large group experience. Search the Quiet Time Ministries Online Store at www.quiettime.org or call Quiet Time Ministries at 1-800-925-6458.

FOR LEADERS

One Holy Passion is a powerful resource for group study including a complete Leader's Guide with Discussion Questions in the Appendix. *One Holy Passion* DVD Leader's Kits or *One Holy Passion* HD 1080p Digital Leader's Kits are available at the Quiet Time Ministries Online Store at www.quiettime.org. You may also call Quiet Time Ministries at 1-800-925-6458. The kit includes the *One Holy Passion* book, *One Holy Passion* 9 video messages, *The Quiet Time Journal*, and the Quiet Time Ministries Signature Tote. Each *One Holy Passion* book is organized into 8 weeks with 5 days of quiet time per week and Days 6-7 for review and meditation. The book also includes 9 Viewer Guides for the group video sessions, Leader's Guide and Discussion Questions, and Journal and Prayer Pages.

QUIET TIME MINISTRIES ONLINE

Quiet Time Ministries Online at www.quiettime.org is a place where you can deepen your devotion to God and His Word. Cath's Blog is where Catherine shares about life, about the Lord, and just about everything else. A Walk In Grace™ is Catherine's devotional photojournal, highlighting her own myPhotoWalk photography, where you can grow deep in the garden of His grace. myQuietTime is an exclusive HD 1080p video presented on YouTube at The Quiet Time Live Channel. myPhotoWalk.com is Catherine's devotional photography website where you can view her nature and landscape photography and order custom prints at CatherineMartin. SmugMug.com. You are also invited to join Catherine on Facebook, Twitter, and GooglePlus.

MY LETTER TO THE LORD

As you begin these quiet times, I'd like to ask, where are you? What has been happening in your life over the last year or so? What has been your life experience? What are you facing and what has God been teaching you? It is no accident that you are in this book of quiet times, *One Holy Passion*. God has something He wants you to know, something that will change the whole landscape of your experience with Him. Watch for it, listen for it, and when you learn it, write it down and never let it go. Will you write a prayer as a letter to the Lord in the space provided expressing all that is on your heart and ask Him to speak to you in these quiet times?

MY LETTER TO THE LORD

Viewer Guide
✤ INTRODUCTION WEEK ✤

Journey To The Heart Of God

Welcome to *One Holy Passion*, a sacred journey in Exodus to God's amazing love. In this study in God's Word, you are going to discover your great God and just how much He loves you. These Viewer Guides are designed to give you a place to write notes from my *One Holy Passion* messages available on DVDs, Digital M4V Video, and Digital MP3 Audio for your computer or mobile device. In our time together today, we are going to look at Exodus 19:4 and God's great desire for an intimate relationship with you.

"You yourselves have seen what I did to the Egyptians, and how I bore you on eagles' wings, and brought you to Myself" (Exodus 19:4).

Some important thoughts as we begin our study in Exodus

1. God always has _____ and intention when He takes us somewhere in Scripture.

Isaiah 55:10-11

2. The book of Exodus is all about the journey to the _____ of God.

Exodus 19:3-6

3. God is most concerned about our intimate _____ with Him.

Exodus 19:4

4. A rescue by God always results in a _____ relationship with God.

Exodus 19:4

5. In Exodus, you will learn to _____.

Exodus 19:4

6. In Exodus, you are going to see one holy _____.

Exodus 19:4

God's passion for His people is His extravagant, immeasurable, unconditional, amazing

_____.

❧ Video messages are available on DVDs or as Digital M4V Video. Audio messages are available as Digital MP3 Audio. Visit the Quiet Time Ministries Online Store at www.quiettime.org.

MEANT FOR MORE

Ephesians 3:20

God loves His people. If you are a believer in Christ Jesus, trusting only in His merits, God loves you as surely as He is God. There is no question about the matter. His divine love is yours as certainly as His power is displayed in creation.

CHARLES SPURGEON

MEANT FOR GOD

…you are Mine.
Isaiah 43:1

PREPARE YOUR HEART

She stood behind the open door, her eyes fixed on the English missionaries who had come to visit her in-laws. Hidden from view, she stared at their gentle faces and felt deep sobs welling up from a place inside she did not care to reveal, not even to herself. *No, I can't entertain the hope I see in these people. How could I have possibly arrived at such a despicable life, with no way of escape? Trapped in this house, forever doomed.* At 19, she was already a widow with a child—a most desperate position for any woman in India in the late 1800s.

Buried in her memories were earlier years of tender love from parents who regarded her as their greatest treasure, naming her Ponnamal, meaning "gold." Her parents showered her with every possible advantage, blessing their bright young daughter with a good education. Then, as was the custom, she was given in marriage to an older man. Clothed in silk, decorated with beautiful jewelry, high-spirited and gentle Ponnamal left the warmth of her father's house to marry a professor at the mission college. Her marriage brought disillusionment, but the birth of a child brought her joy. And then came the sudden, shocking death of her husband only a year after their wedding. Ponnamal had journeyed from safety to sorrow and now to despair. Widows were outcasts in India. What would she do? Where would she go?

Now, standing behind a door, invisible to all but God, she listened intently to Mr. and Mrs. Walker, missionaries committed to sharing Jesus with others in India. They asked about the wild-eyed young girl they had noticed. "Who is the young woman living with you?" "She is the widow of our son," replied Ponnamal's in-laws. "We'd like to invite all of you to attend church," replied the Walkers.

Surprisingly, Ponnamal was allowed to attend church on Sundays. The preacher gave deep, vibrant, Spirit-filled messages with rapid sentences in the complicated Tamil language. He may have thought only the men were understanding and hearing the message. But Ponnamal discerned the meaning of those words better than all others in attendance. *This Jesus is the one I have been longing for all my life. I never have to feel alone again.* Transformed, Ponnamal entered into new life in Christ and was filled with a supernatural joy and peace. Outwardly, she endured the same trapped, hopeless existence, but with newfound serenity, she performed the drudgery of duties in a strength and triumph no amount of reproach could weaken.

One day, Mrs. Walker, with characteristic gentleness, asked, "Could Ponnamal stay an extra hour after the Sunday service to teach Sunday school?" Again, surprisingly, her father-in-law responded, "Yes, she may."

Ponnamal excitedly thought, I can hardly believe I have this open door. But I will walk through it. And walk through it she did, teaching women of all ages. While Ponnamal was teaching one Sunday, she noticed a slight, gentle-faced, dark-haired English woman watching her teach. I wonder who she is? She seems like someone with whom I could pour out my soul.

The English woman watched Ponnamal teach and thought, What strikes me is her power over them. There is something quite unusual about her. Ponnamal is a woman set apart. Later that morning, the woman walked up to her and said, "I'm Amy Carmichael." Ponnamal could have never guessed how one meeting would alter the course of her life.

Amy boldly asked the in-laws, "I would like Ponnamal to join me in ministry and travel throughout India, serving the Lord." Miraculously, they agreed. Thus began the adventures of Amy Carmichael and Ponnamal, coworkers in the missionary work of Dohnavur Fellowship in India.

Perhaps you have felt as Ponnamal did in the beginning of her dark night—helpless, worthless, and so alone. Do you see what really happened? Only God in the whole world could have orchestrated such an amazing rescue. Only God, with one holy passion, motivated by a love greater than she could have imagined, could have so dramatically transformed Ponnamal's life. Very simply, Ponnamal was meant for God Himself. His love moved Him to save her.

And so it is with you, dear friend. God loves you and has a plan for your life. You are meant for God. He created you for Himself. And He will orchestrate circumstances and events to bring you to Himself. As you begin this study of *One Holy Passion*, it is time to get ready for a sacred journey in Exodus to the heart of God and His amazing love. You are meant for more, so much more than you could even begin to imagine. Ponnamal is the perfect example of what it means to move from slavery, oppression, and captivity to freedom, purpose, and love.

As you step into the real life situation of the people of Israel in the book of Exodus, you see a drama of epic proportions. God sees His people in a desperate situation, hears their cries, reaches out of heaven, rescues them, brings them into a life-changing relationship with Himself, and takes them to a new and beautiful place designed just for them.

Begin by writing a simple prayer, asking the Lord to prepare your heart for this journey.

READ AND STUDY GOD'S WORD

1. As you begin this sacred journey you are going to look at the main themes that are seen in Exodus and continued throughout the Bible. This will help in realizing the incredible impact of this amazing book of the Bible. It is as though this week you are studying a travel guide that shows the main things you just don't want to miss on your journey. You are going to pack these main truths in your heart and mind so you have them with you all along the way.

Dr. Ronald Youngblood, Old Testament Professor Emeritus at Bethel Theological Seminary wrote these words about Exodus: "I am becoming increasingly convinced that Exodus is the Old Testament's greatest book…The story of Exodus is the story of how God redeemed His own."[1]

Exodus continues the story of the people of Israel seen in Genesis. At the end of Genesis, the sons of Israel, the descendants of Abraham, Isaac, and Jacob, the patriarchs who dominate the history found in Genesis are settled in Egypt. Joseph, the son of Jacob was a powerful leader in Egypt and all of his family had moved to Egypt, kept safe in his care. Just before he died, Joseph told his brothers, "God surely will come to help you and lead you out of this land of Egypt. He will bring you back to the land He solemnly promised to give to Abraham, Isaac, and Jacob" (Genesis 50:24 NLT). Exodus begins with a king rising to power in Egypt who knows nothing about Joseph. The sons of Israel multiplied in Egypt, causing great fear among the Egyptians. So the Egyptians oppressed the people of Israel, forcing them into slavery and harsh labor. Now begins the discovery of who God is and what He does for His people in their darkest hours. Oh, dear friend, you are in for amazing discoveries in God's Word. There is a theme verse that reveals God's heart for His people and what He does in this oppressive situation. Read the words from God in Exodus 19:3-4 and write out what you learn is going to happen and what you see about God.

2. Exodus 19:4 shows that God set His people free. He rescued His people with great purpose, bringing them to Himself. In these words you see God's desire for an intimate relationship with His people. Rescue by God always results in a deeper relationship with God. Read Deuteronomy 32:9-12, and write out what you learn about God and what He did for His people.

3. As you think about who God is and what He does, it is important to know that God is eternal and unchanging (see Psalm 102:12, 25-28). This is known in theology as the immutability of God. So, you see in Exodus 19:4 and Deuteronomy 32:10-12 that God is passionate about His people and desires an intimate relationship with them. This is who your God is. As He loved

them, so He loves and watches over you. Look at the following verses and underline your favorite words and phrases about God and how He loves us and desires an intimate relationship with us.

"I will be their God" (Genesis 17:8 NIV).

"Be still, and know that I am God" (Psalm 46:10 NIV).

"Do not fear, for I have redeemed you; I have called you by name; you are Mine… Since you are precious in My sight, since you are honored and I love you, I will give other men in your place and other peoples in exchange for your life. Do not fear, for I am with you" (Isaiah 43:1, 4-5).

"I will give them a heart to know me, that I am the LORD. They will be my people, and I will be their God, for they will return to me with all their heart" (Jeremiah 24:7 NIV).

"I have loved you with an everlasting love; therefore I have drawn you with lovingkindness" (Jeremiah 31:3).

"For God so loved the world, that He gave His only begotten Son, that whoever believes in Him shall not perish, but have eternal life. For God did not send the Son into the world to judge the world, but that the world might be saved through Him" (John 3:16-17).

"I heard a loud voice from the throne, saying, 'Behold, the tabernacle of God is among men, and He will dwell among them, and they shall be His people, and God Himself will be among them, and He will wipe away every tear from their eyes; and there will no longer be any death; there will not longer be any mourning, or crying, or pain; the first things have passed away'" (Revelation 21:3-4).

ADORE GOD IN PRAYER

Pray the words of Psalm 139:1-10 NLT: "O LORD, You have examined my heart and know everything about me. You know when I sit down or stand up. You know my thoughts even when I'm far away. You see me when I travel and when I rest at home. You know everything I do. You know what I'm going to say even before I say it, LORD. You go before me and follow me. You place your hand of blessing on my head. Such knowledge is too wonderful for me, too great for me to understand! I can never escape from Your Spirit! I can never get away from Your presence! If I go up to heaven, You are there; if I go down to the grave, You are there. If I ride the wings of the morning, if I dwell by the farthest oceans, even there Your hand will guide me, and Your strength will support me."

YIELD YOURSELF TO GOD

What were we made for? To know God. What aim should we set ourselves in life? To know God. What is the "eternal life" that Jesus gives? Knowledge of God. "This is life eternal, that they might know thee, the only true God, and Jesus Christ, whom thou hast sent" (John 17:3). What is the best thing in life, bringing more joy, delight, and contentment, and than anything else? Knowledge of God.[2]

J.I. PACKER IN KNOWING GOD

Our pursuit of God is successful just because He is forever seeking to manifest Himself to us.[3]

A.W. TOZER IN THE PURSUIT OF GOD

But where do you and I find God? I rejoice to tell you that Christ is our meeting place. The angels long ago announced it when they said that His name should be Immanuel—God with us…When we look up in faith, we see the everlasting face of God revealed in Jesus Christ…Oh, what a delight to know that Jesus Christ is the point at which we experience God! For it was Jesus Himself who told His generation, "He that hath seen me hath seen the Father" (John 14:9). The message remains unchanged.[4]

A.W. TOZER IN MEN WHO MET GOD

ENJOY HIS PRESENCE

The same God who was filled with passion for His people enslaved in Egypt, caring enough to break into human history, deliver His people, and bring them to Himself, is passionate for you. He loves you. Do you see it? Do you see how He reaches out to you and desires you for Himself? Think about these things in depth, dear friend. Sometimes these truths are hard to believe when you are surrounded by difficult people or adverse circumstances. Know this—God's Word is true.

Believe it, receive it, and live it. The Lord has His eye on you. He has revealed Himself in many ways and especially in Jesus Christ, your Savior and Lord. In the days to come you will see His passion for you, His child. And what you see will fill you anew with passion and love for Him. Think about all you have learned today, where you are in your own journey with the Lord, then close this time by writing a prayer to the Lord in your Journal, expressing all that is on your heart.

REST IN HIS LOVE

"I will give them a heart to know me, that I am the LORD. They will be my people, and I will be their God, for they will return to me with all their heart" (Jeremiah 24:7 NIV).

THE PRICELESS PRIVILEGE

The priceless privilege of knowing Christ. Philippians 3:8 WMS
Chapel of the Holy Cross, Sedona, Arizona, USA
Nikon D7000, ISO 100, f11, AEB, Adobe Photoshop, Nik Silver Efex Pro
MYPHOTOWALK.COM—CATHERINEMARTIN.SMUGMUG.COM

MEANT FOR GRACIOUS FREEDOM

It was for freedom that Christ set us free; therefore keep standing
firm and do not be subject again to a yoke of slavery.

GALATIANS 5:1

PREPARE YOUR HEART

As you continue packing and preparing this week for your sacred journey, you discover in God's Word that one of the main themes in Exodus is freedom. And it's a freedom given by God as a gift of grace. He does for you what you cannot do for yourself. God sees the ways people are enslaved and He does what it takes to set them free, and He gives them the power to live in freedom.

What are the things that are potentially holding you captive today—physically, emotionally, or spiritually? Are you struggling with sin in your life? Do you have challenging relationships or oppressive people around you? Are you filled with fear? Have you been overwhelmed with despair or discouragement and find it difficult to believe God or have faith in what He says in His Word? And maybe you are desperately in need of freedom—freedom from worry, fear, guilt, shame, despair, or discouragement. Dear friend, let us begin with the words of Psalm 4:1 (NLT): "Answer me when I call to You, O God who declares me innocent. Free me from my troubles. Have mercy on me and hear my prayer." And then, believe that God has something powerful to teach you about freedom in the book of Exodus as you watch Him set His people free.

As you begin your quiet time today, think about life experience of the psalmist and pray the words back to the Lord: "In my distress I prayed to the LORD, and the LORD answered me and set me free" (Psalm 118:5). Carry those words with you today.

READ AND STUDY GOD'S WORD

1. The book of Exodus begins with slavery for the people of God who were, at that time, living in Egypt. Read Exodus 1:1-22 and describe how the sons of Israel became enslaved and their slavery experience.

2. Where in Exodus 1 can you find proof that God was present in the lives of His people, aware of what was happening, and working on their behalf?

3. Without ruining the excitement of this journey, take a sneak peek at what God determines for His people who are suffering and enslaved in Egypt. Read what God says to Moses, who is going to be instrumental in the deliverance of God's people, in Exodus 3:7-10. What do you learn about God and what is He planning for His people?

4. Read the following verses and underline those phrases that are significant to you related to freedom.

> "I have swept away your sins like a cloud. I have scattered your offenses like the morning mist. Oh, return to Me, for I have paid the price to set you free" (Isaiah 44:22 NLT).

> "The Spirit of the LORD is upon me, for the LORD has anointed me to bring good news to the poor. He has sent me to comfort the brokenhearted and to proclaim that captives will be released and prisoners will be freed" (Isaiah 61:1 NLT).

> "I will show love to the people of Judah. I will free them from their enemies—not with weapons and armies or horses and charioteers, but by My power as the LORD their God" (Hosea 1:7 NLT).

5 Yes, God wants freedom for you, His child. You just read Isaiah 61:1 about captives being released and prisoners being set free. Now you will see that it has great meaning for you because of Jesus. Read Luke 4:14-21 and write out what you learn.

6. Look at the following verses and write what you learn about Jesus and how He sets us free.

John 8:31-36

Romans 8:1-4

Galatians 5:1, 13

Colossians 1:13-14

1 Peter 2:16

ADORE GOD IN PRAYER

Pray the following prayer by Corrie ten Boom: "Thank You, Lord Jesus, for that blessed answer to my sin problem: The cross, where You finished all that was necessary in order to destroy my sin. Keep me close to You, Lord, so that I see Your amazing grace."[6]

YIELD YOURSELF TO GOD

None but Jesus can give deliverance to captives. Real liberty cometh from him only. It is a liberty righteously bestowed; for the Son, who is Heir of all things, has a right to make men free. The saints honour the justice of God, which now secures their salvation. It is a liberty which has been dearly purchased. Christ speaks it by his power, but he bought it by his blood. He makes thee free, but it is by his own bonds. Thou goest clear, because he bare thy burden for thee: thou art set at liberty, because he has suffered in thy stead. But, though dearly purchased, he freely gives it. Jesus asks nothing of us as a preparation for this liberty. He finds us sitting in sackcloth and ashes, and bids us put on the beautiful array of freedom; he saves us just as we are, and all without our help or merit. When Jesus sets free, the liberty is perpetually entailed; no chains can bind again. Let the Master say to me, "Captive, I have delivered thee," and it is done for ever. Satan may plot to enslave us, but if the Lord be on our side, whom shall we fear? The world, with its temptations, may seek to ensnare us, but mightier is he who is for us than all they who be against us. The machinations of our own deceitful hearts may harass and annoy us, but he who hath begun the good work in us will carry it on and perfect it to the end. The foes of God and the enemies of man may gather their hosts together, and come with concentrated fury against us, but if God acquitteth, who is he that condemneth? Not more free is the eagle which mounts to his rocky eyrie, and afterwards outsoars the clouds, than the soul which Christ hath delivered. If we are no more under the law, but free from its curse, let our liberty be practically exhibited in our serving God with gratitude and delight. "I am thy servant, and the son of thine handmaid: thou hast loosed my bonds." "Lord, what wilt thou have me to do?"

CHARLES SPURGEON IN MORNING AND EVENING

ENJOY HIS PRESENCE

We have seen how God intends to set His people free, rescuing them out of Egypt. And oh, what drama and excitement that is going to involve. But then, we have learned there is a much greater rescue that has taken place. When Jesus died on the cross, He died in your place, so that you might have the opportunity to have forgiveness of sins and eternal life. Oh how great a freedom is ours when we know Christ. What is the most important truth you learned today? Close by writing a prayer thanking the Lord for all He has done to set you free.

REST IN HIS LOVE

"So if the Son sets you free, you are truly free" (John 8:36 NLT).

THE GREAT LIGHT

The people who were sitting in darkness saw a great light. Matthew 4:16
Sedona, Arizona, USA

Nikon D7000, ISO 100, f22, AEB, Adobe Photoshop, Nik Silver Efex Pro
MYPHOTOWALK.COM—CATHERINEMARTIN.SMUGMUG.COM

MEANT FOR EXTRAVAGANT LOVE

The proof of God's amazing love is this: that it was while
we were sinners that Christ died for us."
ROMANS 5:8 PHILLIPS

PREPARE YOUR HEART

Many years ago, God gave Dr. Bill Bright, Co-Founder of Campus Crusade for Christ, the idea to write a little booklet entitled *The Four Spiritual Laws*. *The Four Spiritual Laws* contains four principles and accompanying Scripture to help lead a person to Christ. Initially, Dr. Bright wrote the first law about the sin of man and his need for a Savior. He wrote of God's love in the second spiritual law. God then helped him see the need to make an important change in the booklet. He describes what happened: "Just as I was drifting off to sleep, I sat straight up in bed. I thought, There's something wrong about starting this written presentation with the negative note about man's sinfulness. I flung the covers aside, got out of bed, and paced the carpet, repeating those words in my mind. Something's not quite right... Why not start where God Himself starts, with His love? I remembered being drawn to Christ myself when I was overwhelmed with God's love for me. Would other people want to know more if they first hear the positive affirmation that the Creator of the universe loves them personally? How could anyone say no to Christ if they truly understood how much He loves them? We needed to start with the positive! I went to the head of the stairs and called down to Vonette and our associates to reverse the sequence of laws one and two, which they did."[6]

Have you discovered that God loves you and has a wonderful plan for your life? God begins with His love and reaches out to you, His child. You can count on the fact that He will take the initiative to have an intimate relationship with you. As you continue studying the overall themes in Exodus that are seen throughout Scripture, you are going to pack the truth of God's love into your bag to carry with you on your journey. Take a moment now and ask God to speak to you in His Word as you draw near to Him.

READ AND STUDY GOD'S WORD

1. In Exodus you experience firsthand God's rescue of His people as He leads them out of Egypt, through the wilderness, and into the Promised Land. You will never forget what you see about God and what He does for His people. But what motivates God to do things for people who are powerless to help themselves? Read Deuteronomy 7:6-10 and write out everything you learn about God. These verses show why Exodus is all about God's one holy passion for His people.

2. When God spoke to Jeremiah about His people, He said, "I have loved you with an everlasting love; Therefore I have drawn you with lovingkindness" (Jeremiah 31:3). God loves with an unconditional love. By His grace, His people can experience His love, not because of who they are, but because of who He is. And so, in the New Testament, we see this same God with extravagant, immeasurable, unconditional, amazing love, acting in love for you and for me. Look at the following verses and record what you learn about the love of God and why it might be called extravagant and amazing.

John 3:16

Romans 5:5-8

Romans 8:38-39

1 John 3:1, 4:9-10

ADORE GOD IN PRAYER

O most Heavenly Father, send your Holy Spirit to pour into my heart that most excellent gift of love, the bond of peace and of all holiness, that I may love you with all my heart and soul and mind and strength, and my neighbor as myself.[7]

F.B. MEYER IN DAILY PRAYERS

YIELD YOURSELF TO GOD

The bedrock of our Christian faith is the unmerited, fathomless marvel of the love of God exhibited on the Cross of Calvary, a love we never can and never shall merit…Undaunted radiance is not built on anything passing, but on the love of God that nothing can alter. The experiences of life, terrible or monotonous, are impotent to touch the love of God, which is in Christ Jesus our Lord.[8]

OSWALD CHAMBERS IN MY UTMOST FOR HIS HIGHEST

ENJOY HIS PRESENCE

After a lecture in Chicago, Dr. Karl Barth was asked if he could summarize his whole life's work in theology in one sentence. He responded that he could using the words he heard his mother sing to him when he was a child: "Jesus loves me, this I know. For the Bible tells me so." After all you have studied today, what does God's love mean to you? Do you realize that He loves you enough to do for you what you could never do for yourself? Have you entered into a love relationship with Him by asking Him into your life? If not, you can right now, by praying a simple prayer something like this, *Lord Jesus, I need You. Thank You for dying on the cross for me. I ask You now to come into my life, forgive my sins, and make me the person You want me to be. In Jesus' name, Amen.* Do you see even now, how the Lord is reaching out to you with His love? Will you close your time today by writing a prayer and telling the Lord how much His love means to you?

Rest in His Love

"For God so loved the world, that He gave His only begotten Son, that whoever believes in Him shall not perish, but have eternal life" (John 3:16).

Jesus Is The Way

Jesus said to him, "I am the way, the truth, and the life." John 14:6
Sedona, Arizona, USA
Nikon D7000, ISO 100, f11, 1/100sec, Adobe Photoshop, Nik Silver Efex Pro
MYPHOTOWALK.COM—CATHERINEMARTIN.SMUGMUG.COM

MEANT FOR HOPEFUL PURPOSE

Also we have obtained an inheritance, having been predestined according to His purpose who works all things after the counsel of His will.

EPHESIANS 1:11

PREPARE YOUR HEART

How do you view God? Through the lens of the world or the Word of God? This is a most important question for the journey that leads into a more intimate relationship with God. God's Word reveals that God is so much more than we know Him to be right now. It is one thing to know Him as He has revealed Himself, and quite another to act on those truths from God. When you are in the heat of a trial, everything you know to be true about God can be challenged. You can wonder where God is, what He is doing, and who exactly He really is. Such was the case for the people of Israel when they were enslaved in Egypt. The people cried out in their suffering and oh, what an amazing day it was when they heard from God through Moses. Moses was faithful to deliver the message God gave him and the people, according to Exodus 4:29-31, realized that God had a purpose for them, and they believed.

Elisabeth Elliot, a young missionary wife, lost her husband, Jim Elliot, when he was killed by Auca Indians in the jungles of Ecuador. In her book, *A Path Through Suffering*, Elisabeth shared what it was like to speak with her young daughter, Valerie, about God's love and purposes. She wrote, "I still had to give an answer, a truthful answer: I did not know *all* God's reasons. The ones I was quite sure I did know, Valerie could not have understood then. But that He *had* reasons, I was sure. That they were loving reasons I was also sure. The assurance that it was *not for nothing* comforted me and I gave my peace to my child."[9] What allowed Elisabeth to believe that God had reasons and why was that enough for her? It was because of all she knew in God's Word and because His Word was the authority for her belief. And His Word must be the authority for your belief as well.

When you look to God in His Word, you discover that He is a God of purpose. He is not capricious, uncaring, or random in any of His actions. \Take time now to talk with God and ask Him to give you eyes to see and ears to hear Him in His Word. Then pray or sing these words by Joachim Neander:

Praise to the Lord, the Almighty, the King of creation!
Oh my soul, praise Him, for He is thy health and salvation!
All ye who hear, now to His temple draw near;
Join me in glad adoration!

Praise to the Lord, who o'er all things so wondrously reigneth.
Shelters thee under His wings, yes, so gently sustaineth!
Hast thou not seen how all thy longings have been
Granted in what He ordaineth?

Praise to the Lord! O let all that is in me adore Him!
All that hath life and breath, come now with praises before Him.
Let the Amen sound from His people again;
Gladly for aye we adore Him. Amen.

JOACHIM NEANDER

READ AND STUDY GOD'S WORD

1. When God saw His people enslaved and oppressed, He responded with great purpose and a great plan. To get a glimpse into God's response, read Exodus 6:1-8 and write out your insights about God's purpose and plan in all that He has done and is going to do.

2. In Exodus 6:4, God speaks about His covenant that He established with Abraham, Isaac, and Jacob. This covenant is behind what God does in rescuing His people out of Egypt (see Exodus 6:5). So what is a covenant? It is a most solemn, binding agreement between two parties and, according to Kay Arthur, Co-Founder of Precept Ministries, "everything God does for you and me as His children is based on covenant."[10] The word, "covenant" is used approximately 298 times in the Bible. God's covenants are filled with His purpose and His promises. Read His covenant words to Abraham in Genesis 12:1-3 and write out what God promises in this covenant.

3. When God renewed His covenant with Abraham, He took him outside and asked him to try and count the stars. Then He said, "So shall your descendants be" (Genesis 15:5). Then God spoke to Abraham about something in the future that actually occurs in Exodus. Read Genesis 15:13-14 and write out what is going to happen.

4. In the covenant with Abraham, God promises to bless all nations through him. Ultimately the nation of Israel was established through the descendants of Abraham, and through that nation would come the Messiah, who is the Lord Jesus Christ. Read Galatians 3:7-9,13-16, 22, 29 and Romans 4:16-7. Then, write out what you learn about the blessing promised to Abraham and how we are part of that blessing.

5. As you continue looking at how God acts with purpose and a plan, look at some of His great purposes for us. Read the following verses and underline those phrases that speak to His purpose in your life. Be sure to personalize these verses in your mind and heart, knowing He intends these words for you.

"One thing I have asked from the LORD, that I shall seek: that I may dwell in the house of the LORD all the days of my life, to behold the beauty of the LORD and to meditate in His temple" (Psalm 27:4).

"The LORD directs the steps of the godly. He delights in every detail of their lives" (Psalm 37:23 NLT).

"Bring all who claim me as their God, for I have made them for My glory. It was I who created them" (Isaiah 43:7 NLT).

"For as the heavens are higher than the earth, so are My ways higher than your ways and My thoughts than your thoughts" (Isaiah 55:9).

"For as the rain and the snow come down from heaven, and do not return there without watering the earth and making it bear and sprout, and furnishing seed to the sower and bread to the eater; so will My word be which goes forth from My mouth; It will not return to Me empty, without accomplishing what I desire, and without succeeding in the matter for which I sent it" (Isaiah 55:10-11).

"Thus says the LORD, 'Let not a wise man boast of his wisdom, and let not the mighty man boast of his might, let not a rich man boast of his riches; but let him who boasts boast of this, that he understands and knows Me, that I am the LORD who exercises lovingkindness, justice and righteousness on earth; for I delight in these things,' declares the LORD" (Jeremiah 9:23-24).

"'For I know the plans that I have for you,' declares the LORD, 'plans for welfare and not for calamity to give you a future and a hope'" (Jeremiah 29:11).

"And we know that God causes all things to work together for good to those who love God, to those who are called according to His purpose. For those whom He foreknew, He also predestined to become conformed to the image of His Son, so that He would be the firstborn among many brethren" (Romans 8:28-29).

"He did so to make known the riches of His glory upon vessels of mercy, which He prepared beforehand for glory" (Romans 9:23).

"No eye has seen, no ear has heard, and no mind has imagined what God has prepared for those who love Him" (1 Corinthians 2:9 NLT).

"But we all, with unveiled face, beholding as in a mirror the glory of the Lord, are being transformed into the same image from glory to glory, just as from the Lord, the Spirit" (2 Corinthians 3:18).

"Also we have obtained an inheritance, having been predestined according to His purpose who works all things after the counsel of His will" (Ephesians 1:11).

"For we are God's masterpiece. He has created us anew in Christ Jesus, so we can do the good things He planned for us long ago" (Ephesians 2:10 NLT).

ADORE GOD IN PRAYER

Pray the words of Psalm 86:11-13 NLT: "Teach me Your ways, O Lord, that I may live according to Your truth! Grant me purity of heart, so that I may honor you. With all my heart I will praise You, O Lord my God. I will give glory to Your name forever, for Your love for me is very great."

YIELD YOURSELF TO GOD

Many times covenant agreements were extended beyond individuals to their families…This was the covenant that God made with Abraham. It was not to be just a compact between the two of them, but was to extend beyond Abraham to his seed. God would become not only the God of Abraham, but also of Isaac and of Jacob. Those then who were of Abraham's seed would know the benefits of God's covenant with Abraham. And to them would be extended the lovingkindness of covenant…Oh, how God loves to extend the lovingkindness of His covenant promises to Abraham's descendants. "And if you belong to Christ, then you are Abraham's offspring [descendants, seed], heirs according to promise" (Galatians 3:29).[11]

KAY ARTHUR IN HOW CAN I LIVE

To understand covenant is…to discover a promise that has been there all the time, hidden in vague shadows and blurred by the veil of my ignorance. To understand the intimacy and intricate details of God's plan and purpose. To know that because of His covenant of grace I can be assured that I will always be beloved of God. It frees us to bask in His love and to move through every circumstance of life in the security of His promises…To understand covenant is to hear Him say to you, "You are precious in My sight"—and to believe Him.[12]

KAY ARTHUR IN OUR COVENANT GOD

ENJOY HIS PRESENCE

Think about all you've learned today about how God works with purpose and how you are meant for His purposes. God wants you to know that He is the Lord your God. You are God's masterpiece, dear friend. He has amazing things in mind, planned for you long ago. What is your most significant insight about His purpose for your life? What does this show you about God's passion for you—His extravagant, unconditional love? Reflect on God's handiwork in the devotional image. Write your thoughts, then close with a prayer to the Lord.

REST IN HIS LOVE

"For we are God's masterpiece. He has created us anew in Christ Jesus, so we can do the good things He planned for us long ago" (Ephesians 2:10 NLT).

ON FIRE FOR JESUS

They got up and returned at once to Jerusalem. John 24:33 NIV
Sedona, Arizona, USA
Nikon D7000, ISO 100, f11, AEB, Adobe Photoshop, Nik Silver Efex Pro
MYPHOTOWALK.COM—CATHERINEMARTIN.SMUGMUG.COM

MEANT FOR
IMMEASURABLE ABUNDANCE

The thief comes only to steal and kill and destroy; I came that
they may have life, and have it abundantly."

JOHN 10:10

PREPARE YOUR HEART

God's plan for His people as seen in Exodus was to rescue them from the Egyptians. But He did not stop there in His plan. He also made it clear that He wanted to redeem them, deliver them, take them to be His people and be their God, and bring them to a land flowing with milk and honey (Exodus 3:17, 6:5-8). What we see here is that God intends abundance for His people—abundant blessings and abundant life. You, dear friend, as God's beloved child, are meant for more than all the world can offer—an intimate relationship with the God who has created us, a life of freedom that is secure in Him, the moment by moment experience of His everlasting love, the joy of being His masterpiece living out God's plan and purpose for our lives, and experiencing the abundant life of blessing and glory He has for us in Christ. This does not mean that God's people won't face difficulties in this life. But it does mean that they are enabled to thrive in spite of every adversity because of God's presence and power in them.

Today, dear friend, ask the Lord to speak to your heart as you draw near to Him.

READ AND STUDY GOD'S WORD

1. We have spent this week looking at some of the main themes in Exodus that are important for us as we prepare to go on a journey from Egypt to the Red Sea place, into the wilderness, and finally, on into the promised land. It is as though we are leafing through a guidebook and preparing to make some important stops along the way on our sacred journey through Exodus. Today, the final truth that we want to pack into our bags is abundance. God is a God who is generous and has much more in mind for us than we can even realize right now. We tend to measure and define God by what we see in people and things, rather than by all He has revealed of Himself in His Word. When we see who God really is, what God does, and what He says, we are literally astounded and humbled. Just imagine what it must have been like for the people of Israel, who

only knew a life of slavery, to now discover that God had so much for them than they could have imagined. Look at the following verses in Exodus and write out those things that God wanted to give them and do for them that were above and beyond what they could have imagined.

Exodus 3:17

Exodus 6:6-8

Exodus 19:4-6

2. Jesus, the Son of God, who is the radiance of God's glory and the exact representation of His nature (Hebrews 1:3), shows us God's heart in action among us in new and exciting ways. This is why it is so thrilling to read the gospels and watch the Lord in action to see how He always does more than we can imagine. Read the following two events in the life of Jesus and write what you notice about how He does so much more than we can imagine.

Matthew 14:13-21

Mark 10:46-52

3. Read the following verses and underline those phrases and words that show the abundant nature of God's promises.

"He drew me out of many waters…He brought me forth also into a broad place; He rescued me, because He delighted in me" (Psalm 18:16, 19).

"The LORD is my shepherd, I shall not want. He makes me lie down in green pastures; He leads me beside quiet waters. He restores my soul; He guides me in the paths of righteousness for His name's sake. Even though I walk through the valley of the shadow of death, I fear no evil, for You are with me; Your rod and Your staff, they comfort me. You prepare a table before me in the presence of my enemies; You have anointed my head with oil; my cup overflows. Surely goodness and lovingkindness will follow me all the days of my life, and I will dwell in the house of the LORD forever" (Psalm 23:1-6).

"Yet those who wait for the Lord will gain new strength; they will mount up with wings like eagles, they will run and not get tired, they will walk and not become weary" (Isaiah 40:31).

"But you, Israel, my servant, Jacob whom I have chosen, descendant of Abraham My friend, you whom I have taken from the ends of the earth, and called from its remotest parts and said to you, 'You are My servant, I have chosen you and not rejected you. Do not fear, for I am with you; Do not anxiously look about you, for I am your God. I will strengthen you, surely I will help you, surely I will uphold you with My righteous right hand'" (Isaiah 41:8-10).

"Blessed are the poor in spirit, for theirs is the kingdom of heaven. Blessed are those who mourn, for they shall be comforted. Blessed are the gentle, for they shall inherit the earth. Blessed are those who hunger and thirst for righteousness, for they shall be satisfied. Blessed are the merciful, for they shall receive mercy. Blessed are the pure in heart, for they shall see God. Blessed are the peacemakers, for they shall be called sons of God. Blessed are those who have been persecuted for the sake of righteousness, for theirs is the kingdom of heaven. Blessed are you when people insult you and persecute you, and falsely say all kinds of evil against you because of Me. Rejoice and be glad, for your reward in heaven is great; for in the same way they persecuted the prophets who were before you" (Matthew 5:1-12).

"But seek first His kingdom and His righteousness, and all these things will be added to you" (Matthew 6:33).

"I am the door; if anyone enters through Me, he will be saved, and will go in and out and find pasture. The thief comes only to steal and kill and destroy; I came that they may have life, and have it abundantly. I am the good shepherd; the good shepherd lays down His life for the sheep" (John 10:9-11).

"No eye has seen, no ear has heard, and no mind has imagined what God has prepared for those who love Him" (1 Corinthians 2:9 NLT).

"And God is able to make all grace abound to you, so that always having all sufficiency in everything, you may have an abundance for every good deed" (2 Corinthians 9:8).

"Now to Him who is able to do immeasurably more than all we ask or imagine, according to his power that is at work within us" (Ephesians 3:20 NIV).

"And my God will supply all your needs according to His riches in glory in Christ Jesus" (Philippians 4:19).

"Then the angel showed me a river with the water of life, clear as crystal, flowing from the throne of God and of the Lamb. It flowed down the center of the main street. On each side of the river grew a tree of life, bearing twelve crops of fruit, with a fresh crop each month. The leaves were used for medicine to heal the nations. No longer will there be a curse upon anything. For the throne of God and of the Lamb will be there, and His servants will worship him. And they will see His face, and His name will be written on their foreheads. And there will be no night there—no need for lamps or sun—for the Lord God will shine on them. And they will reign forever and ever" (Revelation 22:1-5).

Adore God in Prayer

Pray through your favorite verses from your study of God's Word today, pouring out your heart to the Lord.

YIELD YOURSELF TO GOD

It is not the favorableness of our circumstances, but the fact of the Lord's shepherdship, which is the perpetual pledge that we shall not want. "The Lord is my shepherd therefore can I lack nothing," is the way the prayer-book puts it. Back of all circumstances is God. Circumstances may and do change, but God, never. Neither abundance nor want can affect the fact of shepherdship. The conditions of the sheep may change but the shepherdship of the sheep is eternal. The visible bread may dwindle, but the invisible Bread Maker remains. Your little store of silver and gold may shrink but—you shall not want. Friends may prove you false in the hour of test but—you shall not want. Old age with its limitations and infirmities may be creeping up on you, but—you shall not want. Strength may wane, health fail, earthly supply cut off, but—you shall not want. When you and I say "The Lord is my shepherd," that means the Lord remains my Shepherd amid all the vicissitudes of human favor and fortune.[13]

JAMES McCONKEY

To stand in heaven and look back on earth, and weigh them together in the balance, must transport the soul and make it cry out, "Is this the place that cost so dear as the blood of God? No wonder, O blessed price, and thrice-blessed love! Is this the result of believing? Is this the outcome of the Spirit's work? Have the gales of grace blown me into such a harbour? Is it here that Christ has enticed my soul? O blessed way and end…The Lord had a sweeter purpose and meant better than you would believe."[14]

RICHARD BAXTER

ENJOY HIS PRESENCE

This week we have seen how we are meant for more than all the things this world has to offer. We will see this in much more detail as we continue our sacred journey in Exodus. What is the most significant insight you learned today as you looked at God's abundant provisions for us as His children? How have you seen God's passion for you this week? How does it impact your own love for God? Summarize your insights in 2-3 sentences.

REST IN HIS LOVE

"Now to Him who is able to do far more abundantly beyond all that we ask or think, according to the power that works within us" (Ephesians 3:20).

ABUNDANT LIFE

I came that they may have life, and have it abundantly. John 10:10
West Fork Trail, Sedona, Arizona, USA
Nikon D7000, ISO 100, f11, AEB, Adobe Photoshop, Nik Silver Efex Pro
MYPHOTOWALK.COM—CATHERINEMARTIN.SMUGMUG.COM

DEVOTIONAL READING
BY A.W. TOZER

DEAR FRIEND,

The next two days are your opportunity to review what you have learned this week. You may wish to write your thoughts and insights in your Journal. As you think about preparing for this study in Exodus and how we are *meant for more*, write:

Your most significant insight:

Your favorite quote:

Your favorite verse:

It is a strange and beautiful eccentricity of the free God that He has allowed His heart to be emotionally identified with men. Self-sufficient as He is, He wants our love and will not be satisfied till He gets it. Free as He is, He has let His heart be bound to us forever. "Herein is love, not that we loved God, but that he loved us, and sent his Son to be the propitiation for our sins."[15]

A.W. TOZER IN THE KNOWLEDGE OF THE HOLY

Viewer Guide
❦ WEEK ONE ❧

You Are Meant For More

You have just completed the first week of study in *One Holy Passion*. Today we are going to share together some important themes in Exodus from Exodus 19:3-6. In our time together I want you to see God's extravagant love for you and how He has so much for you than you can imagine.

"Now if you will obey me and keep my covenant, you will be my own special treasure from among all the peoples on earth; for all the earth belongs to me." (Exodus 19:5 NLT).

Where are you?

Where are you in your relationship with God? Where are you in life? Where are you with how you see yourself? What are you thinking about and believing right now?

How we are meant for more because of the Lord in our lives

1. We are meant for _____. Exodus 19:4

2. We are meant for gracious _____. Exodus 19:4

Warren Wiersbe writes: "Freedom isn't the privilege of doing whatever we want to do. It's the opportunity to do whatever God wants us to do."

3. We are meant for extravagant _____. Exodus 19:5

4. We are meant for hopeful _____. Exodus 19:6

"For we are God's masterpiece. He has created us anew in Christ Jesus, so we can do the good

5. We are meant for immeasurable _____. Exodus 19:3-6

Video messages are available on DVDs or as Digital M4V Video. Audio messages are available as Digital MP3 Audio. Visit the Quiet Time Ministries Online Store at www.quiettime.org.

WHEN GOD REMEMBERS HIS PEOPLE

Exodus 1-3

In all our dealings with God, free grace anticipates us with the blessings of goodness, and all our comfort is owing, not to our knowing God, but rather to our being known of him. We love him, visit him, and covenant with him, because he first loved us, visited us, and covenanted with us (Galatians 4:9). God is the Alpha, and therefore must be the Omega.

MATTHEW HENRY

GOD HELPS IN TROUBLED TIMES

And she had pity on him and said, "This is one of the Hebrews' children."

EXODUS 2:6

PREPARE YOUR HEART

Have you ever felt as though if it could go badly, it did? There is a book with the title, *The Worst-Case Scenario Survival Handbook.* And in that book you can find out how to deal with all kinds of worst-case scenarios like what to do if a bird is in your house or how to handle a charging bull. For the people of Israel following the death of Joseph, times became very difficult for them in Egypt. It was a worst-case scenario for them. They grew strong in numbers and their presence became intimidating to the Egyptians. So, the Egyptians conspired to oppress the people of Israel, make them slaves and afflict them with hard labor. According to Exodus 1:14, "they made their lives bitter with hard labor in mortar and bricks and at all kinds of labor in the field." To inflict further control and power over them, the king of Egypt commanded the Hebrew midwives to put to death all Hebrew male babies (Exodus 1:15-16). Where was God in all of this? Exodus 1:17ff reveals that God was very present. The midwives feared God and did not follow the Egyptian king's command. They let the boys live (Exodus 1:17). And God was "good to the midwives, the people multiplied, and became very mighty" (Exodus 1:20). And further, God established households for the midwives.

And so it begins—this sacred journey in Exodus to God's amazing love. For God is only just getting started in carrying out His magnificent plan for His people. God never forgets His people. In fact, He always remembers them (Exodus 2:23-25). And He does it all out of pure, unfailing love. Ask the Lord now to quiet your heart and lead you into a deeper relationship with Him as you take this sacred journey in Exodus.

READ AND STUDY GOD'S WORD

1. Exodus was written by Moses sometime after his 80th year (either 1295 or 1445 BC according to most commentators), and is part of the five books known as the Torah (Genesis, Exodus, Leviticus, Numbers, and Deuteronomy). The title "Exodus" means "departure" or "the way out." Exodus is the record of how God saved the people of Israel and established them as His

people in covenant relationship with Him, and as a nation representing Him, the one true God. To give you an overview and understanding of Exodus, the two main divisions of the book are Exodus 1-18 where we see God coming down, redeeming, rescuing, and delivering His people out of Egypt and Exodus 19-40 where God reveals Himself to His people, brings His people near to Him in a covenant relationship, and is intent on getting Egypt out of the people. The Lord moves His people from groaning and grief to grace and on to glory. The things that happened to the children of Israel are, according to Paul in 1 Corinthians 10:11, an example for us and written for our instruction. You might think of Egypt as the world and all it represents including sin, the flesh, and the devil. In the New Testament, we see that God does indeed rescue and redeem His people, breaking them from sin and the slavery to sin, then giving them power through the Holy Spirit against the world influences of the devil, the flesh and the lustful pride of life. He takes them to the Red Sea place where they must trust Him by faith to make a way through to bring them to Himself in an intimate, personal relationship. The wilderness is very much like our life on earth where the world is present in every aspect of culture and is the place where God matures us in our intimate relationship with Christ so that we are in the world, but not of the world. It seems we can find ourselves at the Red Sea place more than once as we are faced with impossibilities necessitating a deeper faith and trust where God helps us become who we are and possess all He has given us through the power of the Holy Spirit, breaking us from worldly influences and drawing us closer to Himself. We need to realize the truth of our redemption and relationship with God. In Exodus, God opens up His heart in a way that reveals His passion for His people. He does what it takes to rescue them and bring them to Himself. The beauty is seen in the details. Everything God does is significant. In your study of Exodus, some of the most profound truths God has for you will be seen as you slow down, draw near to Him, and look intently at the details. David, the man after God's own heart discovered a very important truth that will guide you in your study: "The LORD directs the steps of the godly. He delights in every detail of their lives" (Psalm 37:23 NLT). Always remember, dear friend, that God has His eye on you and delights in every detail of your life as well. He has something powerful to say to you, even today, as you live in His word.

The sacred journey in Exodus begins with the journey of one—Moses. Read Exodus 2:1-22, Hebrews 11:23-27, and Acts 7:17-29, and describe the most significant details of Moses' life where you see God's hand at work to save him, protect him, lead him, and guide him.

His birth (Exodus 2:1-10, Acts 7:17-21, Hebrews 11:23)

His early life—the first 40 years (Exodus 2:10-15, Acts 7:21-29, Hebrews 11:24-27)

His next 40 years in the land of Midian (Exodus 2:15-22, Acts 7:29)

2. Read Hebrews 11:24-27 again and note all that Moses did "by faith." Corrie ten Boom, survivor of Ravensbruck concentration camp during World War II, was a passenger on a ship guided by radar. The fog was so thick that they couldn't even see the water. But the radar was able to see past the fog and pick up the shape of another ship nearby. Corrie ten Boom writes, "So, also, is faith the radar that sees reality through the clouds."[1] What realities did Moses see through the clouds?

3. The account in Exodus 2 doesn't give us the names of Moses' family. Read Numbers 26:59 and write out the names of Moses' biological father, mother, brother, and sister.

4. Behind the events of Exodus 2 and the journey of Moses, is a faithful, sovereign God at work. He gave Moses faithful parents who were not afraid and He protected Moses from harm. God is always at work in your life, especially in times of trouble. Read the following verses and write out what you learn about how God works in your life and helps you.

Psalm 31:21

Psalm 34:15-19

Psalm 46:1

Philippians 1:6, 2:13

ADORE GOD IN PRAYER

O my refuge, outside you the waves are high and the winds fierce, but in you I have haven, protection, peace, and blessedness. You are my pavilion, my refuge, my strong tower, the house of my defense, my shield and exceeding great reward. In you I make my refuge.

F.B. MEYER IN DAILY PRAYERS

YIELD YOURSELF TO GOD

"By faith Moses, when he was born, was hid three months of his parents, because they saw he was a proper child; and they were not afraid of the king's commandment."

We have often been furnished with a picture depicting the anxiety with which his parents received their newborn babe, the distress of Amram, and the fears of Jochebed. Such a picture may be true of other Hebrew parents, but it is not true of them. "They were not afraid." When it was announced to Jochebed that she had borne a boy, she was enabled to cast the care of him on God, and to receive the assurance that he should come to no hurt…It all happened according to the mother's faith. The princess, accompanied by a train of maidens, came to the river bank to bathe. She saw the ark among the flags, and sent her maid to get it. In the midst of the little group the lid was carefully lifted, and their eyes were charmed with the sight of the beautiful face…The sudden interposition of Miriam, who had eagerly and breathlessly watched the whole scene, with her naive suggestion of fetching a Hebrew nurse, solved the problem of what should be done with the foundling almost as soon as it could have suggested itself…The child's life was secure beneath the powerful protection of Pharaoh's own daughter, who had said, "Nurse it for me." And the wages she had promised would do more than provide for all their need. God had done "exceedingly abundantly." How long the boy stayed in that lowly home we do not know, but it was long enough to know something of the perils and hardships of his people's lot; to learn those sacred traditions of their past, and to receive into his heart the love of the only God, which was to become the absorbing passion and emphasis of his career.[2]

F.B. Meyer

Enjoy His Presence

God clearly intervened from the beginning of Moses' life. He wove quite a story with Moses' life, even having him spend the first forty years in Pharaoh's court. Because he grew up in Egypt, he had firsthand knowledge of the culture and ways of the people. And because he was able to spend the very first part of his life with his own mother in a family that knew and loved God, he learned all about faith in God. Think about the story of your own life. God is at work in unique ways in you though you may not realize it now. He loves you and wants you for Himself. Behind many seemingly haphazard events is the hand of a faithful God who promises to cause "all things to work together for good to those who love God, to those who are called according to His purpose" (Romans 8:28). Think about all you've learned today. How is your faith these days? Have you learned, like Moses, to see Him who is unseen, and look ahead to your reward? How have you seen the Lord at work in your life, behind the scenes, to help you and guide your life? What is your most significant insight? Write a prayer to the Lord expressing all that is on your heart.

REST IN HIS LOVE

"And we know that God causes all things to work together for good to those who love God, to those who are called according to His purpose" (Romans 8:28).

JESUS ANSWERS YOUR NEED

And answering him, Jesus said, "What do you want me to do for you?" Mark 10:51
West Fork Trail, Sedona, Arizona, USA
Nikon D7000, ISO 100, f11, AEB, Adobe Photoshop, Nik Silver Efex Pro
MYPHOTOWALK.COM—CATHERINEMARTIN.SMUGMUG.COM

GOD KNOWS HIS PEOPLE

So God heard their groaning and God remembered His covenant with Abraham,
Isaac, and Jacob. God saw the sons of Israel, and God took notice of them.

EXODUS 2:24-25

PREPARE YOUR HEART

The defining moment in any person's life comes when God reaches through the heavens to help in the impossible circumstance. There are those times when nothing can explain the turn of events, the open door of opportunity, or abundant provision from an unseen source.

One of the most unforgettable scenes in the movie Ben-Hur occurs when Judah Ben-Hur is a condemned prisoner sentenced to a life of forced labor in the galleys of a ship. He is walking in shackles with other prisoners across the barren hot desert on the way to the harbor. They arrive along the dusty road of the small village of Nazareth. Water is given to the prisoners. But the guard in charge says, "Not for that one." And he points his finger at Judah Ben-Hur. Now imagine the most pitiful scene of a man who can barely stand and finally falls to the ground with heat exhaustion and dehydration. With almost his last breath he cries out, "God help me." A hand with a cup of water reaches down to him. You never see the face of this one who helps. The guard yells to the man, "I said he is not to get any water!" The man stands up tall, with a commanding presence. The guard backs up, gazing into the face of this man who appears to have more power than any in the group. The guard stops, turns, and walks away. Judah Ben-Hur cannot take his eyes off of this one who has helped him. And, of course, it is very clear—as Lew Wallace writes in his book, *Ben-Hur*— "And so, for the first time, Judah and the son of Mary met and parted." The man who had helped him there on the road when there was no one to help was Jesus.

Do you need the help and hope of the Lord in your own life today? Do you need something to stop the tears from falling hard in a broken situation. Oh, dear friend, draw near and ask Him to open your eyes and ears to the hope found in His word today. Write a simple prayer to the Lord expressing all that is on your heart.

READ AND STUDY GOD'S WORD

1. One of the most powerful moments in the book of Exodus occurs when the people of Israel, because of their suffering, cry out for help. Read Exodus 2:23-25 and note everything you learn about God's response to their cry.

2. This moment in the life of Israel is pivotal to the sacred journey in Exodus. When God hears the cries of His people, remembers His covenant, sees them, and takes notice of them, God makes things happen. When you see the Lord and cry out to Him, He hears and answers (Psalm 34:4-6). God has His eye on you. In fact, He promises to counsel you with His eye upon you (Psalm 32:8). And, according to 2 Chronicles 16:9 "the eyes of the LORD move to and fro throughout the earth that He may strongly support those whose heart is completely His." He says, "Can anyone hide from me in a secret place? Am I not everywhere in all the heavens and earth?" (Jeremiah 23:24). Dear friend, God hears you. And He has His eye on you. He promises. In Exodus 2:23-35, there are two special words related to God from these verses that are important to understand. The first of these words is "remembered" from the Hebrew "zakar" and means to express concern for a person and visit that person with gracious love.[3] So when God remembered His covenant with Abraham, Isaac, and Jacob, God wanted us to know everything He does is based on the covenant He makes with His people, and He always keeps His promises that make up that covenant. The fact that He "remembered" His covenant demonstrates His intention to act out of concern and visit the people of Israel with gracious love. He never forgets and His timing is always perfect. Read the following verses and write what happened when God "remembered."

Genesis 8:1

Genesis 30:22

Exodus 6:5-8

3. In Exodus 2:25 "God saw the sons of Israel, and God took notice of them." In this verse, the second special word is the Hebrew "yada," translated "took notice" (NASB) and "concerned" (NIV). This word means to know by experience and relationship. The powerful truth here is that God was intimately involved with His people and knew them first before they knew Him. That means that our knowledge of God always begins with His knowledge of us. Read the following verses and write what you learn about what God knows and what He desires you to know.

Exodus 3:7 (translated "aware" NASB and "concerned" NIV)

Psalm 139:1-5

Psalm 46:10

Jeremiah 9:23-24

ADORE GOD IN PRAYER

In Exodus 2:23-25, one thing is certain. When the people of God were in trouble, they cried out to Him. And He heard and responded to their cries. Will you cry out to Him today and take all your needs to Him? In what way do you need God to "remember" you today i.e. to express concern for you and visit you with gracious love? Write out all your prayer requests on one of the Prayer Pages in the back of this book. Then, pour out your heart to Him in prayer.

YIELD YOURSELF TO GOD

God was closely interested in his people and in the process of making himself known to them…God alone was the Israelite's hope in this situation… The best reading of the original, "God looked on them and made himself known to them," sets the scene for what follows. God was initiating the process of deliverance, and the circumstances of both Moses and Israel were about to change. Implicitly, the theological issue here is not whether or how people suffer; the issue is: does suffering go unnoticed? If it does not—and indeed the one doing the noticing is the true, omnipotent, and loving covenant God—his people can properly surmise that their suffering may well be part of a plan, that it is a suffering with a distinct beginning and end, a hardship understood by and watched over by a sovereign who will not let it continue without good purpose and result.[4]

STUART DOUGLAS IN THE NEW AMERICAN COMMENTARY: EXODUS

God's knowledge of you is based upon His own investigative searching (Psalm 139:1). The underlying Hebrew word for "search" means "to dig." The Lord "digs" into you—not with a careless thrust of a shovel, but with the painstaking sifting of an archaeologist probing the layers of your soul. When His digging into you is done, there's nothing about you He doesn't know.[5]

GEORGE O. WOOD IN A PSALM IN YOUR HEART

What ineffable comfort there is in the thought that our hearts closed to all else, are open to Him! Because, as He can detect the secret source of our disease, He can cure it; and as He can read our secret sorrow, He can apply the healing balm…The All-knowing is also the All-present. We are God-encompassed; God-environed. Behind, that none may attack in the rear. Before, that He may search out the way and meet our foes…Neither change of hemispheres, nor distance, nor darkness, can at all alter the soul's proximity to its ever-present God. What bliss this is to those who know Him as Father and Friend!

F.B. MEYER IN CHOICE NOTES ON THE PSALMS

ENJOY HIS PRESENCE

Have you learned the secret of prayer in your most difficult days, and even in your dark night of the soul? Where do you run first when you are in trouble? Allow the tears to fall, dear friend, but then pray. Cry out to your Lord and pour out your heart to Him. Pray big, not small. These verses in Exodus 2:23-25 teach the powerful truth that prayer is the first action to take, not the last resort. Paul told Timothy, "I urge you, first of all, to pray…" (1 Timothy 2:1 NLT).

Think about all you have learned of your God today. He knew all of the sufferings of His people. He saw every act of oppression and insult that His beloved people experienced. He heard their cries. And He remembered His covenant and all the accompanying promises. And so, He now was ready to carry out His plan for His people. And what a plan it was—more than they could have imagined. And soon His people would discover how much He loved them, had His hand on them, and was resolute and determined to deliver them and bring them to Himself. And the same is true with you, dear friend. Oh, how much God loves you and has designs on you. He is the God who remembers you. And He is faithful to keep all His promises in His Word. Close your time today by writing a prayer to the Lord, thanking Him specifically for those insights that were most significant to you today.

REST IN HIS LOVE

"O LORD, You have searched me and known me" (Psalm 139:1).

THE GOD WHO SEES ME

You are the God who sees me. Genesis 16:13 NLT
Sedona, Arizona, USA

Nikon D7000, ISO 100, f11, AEB, Adobe Photoshop, Nik Silver Efex Pro
MYPHOTOWALK.COM—CATHERINEMARTIN.SMUGMUG.COM

GOD CALLS HIS LEADER

When the LORD saw that he turned aside to look, God called to him from the midst of the bush and said, "Moses, Moses!" And he said, "Here I am."

EXODUS 3:4

PREPARE YOUR HEART

One thing you notice as you read the pages of the Word of God is how often God begins with one person. When God does a powerful work in the lives of His people, He often will call one person to be part of His plan. And that one person will often become a leader of others. Again and again, you see God calling out to that one person. He called Joshua in Joshua 1:7-9, Isaiah in Isaiah 6:1-8, and Jeremiah in Jeremiah 1:4-10. And then, in the New Testament, Jesus called those who would become His disciples. He said, "Follow me and I will make you fishers of men" (Matthew 4:19).

Moses was God's man for His great plan for His people when He remembered His covenant. Just think of Moses' journey. He was saved because his parents had a courageous faith to place him in a position in the Nile River where he could be discovered. And then, he grew up in the palace court of Egypt. He had the finest education and learned all the ways of the world and culture of his day. But then, we learn he found himself faced with a choice. And dear friend, we must understand this choice for ourselves as well. He could have lived as a man of the world all his days. But no, that is not the choice Moses made. We see that "by faith he chose rather to endure ill-treatment with the people of God than to enjoy the passing pleasure of sin" (Hebrews 11:25). This section of Hebrews goes on to reveal the heart of Moses. He was looking to an unseen reward he considered of greater value than all the treasures of Egypt. And so, by faith, he left Egypt. What was in his future? He did not know at that time, but Hebrews 11:27 says that he saw Him who is unseen. So, with his eyes on the Lord, by faith, he launched out in the wilderness and the vast unknown. And oh, how fitting this was for a man who was going to lead the people of God into the wilderness for forty years. What a journey of faith. Where would he go? How would he survive with no visible means of support? These, dear friend, are the questions that come to you in the wilderness. There is much to learn in the wilderness and you will have the opportunity to see this more clearly in Week Five. D.L. Moody said that "Moses spent his first forty years thinking he was somebody. He spent his second forty years learning he was a nobody. He spent his third forty years discovering what God can do with a nobody."

Imagine that you are walking with Moses now into the wilderness of Midian. Oh, dear friend, soon you are going to remove your shoes, for you will be standing on holy ground. Draw near to God now, and ask Him to quiet your heart and focus all your attention on Him as you live in these precious words in Exodus. Prepare your heart with the words of this hymn by Clara Scott.

> Open my eyes, that I may see glimpses of truth You have for me;
> Place in my hands the wonderful key that shall unlock and set me free.
> Silently now I wait for You, Ready, my God, Your will to do;
> Open my eyes, illumine me, Spirit divine!
>
> Open my ears, that I may hear voices of truth so sharp and clear;
> And while the message sounds in my ear, everything else will disappear.
> Silently now I wait for You, Ready, my God, Your will to do;
> Open my ears, illumine me, Spirit divine!
>
> Open my mouth, let me declare, words of assurance everywhere;
> Open my heart, and let me prepare Your lovingkindnesses to share.
> Silently now I wait for You, Ready, my God, Your will to do;
> Open my heart, illumine me, Spirit divine! Amen.
>
> CLARA SCOTT

READ AND STUDY GOD'S WORD

1. Moses left Egypt at the age of 40 and settled as a foreigner in the land of Midian (Acts 7:23-29). Read Exodus 2:15-22 to review where Moses went from Egypt and how he began this new phase of his life that would comprise another 40 years (Acts 7:30). Describe his new life and how it differed from life in Egypt. Note: the land of Midian was located in southeastern Sinai in west central Arabia, and was mostly desert.[6]

2. And now, you are going to walk with Moses to the back side of the desert in Midian. Read Exodus 3:1 and describe where Moses was and what he was doing. Note: Horeb is either an alternate name for Mount Sinai or is in the vicinity of Mount Sinai.

3. Imagine yourself with Moses there at the mountain all alone in the remotest part of the desert. Read Exodus 3:2-6 and describe what God did and said, and how Moses responded.

What God did

What God said

How Moses responded

4. And now, God is going to call Moses to something much greater than himself. Read Exodus 3:6-10 and write what you learn about God, what He is going to do, and what He is calling Moses to do.

What you learn about God

What God is going to do

What God is calling Moses to do

5. Imagine this moment. Moses, hiding his face in his hands, hears God calling him to bring the Israelites out of Egypt (approximately 600,000 to 2,000,000 people). Read Exodus 3:11-12 and write your most significant insights about how Moses responded and what God promised.

Moses' response

God's promise

6. Just think, there was Moses in the wilderness, at the age of 80, tending the flock of Jethro, his father-in-law. Nothing special. Just another day on the back side of the desert. What does this teach you about your own wilderness experiences and what can happen? Think about the promise of Hosea 2:14, "I will lead her into the desert and speak tenderly to her there."

7. Notice that when the bush burned and Moses turned aside to look, God spoke and Moses heard God's Word. In Jeremiah 23:29 God describes His word as a fire. Imagine that the bush is burning even now in the Word of God. How important is it to listen to God in His Word? And what is necessary for a person to turn aside to look so that they can hear God speak in His Word?

ADORE GOD IN PRAYER

Take some time now and pray the words of Clara Scott's hymn "Open My Eyes" from the Prepare Your Heart today.

YIELD YOURSELF TO GOD

The vision came in the midst of common toil, and that is where the Lord delights to give His revelations. He seeks a man who is on the ordinary road, and the Divine fire leaps out at his feet. The mystic ladder can rise from the market place to Heaven. It can connect the realm of drudgery with the realms of grace. My Father God, help me to expect Thee on the ordinary road. I do not ask for sensational happenings. Commune with me through ordinary work and duty. Be my Companion when I take the common journey. Let the humble life be transfigured by Thy presence.

MRS. CHARLES COWMAN IN STREAMS IN THE DESERT

Moses' reply revealed that he was somewhere. Readiness means a right relationship to God and a knowledge of where we are at present. We are so busy telling God where we would like to go. The man or woman who is ready for God and His work is the one who carries off the prize when the summons comes...Readiness for God means that we are ready to do the tiniest little thing or the great big thing, it makes no difference. We have no choice in what we want to do; whatever God's programme may be we are there, ready. When any duty presents itself we hear God's voice as Our Lord heard His Father's voice, and we are ready for it with all the alertness of our love for Him...Be ready for the sudden surprise visits of God. A ready person never needs to get ready. Think of the time we waste trying to get ready when God has called! The burning bush is a symbol of everything that surrounds the ready soul, it is ablaze with the presence of God.[7]

OSWALD CHAMBERS IN MY UTMOST FOR HIS HIGHEST

Moses' stay in Midian not only provided him protection, daily provisions, a place to live, a job, and a wife and family, but it also did much to ready Moses for being Israel's emancipator...The many years spent shepherding the flocks would do much to develop that superior meekness in Moses, and it would give him much quiet time to do some serious thinking and meditating and especially to do some communing with God. It would also help him to become well acquainted with the wilderness through which he must lead the Israelites for many years.[8]

JOHN G. BUTLER IN MOSES, THE EMANCIPATOR OF ISRAEL

ENJOY HIS PRESENCE

The wilderness is where you can most clearly hear from God in His Word. So if you happen to be in a wilderness experience right now, then be encouraged. You can have the great hope of hearing from the Lord as you live in His Word. Remember, the bush is burning even now in His Word. Will you turn aside to look? What is your most significant observation today? What are you learning from your Lord? How do you see His heart for His people in the call of Moses? And how do you see His heart for you? Take some time to look at the devotional photography on this page, then close your quiet time with God in prayer.

REST IN HIS LOVE

"'Does not My word burn like fire?' says the LORD" (Jeremiah 23:29 NLT).

THE CALLING OF GOD

When the LORD saw that he turned aside to look, God called to him. Exodus 3:4
Upper Red Rock Loop, Sedona, Arizona, USA
Nikon D7000, ISO 100, f11, AEB, Adobe Photoshop, Nik Silver Efex Pro
MYPHOTOWALK.COM—CATHERINEMARTIN.SMUGMUG.COM

GOD REVEALS HIS NAME

This is My name forever, and this is My memorial-name to all generations.
EXODUS 3:15

PREPARE YOUR HEART

There is always one question to ask in every circumstance, even in wilderness situations or dark nights of the soul. And that is, "Lord, what is Your name?" God wants you to know Him, personally and intimately, in a vibrant, ongoing, dynamic relationship with Him. He has revealed Himself through His names. He doesn't have just one name, but many names. And He gives you His names through the progressive revelation of His Word that you might know who He is, what He does, and what He says. Every day when you open the Bible and read, you can make new discoveries and look for how God is revealing Himself to you.

What a day it was for Moses when the bush burned there on the mountain in the wilderness. Not only did Moses turn aside to look and hear God speak. But he then asked that one question that took him to a new place in his relationship with God. God told Moses that He was sending him to the sons of Israel to bring them out of Egypt. Moses said, "Now they may say to me, 'What is His name?' What shall I say to them" (Exodus 3:13). Oh what a great question. Moses was actually asking God who He is. And this is the question that leads you to a greater trust in God. For He will reveal Himself to you. And you can find great comfort in the promise, "And those who know Your name will put their trust in You" (Psalm 9:10).

And so today, will you ask God who He is? Will you draw near to God now, and have faith in the promise in James 4:8—"Draw near to God and He will draw near to you." And then, will you answer God's great invitation in Psalm 46:10—"Be still and know that I am God."

READ AND STUDY GOD'S WORD

1. Read Exodus 3:13-15 and the encounter of Moses and God. What did Moses ask and how did God respond?

2. When God revealed Himself in His name, I AM WHO I AM, He spoke His name using Hebrew verbs, not nouns. The Hebrew word translated "I AM" is YHWH, transliterated Yahweh. God was saying "I am the one who always is." "Yahweh is so sacred a word in rabbinical writings that it is distinguished with euphemistic expressions such as 'the name,' 'the unutterable name,' and 'the holy name.' Jewish reverence for Yahweh is so great that authors and writers frequently refrained from putting the name into print or speaking the name aloud."[9] Yahweh is used 6823 times in the Old Testament alone and is rendered LORD, usually in small capital letters, befitting its sacred and personal nature.[10] The original pronunciation for YHWH, known to the Patriarchs and to Moses, has been lost following the destruction in AD 70. Some scholars refer to this name of God as Yahweh and others as Jehovah. Since the construct form Yah is most likely part of the original pronunciation, we will refer to YHWH as Yahweh.

The fact that God's name, Yahweh, is a verb instead of a noun implies that He is everything you need for every circumstance of your life. F.B. Meyer, in *My Daily Homily*, writes that it is as though God is presenting you with a blank check in His name, Yahweh, as the provision for every need you face today. Read the following verses and write out everything you learn about Yahweh (LORD).

Psalm 9:7-10

Psalm 18:1-3

Psalm 27:1

Lamentations 3:21-25

3. In the New Testament we find the Greek words, *ego eimi*, used by the Septuagint (the Greek translation of the Hebrew Old Testament) for I AM. The Greek *ego eimi* is used by Jesus Christ Himself. Read the following verses and write what you learn about Yahweh.

John 8:12

John 8:53-59

4. What is your favorite truth from your time studying Yahweh?

5. How do you think Moses' discovery of God as Yahweh was an encouragement to him? How could this knowledge of God impact Moses' life in the days to come?

ADORE GOD IN PRAYER

Turn to your Prayer pages in the back of this book and write out your deep heart prayer needs to the Lord. Be sure to date each request so you can return to see how God answers each prayer. Be encouraged from the words of David prayed to Yahweh, "In the morning, O LORD, You will hear my voice; in the morning I will order my prayer to You and eagerly watch" (Psalm 5:3). Then, as you think about Moses and his wrestling with the call of God in his life, and the times when you are journeying through the wilderness, pray the words of this prayer: "Lord, I am willing. I am willing to receive what You give. I am willing to lack what You withhold. I am willing to relinquish what You take. I am willing to suffer what You require."[11]

YIELD YOURSELF TO GOD

The word "*Yahweh*" is the most intimate term for the living Lord in the Hebrew vocabulary. God was saying, "Moses, when you stand before those elders of Israel, you let them know that the intimate God of Israel has sent you to be His representative."[12]

CHARLES SWINDOLL IN MOSES

What Moses asked was, "What does Your name mean? What kind of a God are You?" God explained that the name Jehovah [Yahweh] is a dynamic name, based on the Hebrew verb "to be" or "to become." He is the self-existent One who always was, always is, and always will be, the faithful and dependable God who calls Himself "I AM." Centuries later, Jesus would take the name "I AM" and complete it: "I am the bread of life" (John 6:35), "I am the light of the world" (8:12), "I am the true vine" (15:1), and so on.[13]

WARREN WIERSBE IN BE DELIVERED

Think about these words by Hannah Whitall Smith as quoted in *Streams In The Desert*: "In order really to know God, *inward stillness* is absolutely necessary. I remember when I first learned this. A time of great emergency had risen in my life, when every part of my being seemed to throb with anxiety, and when the necessity for immediate and vigorous action seemed overpowering; and yet circumstances were such that I could do nothing, and the person who could, would not stir. For a little while it seemed as if I must fly to pieces with the inward turmoil, when suddenly the still small voice whispered in the depths of my soul, 'Be still, and know that I am God.' The word was with power, and I hearkened. I composed my body to perfect stillness, and I constrained my troubled spirit into quietness, and looked up and waited; and then I did 'know' that it was God, God even in the very emergency and in my helplessness to meet it; and I rested in Him. It was an experience that I would not have missed for worlds; and I may add also, that out of this stillness seemed to arise a power to deal with the emergency, that very soon brought it to a successful issue. I learned then effectually that my 'strength was to sit still.'"

MRS. CHARLES COWMAN IN STREAMS IN THE DESERT

ENJOY HIS PRESENCE

Always remember, "The people who know their God shall be strong, and carry out great exploits" (Daniel 11:32 NKJV). "The name of the LORD is a strong fortress; the godly run to Him and are safe" (Proverbs 18:10 NLT). "Those who know Your name will put their trust in You" (Psalm 9:10). These profound verses demonstrate the priceless value of knowing God's names. Take time every day in your quiet time to ask, "God what is your name? What do You want me to know about who You are, what You do, and what You say?" When you take time to know God, your passion for Him will grow, and you will live out His plan and purpose for your life.

What is your most significant insight from your quiet time today? As you stood with Moses before God at the burning bush and heard Him say His name, how did it impact your life? How does knowing that your God is everything you need for every circumstance of life help you today? How does knowing your God as Yahweh change how you go about your day, deal with difficulties, and relate to other people? Write your thoughts and insights. Write a prayer to Yahweh, your LORD, in worship. Then, take some time with the devotional photography on the next page.

Rest in His Love

"The Lord is my light and my salvation; whom shall I fear? The Lord is the defense of my life; whom shall I dread" (Psalm 27:1)?

Surprising Light Of The Lord

The Light shines in the darkness. John 1:5

Bell Rock-Courthouse Butte, Sedona, Arizona, USA
Nikon D810, ISO 400, f6.3, 1/3200sec, Adobe Photoshop, Nik Silver Efex Pro
MyPhotoWalk.com—Catherinemartin.smugmug.com

GOD DECLARES HIS PROMISE

*So I said, I will bring you up out of the affliction of Egypt to the land of
the Canaanite and the Hittite and the Amorite and the Perizzite and
the Hivite and the Jebusite, to a land flowing with milk and honey.*

EXODUS 3:17

PREPARE YOUR HEART

Corrie ten Boom describes a challenging time of ministry when she was part of a team
reaching out to prisoners at a large prison. The team began their time with a song. The
prisoners screamed and yelled to drown out the music. Then they laughed and made more noise.
The sound was so loud that Corrie prayed to God silently, "Must I speak in this place? I cannot."
Immediately, a promise from God's word came to her mind. "I can do all things through Him
who strengthens me" (Philippians 4:13). She was encouraged by the Lord to not be afraid, but
instead to believe. She began giving her message and the noise increased. Then she described her
time in Ravensbruck concentration camp when she was alone in a cell for four months. The room
got very quiet. Soon more and more of the men behind bars gathered to hear Corrie's message.
She spoke for almost an hour in that quiet room as everyone listened. She knew the love of God
was at work. Six men gave their lives to Christ that day.[14]

What gave Corrie strength more than anything? A promise from God applied to her heart
through the power of the Holy Spirit. Oh how powerful are the promises of God! Corrie ten
Boom was a master at relying on God's promises in every situation. And how did she become
so practiced with the promises of God? Through the many wildernesses and dark nights of the
soul in her life. She wrote, "Do you ask, 'Is Jesus able?' I can say, 'Yes, and you have the victory
through Him.' Don't believe what your emotions tell you. Believe what God's Word tells you."[15]

The book of Exodus is filled with promises from God. These promises are the "I will's" of
Scripture—all God says He will do. And those "I will's" are the secret to hope, courage, trust, and
revival as you walk with God.

Draw near to God now, and ask Him to speak to you from His promises today. Then, meditate
on the words of this hymn, "Go To The Deeps Of God's Promise," written by Carrie E. Breck
(1855-1934), author of more than 1400 hymns.

Go to the deeps of God's promise;
Ask freely of Him, and receive;
All good may be had for the asking,
If, seeking, you truly believe.

Refrain
Go to the deeps of God's promise;
There's wideness of meaning untold
In the promises given His people,
And the treasures they ever unfold.

Go to the deeps of God's promise;
And claim whatsoever ye will;
The blessing of God will not fail thee,
His Word He will surely fulfill.
Refrain

READ AND STUDY GOD'S WORD

1. This week you have seen what happens when God "remembers" and how He visits His people with gracious love. You've witnessed the birth of Moses and the early years, and learned that behind these life events were "by faith" decisions as seen in Hebrews 11:24-27. It was in the wilderness experience of Moses that a bush began to burn. And when Moses turned aside to look, God called him by name. It was then that God revealed His plan for His people and called Moses to be part of His work. He told Moses His most intimate name, Yahweh. These are all things that happen when God "remembers." And now, God not only gives Moses His name, Yahweh, but then gives him a list of promises that Moses can stand on. It is one thing to know God's name. But now, Moses learns God's promises and begins to learn to trust God. Read Exodus 3:16-22 and write out all that God promises about Himself and what He will do.

2. God made amazing promises and was about to do something powerful and magnificent in rescuing His people from the Egyptians. Behind everything you read in Exodus, there is something very important to understand about the heart of God—His passionate love for His people. You saw this in Week One, but it is important to see these truths again. Read Deuteronomy 7:6-9 and write what you learn about God.

3. God has given you numerous promises throughout His Word. Read the following verses in the Psalms and underline those words and phrases that are significant to you about God's Word and His promises.

"The LORD's promises are pure, like silver refined in a furnace purified seven times over" (Psalm 12:6 NLT).

"God's way is perfect. All the LORD's promises prove true. He is a shield for all who look to Him for protection" (Psalm 18:30 NLT).

"He will cover you with His feathers. He will shelter you with His wings. His faithful promises are your armor and protection" (Psalm 91:4 NLT).

"Remember Your promise to me; it is my only hope. Your promise revives me; it comforts me in all my troubles" (Psalm 119:49-50 NLT).

"I bow before Your holy Temple as I worship. I praise Your name for Your unfailing love and faithfulness; for Your promises are backed by all the honor of Your name" (Psalm 138:2 NLT).

"For Your kingdom is an everlasting kingdom. You rule throughout all generations. The LORD always keeps His promises; He is gracious in all He does" (Psalm 145:13 NLT).

"But joyful are those who have the God of Israel as their helper, whose hope is in the LORD their God. He made heaven and earth, the sea, and everything in them. He keeps every promise forever" (Psalm 146:5-6 NLT).

4. You have read about the power of God's promises today. Look up the following verses and write out what God is promising to you.

Matthew 11:28-30

Ephesians 3:20

Philippians 4:13

Philippians 4:19

Hebrews 13:5-6

ADORE GOD IN PRAYER

Thank God for His promises in your life. Then, pray through those promises that are most significant to you today as you bring your praises and requests before Him.

YIELD YOURSELF TO GOD

"My expectation is from Him" (Psalm 62:5). It is the believer's privilege to use this language. If he is looking for aught from the world, it is a poor "expectation" indeed. But if he looks to God for the supply of his wants, whether in temporal or spiritual blessings, his "expectation" will not be a vain one. Constantly he may draw from the bank of faith, and get his need supplied out of the riches of God's lovingkindness. This I know, I had rather have God for my banker than all the Rothschilds. My Lord never fails to honour his promises; and when we bring them to his throne, he never sends them back unanswered. Therefore I will wait only at his door, for he ever opens it with the hand of munificent grace. At this hour I will try him anew.

CHARLES HADDON SPURGEON

It is the everlasting faithfulness of God that makes a Bible promise "exceeding great and precious." Human promises are often worthless. Many a broken promise has left a broken heart. But since the world was made, God has never broken a single promise made to one of His trusting children.

WILLIAM GURNALL

ENJOY HIS PRESENCE

Do you see how God revealed Himself to Moses in the wilderness and gave Him magnificent promises that he could stand on in the face of any future challenge? Soon Moses is going to come down from the mountain in obedience to his call from God. And he will face much adversity and many tests of faith, leading him to a greater trust in God. According to Numbers 12:3, Moses "was very humble, more than any man who was on the face of the earth." A great view of God brings a man or woman low to the ground in humble worship. Over the course of his life, Moses would never forget that day on the mountain when the bush burned and God spoke. Your view of God and your growing relationship with Him will give you a deeper trust in Him as you face your own adversity and tests of faith. Think about the promises you read today. What promise does God want you to hold on to as you walk with Him today? As you close your quiet time with the Lord, what is the most significant truth you have learned today from the Lord? Write it out and then thank the Lord for all He is teaching you.

Rest in His Love

"Remember Your promise to me; it is my only hope. Your promise revives me; it comforts me in all my troubles" (Psalm 119:49-50 NLT).

FAITHFUL PROMISES

The LORD always keeps His promises. Psalm 145:13 NLT
Bell Rock, Sedona, Arizona, USA
Nikon D800E, ISO 100, f16, 1/15sec, Adobe Photoshop, Nik Silver Efex Pro
MYPHOTOWALK.COM—CATHERINEMARTIN.SMUGMUG.COM

DEVOTIONAL READING
BY CHARLES SWINDOLL

DEAR FRIEND,

This week has been a deep time of study and learning about what happens when God "remembers." Take some time now to write about all that you have learned this week. What have you learned about God and His passion for His people that draws you to Him in love and trust? What has been most significant to you? Close by writing a prayer to the Lord.

What were your most meaningful discoveries this week as you spent time with the Lord?

Most meaningful insight:

Most meaningful devotional reading:

Most meaningful verse:

As you think about all that you have learned this week, meditate on these words by Charles Swindoll: "The Lord was reassuring Moses, 'I've been watching this situation. I'm aware of what's happening. I've seen My people weeping at night. I've heard the crack of the whip and the cries of the little ones. I've seen the bodies along the road, or flung into the Nile like so many beasts of burden. None of it escapes my notice. Now, behold, the cry of the sons of Israel has come to Me; furthermore, I have seen the oppression with which the Egyptians are oppressing them' (Exodus 3:9). God knows, right down to the final nub, exactly where you are in life. He sees. He cares. He is aware. And best of all, He is touched by it."[16]

CHARLES SWINDOLL IN MOSES

Charles Swindoll describes God's choice of Moses. He writes: "What was God's larger message to Moses in that moment? Release your imagination for a few moments. It might have included some thoughts such as these: 'I want use you, Moses. Stand still, and let Me set you on fire!'…You have to be burnable. God is looking for flammable bushes…The truth is, any old bush will do as long as God is in the bush.' That's what He was saying to Moses. 'I want you to burn for Me as no man has burned before. '"[17]

CHARLES SWINDOLL IN MOSES

Viewer Guide
❧ WEEK TWO ❧

Living In The Audience Of One

In our time together in this message, we are going to look at the life of Moses and how he met God in Exodus 3:1-10 and learned to live in the audience of One. Our goal is to learn from Moses how we can cultivate a life in the audience of One.

"When the LORD saw that he turned aside to look, God called to him from the midst of the bush…" (Exodus 3:4).

Every life and ministry begins and continues in one place — in the audience of One — where the focus of life is on an intimate, ongoing, vibrant relationship with God that is nurtured and cultivated through quiet time alone with Him.

How to cultivate a life in the audience of One

1. Turn aside to _____ at the Lord. Exodus 3:3

2. Listen to the Lord and _____ what He has to say to you. Exodus 3:4

3. Remove your _____. Exodus 3:5

4. Share God's _____. Exodus 3:7-9

5. Hear and respond to God's _____ in your life. Exodus 3:10

6. _____ honestly with God. Exodus 3:11

7. Hold on to God's _____. Exodus 3:12

8. Ask one question from God. What is Your _____. Exodus 3:13

9. _____ God more and more as He reveals Himself to you. Exodus 3:14

10. Live according to God's _____ perspective. Exodus 3:16-20

The eternal perspective is the ability to see all of life from God's point of view, and to have what you see affect how you live in the present.

Video messages are available on DVDs or as Digital M4V Video. Audio messages are available as Digital MP3 Audio. Visit the Quiet Time Ministries Online Store at www.quiettime.org.

THAT ALL MAY KNOW

If men know God, it is because He has made Himself known to them. This knowledge is due to what He does, not to what men themselves achieve…If man has anything of God, he has received it from God, who communicates Himself in love and grace…God speaks, He appears, man listens and beholds. God brings Himself nigh to men; He enters into a covenant or personal relation with them; He lays commands on them…The Unseen manifests itself before them, and they know it.[1]

A.B. DAVIDSON

HE GIVES YOU HOPE

So the people believed; and when they heard that the LORD was concerned about the sons of Israel and that He had seen their affliction, then they bowed low and worshipped.

Exodus 4:31

PREPARE YOUR HEART

What is this sacred journey in Exodus all about? While it involves the people of Israel and God's rescue and redemption of them, it also involves you. Paul tells us in 1 Corinthians 10:11 that the things that happened to the people of Israel "happened to them as an example, and they were written for our instruction, upon whom the ends of the ages have come." He makes a similar statement in 1 Corinthians 10:6 where he concludes, "Now these things happened as examples for us…" This means that the events in Exodus are not only history, but were actually written down and included in Scripture for our own instruction. This instruction includes who God is, what He does, and what He says. Ultimately, God can use what we learn in Exodus to literally transform our lives. The Holy Spirit takes the Word of God and applies it to our hearts and minds, and uses it to change us, making us more and more like Christ.

This application of Old Testament truths in our lives is important to emphasize. As you read and study, always ask God what He wants you to know, what He wants you to learn, and how He wants to apply it to your life. Good rules of interpretation are imperative and must include the whole counsel of God's Word. So as we study Exodus, we will also include important New Testament verses that will help reveal what God is teaching us in His Word. Draw near to the Lord now and ask Him to speak to you in His Word.

READ AND STUDY GOD'S WORD

1. Moses is now standing in the presence of Yahweh and has just received the promises and the plan of what God is going to do for His people. He also has heard the call of God and how God wants to use Him. What is Moses' response? Read Exodus 4:1 and record your most significant observation.

2. How does God respond to Moses' question? Read Exodus 4:2-9 and write your insights about the signs God gives to Moses. What is the ultimate goal with the signs?

3. God is resolute and steadfast in His love and His plan of rescue for His people. Nothing is going to deter God in carrying out His plan, not even a person's fears, excuses, or objections. What a comfort, especially if we are overcome with fear and worry today. In Exodus 4 God's determination is clear in His responses to Moses' early objections. Interestingly, in the beginning Moses protested with a number of questions and excuses as to why he should not be God's choice and why the plan of God was seemingly flawed. You will read them in the next number of chapters, but then, almost suddenly, you notice that Moses no longer wrestles with God about His plan. Why? Because Moses has seen God in action, fulfilling His promises and displaying His power, and as a result, he trusts God in a new and deeper way. And so it is with you. The more you see God in action, responding to your prayers, fulfilling His promises in your life, the more you will be filled with belief in Him. You will find hope in His promises. And you will learn to "trust in the LORD with all your heart and lean not on your own understanding" (Proverbs 3:5).

Moses begged God not to choose him because he wasn't eloquent in speech. How in the world could he possibly take God's message to the people of Israel or to Pharaoh (Exodus 4:10)? Read Exodus 4:10-17 and take note of the exchange between Yahweh and Moses. What is your favorite promise from God in these verses and how would such a promise give hope and confidence to Moses?

4. God gave the vision to Moses on the mountain. And there on the mountain alone in the presence of Yahweh, it would be easier to have faith in all God promises. But then there is the day when we come down from the mountain into the valley to live by faith in what God has shown us. Oswald Chambers makes the following observation about the mountain and the valley: "If we prefer to loll on the mount and live in the memory of the vision, we will be of no use actually in

the ordinary stuff of which human life is made up. We have to learn to live in reliance on what we saw in the vision, not in ecstasies and conscious contemplation of God, but to live in actualities in the light of the vision until we get to the veritable reality."[2] Moses came down from the mountain and went back to his home. Read Exodus 4:18-23 and note how Moses responds to God's plan and promises. And observe the heart, passion, and purpose of God for His people.

Moses' response to God (Exodus 4:18-20)

God's passion for His people (Exodus 4:21-23)

God's purpose for His people (Exodus 4:23)

5. Obedience to God is imperative in the life of those who are His leaders. Nowhere was this more true than with Moses. In Exodus 4:24-26 there is a seemingly strange meeting between God and Moses. This meeting has to do with circumcision, part of God's covenant with Abraham (Genesis 17:9-14, 23-27). Dr. Ronald Youngblood explains, "Before Moses could return to Egypt to rescue the covenant people as their acknowledged leader, he himself must obey the covenant in every detail."[3] Zipporah, the wife of Moses, understood this, and used a flint knife to cut off her son's foreskin. As you read Exodus 4:24-26, think about how God sees everything. Nothing escapes His notice in your life. Everything is important to Him. As you read about this event, how important is our obedience to God? Where do you need to be obedient to Him today?

6. Think now about the people of Israel. Remember where they are right now. Enslaved and oppressed in Egypt, they are suffering greatly at the hands of taskmasters. Their suffering was so bitter that they cried out in desperation to God. They had no idea of God's plan that is beginning to unfold behind the scenes. And at the appointed time, God's perfect time, He is going to act.

And now it begins. Read Exodus 4:27-31. How did the elders of the people of Israel respond and what was it that meant so much to them?

7. You can just imagine how the Word of God spread among the people of Israel, "from hut to hut, and from slave to slave among the brick kilns" according to F.B. Meyer. And how did they respond? The people believed according to Exodus 4:31. That word, "believed," in Hebrew is "aman" and means assurance in the sense of receiving something as true and sure. They had a new certainty and confidence, something they had not experienced perhaps ever before in their lives because of their oppression and slavery. In the New Testament, Hebrews 11:1 defines faith as "the assurance of things hoped for, the conviction of things not seen." In Exodus 4:31, the people learned that God was concerned about them and that He had seen all their affliction. They took God at His Word, bowed low and worshipped God. This was a new day for the people. It was a day of hope because they had received the promises from God and believed those promises. God wants you to know this day of hope as well. We learn from Romans 15:4 "whatever was written in earlier times was written for our instruction, so that through perseverance and the encouragement of the Scriptures we might have hope." Your God is a God of hope, and wants to "fill you with all joy and peace in believing, so that you will abound in hope by the power of the Holy Spirit" (Romans 15:13). In light of what you see in their new day of hope, how do you need hope today, and what promise made to them about God can be a source of hope for you?

ADORE GOD IN PRAYER

Pray the prayer of F.B. Meyer today remembering that God sees you, knows you, is concerned about you, and loves you.

> Father, you have loved us; you love us now; you will love us forever. Your love passes knowledge. It is like a warm, sunlit ocean enfolding the tiny islet of my life; I swim in it, but can never reach its limits. I thank you for the depth and length of your love.

YIELD YOURSELF TO GOD

Meditate on these words by H.E. Govan in his book, *Discoveries of God*, about the ramifications of who God has revealed Himself to be in the name Yahweh (or Jehovah) and think about how Moses and the children of Israel could have hope because of who He is—and how you also can have hope in Him:

> This name, Jehovah [Yahweh], in all significance, is God's memorial, God's "forget-me-not." Let our faith treasure it and hold it fast against all the World's attempts to filch it from us. He is the God of the blank cheque; we shall never be confronted by a claim that He cannot meet. Through all life's years, with all their needs, His wealth is open to our demands if only these are made within the terms of His will. Eternity itself will furnish us with ever-new discoveries of His sufficiency.[4]

H.E. GOVAN IN STUDIES IN THE SACRED NAME

> It is astonishing—something beyond human conception, this "comfort of the Scriptures!" We have all seen saints poor in purse, accounted nothing at all by men, and perhaps suffering constant physical pain, sad bereavement of loved ones, and complete lack of understanding by other professing Christians: yet comforted by poring over the Scriptures! Hearts happy and hopeful, despite it all! You can step from any state of earthly misery into the glorious halls of heavenly peace and comfort! Praise God for this…It is ever good to be going over God's dealings, not only with Christ, but with His Old Testament saints; marking how He is continually bringing them into hard places, where they learn to trust Him more!

WILLIAM NEWELL IN ROMANS VERSE-BY-VERSE

> God keeps His choicest cordials for our deepest faintings.

MRS. CHARLES COWMAN IN STREAMS IN THE DESERT

> The LORD is God. Underlying the universe and your own personal world is His reality. You have a floor of hope, a foundation of sureness. No matter what stage you are passing through, whether you are at the peak or in the pit, the Lord reigns eternal.[5]

GEORGE O. WOOD IN A PSALM IN YOUR HEART

ENJOY HIS PRESENCE

How have you seen that you can have hope in God by what you learned about Him today? Close by writing a prayer to Him expressing all that is on your heart.

REST IN HIS LOVE

"For whatever was written in earlier times was written for our instruction, so that through perseverance and the encouragement of the Scriptures we might have hope" (Romans 15:4).

ALWAYS HOPE

I have hope in Him. Lamentations 3:24
Oak Creek Canyon, Sedona, Arizona, USA
Nikon D800E, ISO 1000, f11, 1/25sec, Adobe Photoshop, Nik Silver Efex Pro
MYPHOTOWALK.COM—CATHERINEMARTIN.SMUGMUG.COM

HE DEFENDS YOU

Let My people go...
EXODUS 5:1

PREPARE YOUR HEART

Is your heart beating just a bit faster right about now on this sacred journey in Exodus? Now you will see your God in action. Oh, what an amazing day it is when you see God step out of heaven and accomplish a miraculous rescue. David, the man after God's own heart, described his own rescue in Psalm 18 when he wrote, "He sent from on high, He took me; He drew me out of many waters. He delivered me from my strong enemy, and from those who hated me, for they were too mighty for me" (Psalm 18:16-17).

The people of Israel are about to experience a rescue of epic proportions, one that can only be accomplished by Yahweh. How else could approximately 600,000 to 2,000,000 people who are enslaved by the powerful Pharaoh and the Egyptians be set free? In Exodus 5-12 we are going to see God step in and rescue His people. The battle includes plagues, signs, and wonders. In our study of this section, we will look at specific repeated phrases and themes that help us see the greatness and glory of our God.

Are you in a place where you need God's rescue? Do you feel as though everything is against you even now? Have you been living in despair and discouragement, where you have given up on God? You can know that your hope is in Him alone. He alone is your rock and your salvation (Psalm 62:5-6). Dear friend, take heart, for today you are going to see that God is your defense. And He is the One who will deliver you. Turn to Psalm 18:1-19 and pray through these words, asking God to quiet your heart that you may realize that He is your defender and your deliverer.

READ AND STUDY GOD'S WORD

1. God told Moses to go to Pharaoh with His words. Imagine this scene. Pharaoh is the ruler of the Egyptians and the most powerful man in the world. No one was greater than Pharaoh. And his word ruled. If he commanded it, it was done. God gave Moses His words to speak to Pharaoh. Read the following verses and write what God wanted and why. (Note: Tr. "Let my people go, that they may worship me" NIV, "Let My people go, that they may serve Me" NASB).

Exodus 5:1

Exodus 6:11

Exodus 7:16 (see also in 8:1, 20, 9:1, 13, 10:3)

2. Now a great battle takes place between Pharaoh and God. Can you imagine a man of any stature or earthly power deciding to take on Yahweh, the God of all creation? Look at the following verses and write what you learn about Pharaoh and his response to God. Some of Pharaoh's responses occur after plagues sent to convince him of God's power. We will look at those plagues in more detail later.

Exodus 5:2-9

Exodus 7:10-14

Exodus 8:32

Exodus 9:35

Exodus 10:27-29

3. In Exodus 7:3-4 God told Moses, "But I will harden Pharaoh's heart that I may multiply My signs and My wonders in the land of Egypt. When Pharaoh does not listen to you, then I will lay my hand on Egypt and bring out My hosts, My people the sons of Israel, from the land of Egypt by great judgments." Dr. Ronald Youngblood points out in his commentary on Exodus that this hardening of Pharaoh's heart has been a subject of theological debate for centuries. He writes:

> God, though sovereign, does not violate a person's free will. Exodus tells us that God hardened the pharaoh's heart, but it also tells us that the pharaoh hardened his own heart and did so willfully and repeatedly…God, on the basis of His foreknowledge, predicted (4:21; 7:3) and announced that He would harden the pharaoh's heart, but only after the pharaoh had hardened his own heart (the next ten references)… In the pharaoh's case God foreknew that Egypt's king would harden his heart, and the pharaoh proceeded to do so—knowingly, willfully, and sinfully (Exodus 9:34). God then confirmed the pharaoh's action through His own judicial hardening of the pharaoh's heart. Paul reasoned that God hardened the pharaoh's heart in a free and sovereign manner but not in a capricious or arbitrary manner (Romans 9:14-18).[6]

Because Pharaoh's heart was hardened, everything escalated, including the signs and wonders performed by God. We see in Exodus 7:3-4 that God wanted to multiply His signs and wonders in the land of Egypt. What do you think this demonstration of signs and wonders by God would mean to Pharaoh and the Egyptians? Read the words of Pharaoh's servants spoken to Pharaoh in Exodus 10:7 for insight into the impact of God's power on display in Egypt.

4. From these verses in Exodus you can see that God is serious about His defense of you. When He says, "Let My people go," He means it. Read the following verses and underline those words and phrases that help you understand more clearly how He defends you and is your deliverer.

"He found them in a desert land, in an empty, howling wasteland. He surrounded them and watched over them; He guarded them as He would guard His own eyes.

Like an eagle that rouses her chicks and hovers over her young, so He spread His wings to take them up and carried them safely on His pinions" (Deuteronomy 32:10-11 NLT).

"God is to us a God of deliverances; and to God the Lord belong escapes from death" (Psalm 68:20).

"The Lord is my strength and my defense; he has become my salvation" (Psalm 118:14 NIV).

"But the LORD is with me like a dread champion" (Jeremiah 20:11).

"He who touches you touches the apple of His eye (Zechariah 2:8).

"If God is for us, who is against us…in all these things we overwhelmingly conquer through Him who loved us" (Romans 8:31, 37)

ADORE GOD IN PRAYER

Talk with God about His defense of His people and His defense of you. Take each one of the verses on this page and pray them back to the Lord, personalizing them, and thanking God for who He is in your life. For example, "Lord, thank You that You are with me like a dread champion and that the one who touches me touches the apple of Your eye." Then, lay every need and desire before Him. Pour out your heart to Him today.

YIELD YOURSELF TO GOD

It is always our peril to think that the visible field reveals all the factors in the campaign. We are bondslaves to our sight, and we are therefore its victims. We make a survey of our circumstances, and we are appalled because the opposing forces appear overwhelming. We do not see the armies of the air, the invisible legions which fill the mountains with their horses and chariots. We leave out the hosts of the Lord…When we go out upon a righteous way, even though our enemies are massed in fierce hostility, the mountains shall be full of invisible horses and chariots, for the Lord of Hosts shall be with us, the God of Jacob shall be our refuge.[7]

JOHN HENRY JOWETT IN THE EAGLE LIFE

ENJOY HIS PRESENCE

Today in the sacred journey in Exodus, you had the opportunity to see firsthand the heart of God for His people, when He said again and again to Pharaoh, "Let My people go." This is God's resolute heart and His determination to rescue His people and set His people free. But there is something more to notice here. Again and again, God says, "Let My people go that they may worship me" (NIV) and "Let My people go that they may serve me" (NASB). His words imply that while His people were in Egypt enslaved to the Egyptians and controlled by their evil worldly ways, they could not serve God in the way He intended or worship Him in the way He desired. And in the same way, the things that enslave us and hold us captive are keeping us from serving the Lord and worshiping Him. Think about it. If you are held captive by something or someone, you are not able to serve the Lord using your gifts given by the Holy Spirit. Someone's actions or something else may be inhibiting the free move of the Holy Spirit. This oppression can be present in the form of sin. It can be a fascination with the things of the world including money and possessions that have a hold on you. But it can also be at work in the actions of people against us such as rejection, bullying, shaming, or even persecution to exercise power and achieve a particular agenda. Be aware that these things are all around us in the world and even in the church. The enemy wants to keep you oppressed, discouraged, afraid, and defeated. The Lord wants your freedom to love and serve Him. So when you cry out to Him, He will rescue you in His way and in His time according to His plan and will for your life. When the Lord sets you free, He does it with the intention of giving you a new ability to love and serve Him. God is faithful to convict of sin through the power of the Holy Spirit, so that you might walk in newness of life. Sometimes God will rescue you by closing a door to one thing in order to open another in a new direction. Other times He works an absolute miracle with His mighty hand in your life and you will know that He is the LORD accomplishing a mighty work. Always remember that God is sovereign, man's actions play into the hands of God, and God causes all things to work together for good to those who love Him and are called according to His purpose (Romans 8:28). Nothing can come against you that has more power than the LORD your God. "Greater is He who is in you than he who is in the world" (1 John 4:4). Count on that promise today.

Where are you, dear friend? How do you need a rescue today? Will you cry out to God? What is your most significant insight from your study and how does it help you grow in an intimate relationship with your Lord?

REST IN HIS LOVE

"The LORD is my strength and my defense; he has become my salvation" (Psalm 118:14 NIV).

HOLDING ON TO THE LORD

The LORD is my strength and my defense. Psalm 118:14 NIV
Sedona, Arizona, USA
Nikon D810, ISO 400, f5.6, 1/1600sec, Adobe Photoshop, Nik Silver Efex Pro
MYPHOTOWALK.COM—CATHERINE MARTIN.SMUGMUG.COM

HE IS THE LORD YOUR GOD

Then I will take you for My people, and I will be your God; and you shall know that I am the LORD *your God, who brought you out from under the burdens of the Egyptians.*

EXODUS 6:7

PREPARE YOUR HEART

Holy ground may be just a step away from where you are right now. For wherever God is, that place is filled with His presence. Then, you are standing on holy ground. One night Jacob dreamed about a ladder reaching from earth to heaven with angels of God ascending and descending on it. Yahweh stood above the ladder, and spoke, promising He would be with Jacob wherever he went, and that He would bring Jacob back to the land. When Jacob awoke from his sleep he said, "Surely the LORD is in this place, and I did not know it" (Genesis 28:16). Knowing that God was with him gave Jacob strength for the long journey ahead and trust that the Lord would watch over him. Realizing the presence of the Lord has altered the course of countless lives throughout history. John Newton realized the existence and power of God while on a slave ship, gave his life to the Lord, and wrote the blessed hymn, "Amazing Grace." C.S. Lewis spent years as an atheist, but came to the realization that God existed and knelt and gave his life to Christ. In his book, *The Problem of Pain*, C.S. Lewis talked about the value of trials in giving us a new awareness of the presence of God. He wrote, "God whispers to us in our pleasures, speaks to our conscience, but shouts in our pains: it is His megaphone to rouse a dead world." Today, as you draw near to the Lord, ask Him to take you onto holy ground and show you that He is the LORD your God.

READ AND STUDY GOD'S WORD

1. Have you ever noticed that way up seems to be down and that sometimes things get worse before they get better. Once Moses went to Pharaoh with the words of God, "Let My people go," things became worse for the people of Israel. Pharaoh lashed out and made their circumstances move from difficult to desperate and finally, to impossible. But with God nothing is impossible. And you, dear friend, are going to develop a passion for the impossible. Read Exodus 5:19-23 and describe how Moses must have felt in these moments in light of what he said to God.

2. And now, God expands on His plan and purpose for His people in His response to Moses. Read Exodus 6:1-13 and note how many times God says "I am the LORD." Then list the promises God makes in response to Moses' cry of discouragement to the LORD.

3. Read the following verses and note all the people God wants to know that He is the LORD.

Exodus 6:6, 6:29, 7:5, 7:16-17

4. What does it mean to know that He is the LORD? Read Exodus 9:14-16 for insight and write your observations. How do demonstrations of God's power help a person know that He is the LORD?

5. God wants you to know that He is the LORD your God. Read Exodus 6:7 again. What does this verse teach you about the kind of relationship God desires with you?

6. In Jeremiah 9:23-24, God says, "Let not a wise man boast of his wisdom, and let not the mighty man boast of his might, let not a rich man boast of his riches; but let him who boasts boast of this, that he understands and knows Me, that I am the LORD who exercises lovingkindness, justice and righteousness on earth; for I delight in these things." How are you living your life? Do you value what God values? Is your greatest desire to know the Lord? Jesus Himself said, "This is eternal life, that they may know You, the only true God, and Jesus Christ whom You have sent" (John 17:3). Write your thoughts from all you have learned today about the heart of God and His passion for His people.

ADORE GOD IN PRAYER

Pray through the following prayer by A.W. Tozer, thinking through every word and what it means for you in your relationship with the Lord: "Father, I want to know Thee, but my cowardly heart fears to give up its toys. I cannot part with them without inward bleeding, and I do not try to hide from Thee the terror of the parting. I come trembling, but I do come. Please root from my heart all those things which I have cherished so long and which have become a very part of my living self, so that Thou mayest enter and dwell there without a rival. Then shalt Thou make the place of Thy feet glorious. Then shall my heart have no need of the sun to shine in it, for Thyself wilt be the light of it, and there shall be no night there. In Jesus' name. Amen."[8]

YIELD YOURSELF TO GOD

God's way is to bring men to an end of themselves before he arises to their help. Our efforts to deliver ourselves only end in increasing our perplexities. The quota of bricks is doubled; the burdens augment; the strength of our purpose is broken; we are brought to the edge of despair. Probably this was the darkest hour in the life of the great leader (Exodus 5:22-23). But from all the obloquy [blame] that was heaped on him, he took refuge in God. There is no other refuge for a limited man than "to return unto the Lord," v.22. Return unto the Lord with your story of failure. Return unto him for fresh instructions! Return unto him with your appeal for his interposition [intervention]! Be perfectly natural with your Heavenly Father! Humble yourself under his mighty hand! Even dare to reason with him, saying: "Why!" Then the Lord will say to you, as to Moses: "Now thou shalt see what I will do."

F.B. MEYER IN THE DEVOTIONAL COMMENTARY

ENJOY HIS PRESENCE

And now, dear friend, we shall see what God will do. He is the LORD our God! Are you ready to see the God of the impossible at work? And are you ready to grow in your own passion for the impossible as you watch God do what only He can do? There comes a point in time where enough is enough and God is going to display His power and glory in a supernatural way. He is going to accomplish a great rescue and do something that will clearly be His work in the midst of impossible circumstances and powerful enemies. What do you see about the heart of God and

His great love for you in all you have studied and how does it encourage you to know and trust Him? Close by writing a prayer expressing all that is on your heart.

REST IN HIS LOVE

"This is eternal life, that they may know You, the only true God, and Jesus Christ whom You have sent" (John 17:3).

THE ONLY TRUE GOD

That they may know You, the only true God. John 17:3
Sedona, Arizona, USA
Nikon D810, ISO 1000, f5.6, 1/2000sec, Adobe Photoshop, Nik Silver Efex Pro
MYPHOTOWALK.COM—CATHERINEMARTIN.SMUGMUG.COM

HE FIGHTS YOUR BATTLE

For this time I will send all My plagues on you and your servants and your
people, so that you may know that there is no one like Me in all the earth.

Exodus 9:14

PREPARE YOUR HEART

Samuel Trevor Francis was born in 1834 in London, and grew up in the city of Hull along the English coast. When he moved to London to work, he struggled spiritually and knew things just weren't right in his life. One night while walking home from work, he crossed the Hungerford Bridge to the south of the Thames. It was winter and the wind was raging and rain was falling hard. He stood at the bridge in the midst of the storm and watched the mighty power of the flowing dark waters. He was in such despair he was tempted to throw himself into the water. And then, the thought came to him, "Do you believe in the Lord Jesus Christ?" Immediately, he prayed, "Yes, I do believe" and at once he trusted in Christ as his personal Savior. Life changed dramatically for him as he was filled with a passion to serve the Lord. He wrote hymns, traveled around the world, and preached outside in the open air for the next seventy-three years of his life. One of his most memorable hymns is "O the Deep, Deep Love of Jesus," an incredible picture of the power of God's love.

Open your quiet time with the Lord meditating on the words of this beautiful hymn. If you know the melody, you may even want to sing these words to the Lord.

> O the deep, deep love of Jesus, vast, unmeasured boundless, free!
> Rolling as a mighty ocean in its fullness over me!
> Underneath me, all around me, is the current of Thy love—
> Leading, onward, leading homeward, to Thy glorious rest above!
>
> O the deep, deep love of Jesus—spread His praise from shore to shore!
> How He loveth, ever loveth, changeth never, nevermore!
> How He watches o'er His loved ones, died to call them all His own;
> How for them He intercedeth, watcheth o'er them from the throne!

O the deep, deep love of Jesus, love of every love the best!
'Tis an ocean full of blessing ,'Tis a haven giving rest!
O the deep, deep love of Jesus—'Tis a heaven of heavens to me;
And it lifts me up to glory, for it lifts me up to Thee!

SAMUEL TREVOR FRANCIS

READ AND STUDY GOD'S WORD

1. As you continue this sacred journey in Exodus, take a moment to put yourself in the position of the people of Israel. There they are in Egypt, living with the promise of God's rescue, yet still they are enslaved and suffering. Perhaps they are afraid of the future, moving from the security of the known to the insecurity of the unknown. Maybe they are frustrated, anxious, and discouraged as they still feel trapped in an impossible situation. In the meantime, God is going to rescue them and is carrying out His plan, whether they realize it or not. Summarize what has occurred behind the scenes, so to speak, with Yahweh, Moses, and Pharaoh in Exodus 5-6.

2. Now God promised in Exodus 7:3 that He would multiply His signs and wonders in the land of Egypt. Read Exodus 7:4-5. What is God promising to do here?

3. And now begins what has been called the plagues that demonstrate the power of Yahweh as He fights the battle for the rescue of His people. His people were helpless to save themselves. Only God could fight the battle. There are ten plagues and you will look at nine of them today. Read the following verses and summarize with short phrases each of these plagues and their purpose.

Exodus 7:17

Exodus 8:1-10

Exodus 8:15-19

Exodus 8:20-23

Exodus 9:1-4

Exodus 9:8-9

Exodus 9:14-21, 27-30

Exodus 10:1-8,16-20

Exodus 10:21-23, 27-29

4. How do you see the passion and power of God as He is fighting the battle on behalf of His people through the plagues?

5. Remember that the things that happened to Israel are an example for us and serve as instruction. Read Romans 5:6-10 and write in 2-3 sentences what you learn about how God has rescued you and fought your battle.

6. How is it that we can live supernaturally with God's power at work in our lives? Very simply, it is by living in the power of the Holy Spirit dwelling within us. We are to be filled (controlled and empowered) with the Holy Spirit (Ephesians 5:18). And when God's power is at work in and through us, God fights our battles. Read Romans 8:31, 37 and write what you learn from these promises about the Lord.

ADORE GOD IN PRAYER

When you think about the helplessness of the people of Israel and your own helplessness and inability to save yourself, think of the word "grace." Grace is the unmerited favor of God. Grace gives us what we need and does for us what we cannot do for ourselves. Grace is a gift and cannot be earned but it can be received. Just think, God demonstrates His love and exercises His power on your behalf to rescue and save you, all as a gift of His grace. Will you take some time now and commune with your Lord about His love for you and how He fights your battle? Pray through the words of Paul in Ephesians 1:18-23.

> I pray that the eyes of your heart may be enlightened, so that you will know what is the hope of His calling, what are the riches of the glory of His inheritance in the saints, and what is the surpassing greatness of His power toward us who believe. These are in accordance with the working of the strength of His might which He brought about in Christ, when He raised Him from the dead and seated Him at His right hand in the heavenly places, far above all rule and authority and power and dominion, and every name that is named, not only in this age but also in the one to come. And He put all things in subjection under His feet, and gave Him as head over all things to the church, which is His body, the fullness of Him who fills all in all.

YIELD YOURSELF TO GOD

One cannot help but be touched with the sorrow that must have existed in the thousands of homes throughout Egypt. Those who had labored long and hard in the hot sun witnessed in a few moments the total destruction of their crops. Their desperate cries to their deities had not brought relief. We know from Egyptian documents that the loss of crops was one of the greatest disasters in this country. The economy and the life of the people were very much involved in agricultural success. Failure brought not only economic desperation but led to social disruption and great sorrow…The pain, death and loss suffered by the thousands of Egyptians would have ended the many songs of merriment and the hymns of praise sung to their gods, at least for the time being. Who would have expected in an age of unparalleled prosperity and military prestige, such as that which characterized the Eighteenth Dynasty, the people of Egypt would find themselves on their knees humbled before Jehovah [Yahweh], the God of the enslaved Hebrews? They who had beaten others were now the oppressed and the humiliated. The power of God as expressed in these plagues is a mighty witness to His sovereign intervention in the affairs of men and to the fact that His purposes will be accomplished.[9]

JOHN J. DAVIS IN MOSES AND THE GODS OF EGYPT

These verses (Romans 5:6-10) describe the incomprehensible love that motivated God to send Christ to die for our sins. The emphasis is that God does not wait for us to become righteous before bringing about our redemption. God saves us when we are ungodly and totally impotent in our bondage to sin.[10]

R.C. SPROUL IN BEFORE THE FACE OF GOD

ENJOY HIS PRESENCE

Today is the day for you to know that God is all-powerful and will do whatever it takes to set you free. How does His power seen in the way He fought the battle for His people encourage you today? How does this grow in your heart a great desire to see God do something only He can do in your own life? If you find such a desire in your heart, then you are developing a passion for the impossible. Our Lord Jesus says that "all things are possible to him who believes" (Mark 9:23). Where in your own life do you need to see and believe God's power to fight a battle, His love to comfort your heart, and His rescue to free you from oppression, worry, fear, despair, or discouragement? Will you surrender to Him, cry out to Him, believe Him, and be filled with His Holy Spirit?

REST IN HIS LOVE

"For while we were still helpless, at the right time Christ died for the ungodly" (Romans 5:8).

LOVE FOR THE HELPLESS

While we were still helpless, at the right time Christ died for the ungodly. Romans 5:8
Sedona, Arizona, USA
Nikon D810, ISO 64, f2.8, 1/320sec, Adobe Photoshop, Nik Silver Efex Pro
MYPHOTOWALK.COM—CATHERINEMARTIN.SMUGMUG.COM

HE REDEEMS YOU

The blood shall be a sign for you on the houses where you live; and when I see the blood I will
pass over you, and no plague will befall you to destroy you when I strike the land of Egypt.

EXODUS 12:13

PREPARE YOUR HEART

The story is told of two boys who grew up in the same neighborhood and were close friends through high school. But when they went to different colleges, they drifted apart. The one boy, Doug, graduated from law school with honors and went on to be a judge. The other, Henry, dropped out of college after his father died. Moving from one job to another, Henry eventually turned to crime. He was an expert in embezzlement and information theft through the computer. He was eventually caught stealing secrets from the military. The mandatory penalty for treason was death. When he was tried, the judge was none other than his boyhood friend, Doug. But there was no sign of familiarity and when the judge tried the case he was fair and impartial. He delivered the verdict and sentence—guilty with the penalty of death. Then, the judge's face changed expression, and tears welled up in his eyes. "My friend, today I choose to take your penalty upon myself so that you may go free and live." At those words, the judge took off his robes, stepped down from the bench, walked over to the bailiff, and held out his hands to be cuffed, and then was led away to the cell, where he would await the carrying out of the sentence.[11]

This story is a picture of redemption that is made by paying the purchase price to set a person free from their bondage. Redemption is part of the theological doctrine of atonement (meaning "at one with" where we are put back into a right relationship with God through Christ's sacrifice for our sin). In Exodus, God promised to deliver His people and redeem them from their bondage (Exodus 6:6). And this points to an even greater redemption—the redemption Christ accomplished for us (Romans 3:24, 1 Corinthians 1:30, Ephesians 1:7,14, Colossians 1:14, Hebrews 9:12,15, 1 Peter 1:18-19). God is resolute about His people knowing and understanding redemption when He says, "Do not fear, for I have redeemed you; I have called you by name; you are Mine" (Isaiah 43:1).

Now the sacred journey gets underway in earnest. In fact, at the beginning of Exodus 12, the Lord says "This month shall be the beginning of months for you..." (Exodus 12:1). It is a time of new beginnings, as God is now going to set His people free, rescue them, redeem them, and lead them out of Egypt. Ask God now to prepare your heart for this exciting journey out of Egypt.

READ AND STUDY GOD'S WORD

1. The tenth plague in Egypt would be the final plague. And for the people of Israel, it involved the "Passover," a term you may have heard before. Today as you study, you will understand its origins. Read Exodus 12:1-13 and describe the following:

What God wants the Israelites to do

What He calls the meal they will eat

What God is going to do

What value there is in the blood

2. Not only did God redeem His people, but He took them out of Egypt. He planned to give them a new life as His holy people, separate from the world. This is the idea behind The Feast of Unleavened Bread (Exodus 12:14-27). Leaven belonged to Egypt, the world, and the old life. Unleavened bread was part of the new life. When the Feast of Unleavened Bread was celebrated as a memorial in future years, the people prepared with a time of spring cleaning. This was a reminder to them that they had new life and belonged to the Lord. In the same way, we are given new life through Christ and are to be holy and separate to Him as His children (2 Corinthians 6:16-18). We belong to Him. We are encouraged to not love the world or be conformed to the world (1 John 2:15, Romans 12:2). And now, read about what God does to set His people free in Exodus 12:29-42, 50. What is your favorite part of this great and daring rescue?

3. When God saw the blood He passed over that house, sparing the firstborn child. Thus, He redeemed that child through the blood of the lamb. And later, in Exodus 13:2, God commanded the people to set apart the firstborn son to Him, for he belonged to Him. Whatever God redeems belongs to Him. Never forget that. In the same way, there is Jesus, the "Lamb of God who takes away the sin of the world" according to John the Baptist in John 1:29. He died in our place, paying the purchase price as the Lamb of God, through the shedding of His own blood, so that we could be set free from the penalty of sin and death. He took that penalty upon Himself when He died on the cross. His was no ordinary death. He was sinless, yet took upon Himself all our sins, and paid the penalty so that we might be forgiven, redeemed, justified, and given eternal life. Even in heaven the Lord Jesus Christ is called the Lamb. Once we receive Him and enter into a personal relationship, we belong to Him forever. We receive forgiveness of sins, redemption, justification, and sanctification. All that is His is ours. Oh what a Savior! Hallelujah! Read the following verses and write what you learn about Jesus and all He has done for you.

Romans 3:24-25

1 Corinthians 5:7

Ephesians 1:7-14

Hebrews 10:19-23

1 Peter 1:18-19

4. Meditate on the words of Romans 5:6-10 (Phillips translation) and underline those words and phrases that mean the most to you, speak of your own redemption, and of God's love for you.

And we can see that it was while we were powerless to help ourselves that Christ died for sinful men. In human experience it is a rare thing for one man to give his life for another, even if the latter be a good man, though there have been a few who have had the courage to do it. Yet the proof of God's amazing love is this: that it was while were sinners that Christ died for us. Moreoever, if he did that for us while we were sinners, now that we are men justified by the shedding of his blood, what reason have we to fear the wrath of God? If, while we were his enemies, Christ reconciled us to God by dying for us, surely now that we are reconciled we may be perfectly certain of our salvation through his living in us.

ADORE GOD IN PRAYER

Take my life and let it be consecrated, Lord, to thee.
Take my moments and my days; let them flow in endless praise,
let them flow in endless praise.
Take my hands and let them move at the impulse of thy love.
Take my feet and let them be swift and beautiful for thee,
swift and beautiful for thee.
Take my voice and let me sing always, only, for my King.
Take my lips and let them be filled with messages from thee,
filled with messages from thee.
Take my silver and my gold; not a mite would I withhold.
Take my intellect and use every power as thou shalt choose,
every power as thou shalt choose.
Take my will and make it thine; it shall be no longer mine.
Take my heart it is thine own; it shall be thy royal throne,
it shall be thy royal throne.
Take my love; my Lord, I pour at thy feet its treasure store.
Take myself, and I will be ever, only, all for thee,
ever, only, all for thee.

FRANCES RIDLEY HAVERGAL

YIELD YOURSELF TO GOD

At the first Passover, the Jewish people were delivered not only from the tyranny of Pharaoh, but also from the judgment of God on their idolatry. It was through the substitutionary death of a lamb, whose blood marked out the Israelite households, that their firstborn sons were spared. These events occurred at a key turning point in salvation history, and were integral to God's faithfulness to his covenant with Abraham. Moreover, the ongoing celebration of the Passover served to implant the notion of salvation through penal sacrifice in every faithful Israelite mind. The New Testament writers see Jesus' death as the fulfilment of the Passover; he suffered in the place of his people in order that they might be marked out by his blood and thus spared from God's wrath.[12]

STEVE JEFFERY, MICHAEL OVEY, ANDREW SACH IN PIERCED FOR OUR TRANSGRESSIONS

God is able to come forth to us now in absolute grace, sending out His messengers "preaching peace by Jesus Christ";—nay, preaching much more than peace. In effect, God says, "Utter and infinite oceans of grace shall roll over the place where judgment and condemnation were!" Forgiving us all our trespasses, He goes further: having raised up Christ from the dead. He says, I will now place you in my Son. I will give you a standing fully and only in Him risen from the dead! Not only did He bear your sins, putting away your guilt, but in His death I released you from your standing and responsibility in Adam the first. You who have believed are now new creatures in Christ: for I have created you in Him…In the book of Romans, Paul is describing God's action toward a believing sinner in view of the shed blood of Christ. It is as if God were holding court with the infinite value and benefit of the propitiatory sacrifice and resurrection of Christ only and ever before Him.

WILLIAM NEWELL IN ROMANS VERSE-BY-VERSE

ENJOY HIS PRESENCE

What a week of study in Exodus! God wants you to know that He gives you hope, defends you, is the Lord your God, fights your battle, and redeems you. Oh how God loves us. Paul says "we may hold our heads high in light of God's love" (Romans 5:11). What have you learned today that is most significant to you? Write your thoughts, then close in prayer to your Lord.

REST IN HIS LOVE

"You were not redeemed with perishable things like silver or gold from your futile way of life inherited from your forefathers, but with precious blood, as of a lamb unblemished and spotless, the blood of Christ" (1 Peter 1:18-19)

YOU CAN BELIEVE

Unless one is born again, he cannot see the kingdom of God. John 3:3
Sedona, Arizona, USA
Nikon D7000, ISO 100, f11, AEB, Adobe Photoshop, Nik Silver Efex Pro
MYPHOTOWALK.COM—CATHERINEMARTIN.SMUGMUG.COM

DEVOTIONAL READING
BY CHARLES SPURGEON

DEAR FRIEND,

The next two days are your opportunity to review what you have learned this week. Thank the Lord for all you have seen thus far about His one holy passion for you. As you think about your sacred journey in Exodus this week, record your:

Most meaningful insight:

Most meaningful devotional reading:

Most meaningful verse:

We were chosen from before the foundations of the world. Everlasting love went with the choice, for it was not a bare act of divine will by which we were set apart, but the divine affections were concerned. The Father loved us in and from the beginning. Here is a theme for daily contemplation. The eternal purpose to redeem us from our foreseen ruin, to cleanse and sanctify us, and at last to glorify us, was of infinite antiquity, and runs side by side with immutable love and absolute sovereignty. The covenant is always described as being everlasting, and Jesus, the second party in it, had his goings forth of old; he struck hands in sacred suretyship long ere the first of the stars began to shine, and it was in him that the elect were ordained unto eternal life. Thus in the divine purpose a most blessed covenant union was established between the Son of God and his elect people, which will remain as the foundation of their safety when time shall be no more.

A monument of grace,
A sinner saved by blood;,
The streams of love I trace
Up to the Fountain, God;
And in his sacred bosom see
Eternal thoughts of Love to me.

CHARLES SPURGEON IN MORNING AND EVENING

Viewer Guide
❧ WEEK THREE ❧

A Passion For The Impossible

This week we studied Exodus 4-12 and experienced the sacred journey to God's amazing love in a powerful way as we watched God at work on behalf of His people. And today in our time together, we are going to see how God has a passion for the impossible and is developing in us that same passion for the impossible. So grab your Bible, and let's get into the Word of God together.

"So the people believed; and when they heard that the Lord was concerned about the sons of Israel and that He had seen their affliction, then they bowed low and worshipped (Exodus 4:31).

What we see in Exodus 4:1 - 5:2:

1. God has a passion for the _____. He loves to do God-sized things.

2. God calls us to _____Him for the impossible.

3. An _____ circumstance is the context for God to do the impossible.

How can you develop a passion for the impossible?

1. _____ your God.

"Now to him who is able to do immeasurably more than all we ask or imagine, according to his power that is at work within us" (Ephesians 3:20 NIV).

2. _____ your God.

3. Rely on your God's _____.

4. _____your God.

Lilias Trotter writes: "Let us dare to test God's resources…Let us ask Him to kindle in us and keep aflame that passion for the impossible that shall make us delight in it with Him, till the day when we shall see it transformed into a fact."

Video messages are available on DVDs or as Digital M4V Video. Audio messages are available as Digital MP3 Audio. Visit the Quiet Time Ministries Online Store at www.quiettime.org.

THE RED SEA PLACE

Exodus 13-15

If we have the faith that believes to see, it will keep us from growing discouraged. We shall "laugh at impossibilities," we shall watch with delight to see how God is going to open up a path through the Red Sea when there is no human way out of our difficulty. It is just in such places of severe testing that our faith grows and strengthens. [1]

STREAMS IN THE DESERT

GOD LEADS THE WAY

God led the people around by the way of the wilderness to the Red Sea; and the sons of Israel went up in martial array from the land of Egypt.

EXODUS 13:18

PREPARE YOUR HEART

Richard Halverson went to Hollywood at the age of 19, filled with ambition for success in the entertainment industry. He lived carelessly, was unsuccessful in his endeavors, and after six months, decided to check out a church near where he lived. As a result, he gave his life to Christ. That decision altered the course of his life. But following that time, he experienced more than one crisis of faith that led him to a deeper, more intimate relationship with Christ. At a youth meeting one day, he realized that the Lord wanted full surrender of his life. He wrestled with that commitment, but got alone with the Lord, and utterly yielded all areas of his life to the Lord. He experienced a new power through the Holy Spirit for life and ministry. Following that time he went to seminary and upon graduation, accepted an assistant pastorate at a church in Kansas City, and then, later, to a church in Coalinga, California. After two years in Coalinga, he became so disillusioned that he almost left the ministry. He felt as though he was on the far side of the earth and wasn't accomplishing anything. He could not see the answers, felt trapped, and did not know the way out. It was a crisis for him involving his entire future. The Lord brought him to a profound decision. He describes it in his own words, "I finally told the Lord I was going to continue to serve Him the rest of my life whether there were any fruit or blessing in that service…I was willing to be buried for the rest of my life in Coalinga and serve in obscurity there or anywhere. This was a tremendous hurdle for me for I had become very ambitious. When this was settled, I took a completely new lease on life."[2] That was a defining moment, and some time later, God led Halverson to resign his position in Coalinga and serve as youth pastor, and then assistant pastor at First Presbyterian Church of Hollywood. Later, he became the Senior pastor of the Fourth Presbyterian Church in Bethesda, Maryland and Chaplain of the U.S. Senate.

Richard Halverson experienced a Red Sea place in Coalinga where he could not see any way out or through. And yet, drawing near to God, the waters seemingly parted as he was led to surrender and new commitment of faith. He was able to move forward, and God led the way into His plan and purpose for his life.

That is only one example of how a person is led to a Red Sea place in life where there is no way back, no way forward, only through. The Red Sea place is the place where your faith is tested, and you experience what might be called a crisis of the heart. The questions in front of you are very real: "How am I going to make it? Where is the answer? Is God real? How can I believe God's Word?" The Red Sea place comes at many defining moments in life—a need for salvation and forgiveness of sin, times of financial struggle, difficulties in a job, loss of career, difficult relationships, illness, and loss of loved ones.

Mrs. Charles Cowman, author of *Streams in the Desert* and *Springs in the Valley*, experienced a Red Sea place when she heard a doctor's report, "No more public services for you. Your heart is gone. To disobey may be to drop dead."[3] She knew that nothing was impossible for God. As she drew near to God, she received a profound promise from Him—that He is the resurrection and the life (John 11:25), and that her life belonged to Christ, and that He lived in her (Galatians 2:20). She was encouraged to depend on His life in her for all that He called her to do until the day she stepped into heaven.

Take My life and let it be
Everything, My child, to thee!
Take Me for thy spirit's wealth,
Take Me for thy body's health.

At the Lord's urging for a new and greater dependence on Him, she decided to launch out trusting Him for His strength. She experienced His power as she spoke and no longer felt weak and sick. She continued to serve in ministry, finishing the manuscript for *Springs in the Valley*, and ministering at many other speaking engagements. At her Red Sea place, Mrs. Cowman was led to a new and deeper trust in God.

God accomplishes some of His most powerful displays of greatness and glory at every Red Sea place. If you are experiencing the Red Sea place even now, take heart, dear friend. God is sovereign and in control and He has a plan and a purpose, even in the Red Sea place. You are not there by accident but by His design. God is the One who leads the way for you.

Draw near to God now, and ask Him to quiet your heart, and give you ears to hear and eyes to see as you continue this sacred journey in Exodus.

READ AND STUDY GOD'S WORD

1. In Week 3 we saw the Lord lead His people out of Egypt with great power and force, so that both the Egyptians and the people of Israel knew that He is the LORD. Now the Lord gave

instructions to His people about consecrating the firstborn to Him and the feast of Unleavened Bread. God had spared their firstborn and so that firstborn was dedicated to Him, set apart for His service. Then, the feast of Unleavened Bread, as we discovered last week, was a reminder of God's deliverance with a purpose—that they were His and separate from the world. Read Exodus 13:1-16 keeping in mind the children of Israel have just been led out of Egypt, God is their God, and they are His people. In Exodus 13:3 God tells His people to remember (commemorate NIV) the day that their powerful God brought them out of Egypt.

Why is remembering what God has done and how He did it so valuable for us in our relationship with Him?

2. God was the One who led the people out of Egypt. Read Exodus 13:17-22 and write everything you learn about how He led His people. Keep in mind that God "makes everything work out according to His plan" (Ephesians 1:11 NLT).

3. What a profound discovery to learn that God is the One who led His people to the Red Sea place! So what is it like when you get to the Red Sea place? Read Exodus 14:1-12 and describe what their Red Sea place was like.

4. Read Exodus 14:10-12 again and describe the response of the people of Israel when they realized the impossibility of the situation.

5. Think about the impossible place where the people of Israel found themselves. They were so afraid that they told themselves the story that it would have been better to still be in Egypt serving the Egyptians. Write out what you think God wanted them to see and learn here at the Red Sea place. How was their faith being tested and how was this a crisis of faith for them?

6. Read the promise of Ephesians 3:20-21 and write what you learn about God that encourages you at your own Red Sea place.

ADORE GOD IN PRAYER

Pray the words of Amy L. Person today: "Thy will be done whether on pleasant paths I walk along, or crouch amid the lightnings of the storm, whether for me the larks of springtime sing, or winter's icy blasts my being sting; whatever Thou dost send is best for me, with joyful heart I take it all from Thee, rejoicing in Thy sovereignty, and pray that Thou wilt lead me on my upward way; the road grows smoother as I travel on. Thy will be done."[4]

YIELD YOURSELF TO GOD

Take a deep breath and recall this deeper secret of the Christian life: when you are in a difficult place, realize that the Lord either placed you there or allowed you to be there, for reasons perhaps known for now only to Himself. The same God who led you in will lead you out...Our whole perspective changes when, finding ourselves in a hard place, we realize the Lord has either placed us there or allowed us to be there, perhaps for reasons presently known only to Himself...God allows our faith to be tried, and He permits troubles to crowd into our lives. Sometimes they seem more than we can bear, but Christ can bear them. The first step toward "parted waters" is to frequently remind ourselves that the Lord has either put us in this difficult place or has allowed us to be there for reasons perhaps only He knows.[5]

ROBERT MORGAN IN THE RED SEA RULES

Pressed out of measure and pressed to all length
Pressed so intently, it seems beyond strength,
Pressed in the body, and pressed in the soul,
Pressed in the mind till the dark surges roll,
Pressed by foes, and pressure by friends,
Pressure on pressure till life nearly ends.
Pressed into knowing no helper but God,
Pressed into loving the staff and the rod,
Pressed into liberty where nothing clings,
Pressed into faith for impossible things,
Pressed into living a life to the Lord,
Pressed into living a Christ-life outpoured.[6]

V. Raymond Edman in The Disciplines Of Life

Enjoy His Presence

Have you discovered that the Red Sea place is not an accident? God is sovereign and sometimes He leads us up to the shore of the impossible. For the people of Israel, their response makes it clear that they were out of Egypt, but there was still a lot of Egypt in them. They were being brought to a new and deeper dependence on their God. They had convinced themselves with a story that Egypt was better than freedom, and that the known was better than the unknown. God has a purpose for you in your Red Sea place as well. James encourages us to "Consider it pure joy, my brothers and sisters, whenever you face trials of many kinds, because you know that the testing of your faith produces perseverance. Let perseverance finish its work so that you may be mature and complete, not lacking anything" (James 1:2-4 NIV). How is God bringing about perseverance and maturity in your life even now? How have you experienced the Red Sea place and what stories are you telling yourself that are not true? How does it encourage you to know that God leads us to Red Sea places where we see Him do great and mighty things, grow in our trust, and become stronger and more mature in Him? What are you learning that is most significant to you? Close your time by writing a prayer to the Lord expressing all that is on your heart.

REST IN HIS LOVE

"'Thus I will harden Pharaoh's heart, and he will chase after them; and I will be honored through Pharaoh and all his army, and the Egyptians will know that I am the LORD.' And they did so" (Exodus 14:4).

A WALK WITH GOD

He set my feet on solid ground, and steadied me as I walked along. Psalm 40:2 NLT
Bell Rock-Courthouse Butte, Sedona, Arizona, USA
Nikon D800E, ISO 100, f16, 1/20sec, Adobe Photoshop, Nik Silver Efex Pro
MYPHOTOWALK.COM—CATHERINEMARTIN.SMUGMUG.COM

GOD ANSWERS YOUR FEAR

But Moses said to the people, "Do not fear! Stand by and see the salvation
of the LORD which He will accomplish for you today; for the Egyptians
whom you have seen today, you will never see them again forever.

Exodus 14:13

PREPARE YOUR HEART

Who can come to your aid when you are at the Red Sea place? You have One who loves you and who is intimately acquainted with the Red Sea place. Jesus, knowing He was going to the cross, asked His Father, "My Father, if it is possible, may this cup be taken from me. Yet not as I will, but as you will" (Matthew 26:39 NIV). And while He was on the cross, He cried out, "My God, my God, why have you forsaken me" (Matthew 27:46 NIV). The Red Sea place is the time when you feel abandoned by God and don't see how you will make it through. Jesus knows that place and is with you there. He knows the way through and will never leave you or forsake you. He promises. The writer of Hebrews gives these encouraging words about Jesus, " For we do not have a high priest who cannot sympathize with our weaknesses, but One who has been tempted in all things as we are, yet without sin. Therefore let us draw near with confidence to the throne of grace, so that we may receive mercy and find grace to help in time of need" (Hebrews 4:15-16).

Fear is a very real emotion in impossible situations that test your faith. In fact, fear is the opposite of faith. Faith is taking God at His Word and calculating God's promise as the truth instead of sight or circumstances. Have you learned this secret? What is greater in your life—fear or faith? The Red Sea place always tests your faith, showing its strength or weakness, and then grows faith to take God at His Word more and more.

Ask God now to teach you how to walk by faith as you continue on this sacred journey in Exodus.

READ AND STUDY GOD'S WORD

1. The people of Israel have now left Egypt and are in a new and unfamiliar position. They are following God's leading out into an unknown place. They have been given assurance through the promises of God. However, they have not yet learned to walk by faith, and are instead living

by sight. We are to walk by faith, not by sight (2 Corinthians 5:7). Read Exodus 14:1-12 again. Write your insights about the following questions:

What did God promise (Exodus 14:4)

What did the people of Israel trust (Exodus 14:10-12)

How did they respond as a result (Exodus 14:10-12)

2. Read Exodus 14:13-14 and write your insights about how Moses encouraged the people? What did they learn about God that could strengthen them at the Red Sea place?

3. How is it possible to be courageous instead of afraid when you are in the impossible situation? Read the following verses and write out what you learn that will give you courage at the Red Sea place.

Psalm 34:4

Psalm 46:10

Isaiah 41:10

Philippians 4:6-7

Hebrews 10:35-38

1 Peter 1:6-7

1 Peter 4:12-13, 19

1 John 5:4

4. What is the most important truth you learned that will help you have faith when you are filled with fear?

ADORE GOD IN PRAYER

Is there no other way, O God,
Except through sorrow, pain and loss,
To stamp Christ's image on my soul?
No other way except the Cross?
And then a voice stills all my soul,
As stilled the waves on Galilee:
Canst thou not bear the furnace heat:
If 'mid the flames I walk with thee?
I bore the Cross, I know its weight,
I drank the cup I hold for thee;
Canst thou not follow where I lead?
I'll give the strength—
lean thou on Me.[7]

MRS. CHARLES COWMAN IN SPRINGS IN THE VALLEY

YIELD YOURSELF TO GOD

Read through these words written by Annie Johnson Flint who intimately knew the Red Sea place and wrote about it. She suffered from crippling arthritis and was unable to live out her dream of being a concert pianist. Instead, she was bedridden and homebound for most of her life. Yet, the Lord gave her the gift of poetry and she wrote words that were beloved by many. Find hope and encouragement in these words today.

Have you come to the Red Sea place in your life
Where, in spite of all you can do,
There is no way out, there is no back,
There is no other way but—through?
Then wait on the Lord with a trust serene
Till the night of your fear is gone;
He will send the wind, He will heap the floods,
When He says to your soul, "Go on."

And His hand will lead you through—clear through—
Ere the watery walls roll down,

No foe can reach you, no wave can touch,
No mightiest sea can drown;
The tossing billows may rear their crests,
Their foam at your feet may break,
But over their bed you shall walk dry shod
In the path that your Lord will make.

In the morning watch, 'neath the lifted cloud,
You shall see but the Lord alone,
When He leads you on from the place of the sea
To land that you have not known;
And your fears shall pass as your foes have passed,
You shall be no more afraid;
You shall sing His praise in a better place,
A place that His hand has made.[8]

ANNIE JOHNSON FLINT

ENJOY HIS PRESENCE

Imagine being the people of Israel who have just been led by the Lord to the shore at the Red Sea. Remember these things in Exodus are written as an example for us and for our instruction. What is God teaching you? Write your thoughts and a prayer in response to all that God is teaching you.

REST IN HIS LOVE

"For we walk by faith, not by sight" (2 Corinthians 5:7).

HOPE IN RIVERS OF DIFFICULTY

When you go through deep waters, I will be with you. Isaiah 43:2 NLT
West Fork Trail, Sedona, Arizona, USA
Nikon D7000, ISO 100, f11, AEB, Adobe Photoshop, Nik Silver Efex Pro
MYPHOTOWALK.COM—CATHERINEMARTIN.SMUGMUG.COM

GOD CALLS YOU TO TRUST

Then the LORD said to Moses, "Why are you crying out to Me? Tell the sons of Israel to go forward. As for you, lift up your staff and stretch out your hand over the sea and divide it, and the sons of Israel shall go through the midst of the sea on dry land."

Exodus 14:16

PREPARE YOUR HEART

Isaiah, the great prophet of God was called by God during his lifetime to speak for Him to His people. Isaiah soon learned that God had a different plan than he expected. God told him that the people wouldn't listen to what he had to say (Isaiah 6:1-13). And still, God wanted him to speak. Isaiah learned a powerful truth from God that helped him in trusting God. God said, "For My thoughts are not your thoughts, nor are My ways My ways," declares the LORD. For as the heavens are higher than the earth, so are My ways higher than your ways and my thoughts than your thoughts" (Isaiah 55:8-9).

Luis Palau trusted Christ at the age of twelve and dedicated his life to the Lord when he was seventeen. He started preaching in Argentina, then was invited by Ray Stedman to come to the United States. Palau stayed with the Stedmans and served for the summer as a pastoral intern at Peninsula Bible Church in Palo Alto, California. He then enrolled in graduate school at Multnomah School of the Bible. But deep inside, Palau was frustrated and exhausted with trying to live the Christian life. He was weary of the struggle to the point of almost giving up. All of that changed when he attended a chapel service where he heard a powerful message by Major Ian Thomas entitled "Any Old Bush Will Do." The message centered around the truth that Christ is your life and trusting in Christ for your life is the secret to victory in the Christian life. Luis Palau had discovered an important secret and went back to his room and fell on his knees before God. He prayed to the Lord, telling Him that now he realized it was "not I, but Christ." He saw that it wasn't what he would do for the Lord but what the Lord was going to do in and through him.[9] Luis Palau became one of the greatest evangelists of all time, preaching to millions of people worldwide.

Have you discovered the secret of trusting the Lord and realizing that it's not your life, but His life? Ask Him now to speak to you in His Word.

READ AND STUDY GOD'S WORD

1. The last thing the people of Israel probably expected was to find themselves at the Red Sea place, hemmed in on every side and seemingly no way out. What is the answer for you when you are in this place? Trust in the Lord. It sounds simple, but only God makes this possible. Read Exodus 14:15-18 and write out your observations about what God wanted the people to do and what He wanted Moses to do.

The people

Moses

2. Proverbs 3:5-6 encourage you to "trust in the LORD with all your heart and do not lean on your own understanding. In all your ways acknowledge Him and He will make your paths straight." Trust may be understood as "total reliance under stress and trial." As you think about trust in this situation, write out your responses to these questions:

How were both Moses and the people of God being asked to trust?

What do you think was the greatest challenge for them in what God was asking of them?

What did they have to believe in order to trust?

3. Luis Palau discovered that Christ was his life and strength in every situation. It changed everything for him because he realized that Christ wanted to live His life in and through Luis

Palau. What are the implications for you at the Red Sea place if Christ lives in you and is your very life? Read the following verses and write out what you learn that you can trust in and rely on at every Red Sea place.

Romans 8:37

2 Corinthians 5:14-17

Galatians 2:20

Philippians 4:13

4. The people of Israel had been set free from the Egyptians and now belonged to God. And now the Lord was telling them to go forward. They had to believe God was going to make a way. And He promised to make a way. They had to take Him at His Word. They were walking in newness of life and were about to experience their first real steps of freedom. And so it is for you, dear friend. Paul encourages you in Galatians 5:1 "It was for freedom that Christ set us free; therefore keep standing firm and do not be subject again to a yoke of slavery." You have been set free to love and serve the Lord. You can be brave and courageous even at your Red Sea place because Christ is in you and He is enough for anything you face today. He has a plan and purpose He desires to accomplish in and through you. He is at work making your trust in Him stronger than ever before. You can say, along with Job, who experienced his Red Sea place, "Though He slay me, yet will I trust Him" (Job 13:15 NKJV). The words of the hymn writer can be yours even at the Red Sea place when you trust God: "It is well with my soul." The Red Sea place is not an obstacle, but your opportunity for a great faith and trust. Launch out, dear friend, with a heart set free. Make a decision now to only believe God's Word—it is the authority for your belief— not emotions, not circumstances, not what people say, not what you're afraid will happen—only

listen to what God says and take Him at His Word. Trust—total reliance under stress and trial. That is your big decision at the Red Sea place. Summarize what you have learned today that helps you trust God and live in freedom.

ADORE GOD IN PRAYER

Make me, O blessed Master, strong in heart, full of courage, fearless of danger, holding pain and peril cheap when they lie in the path of duty. May I be strengthened with all might by your Spirit in my inner being.

F.B. MEYER IN DAILY PRAYERS

YIELD YOURSELF TO GOD

Faith brings us into right relationship with God and gives God His opportunity. God has frequently to knock the bottom board out of your experience if you are a saint in order to get you into contact with Himself. God wants you to understand that it is a life of faith, not a life of sentimental enjoyment of His blessings. Your earlier life of faith was narrow and intense, settled around a little sun-spot of experience that had as much of sense as of faith in it, full of light and sweetness; then God withdrew His conscious blessings in order to teach you to walk by faith. You are worth far more to Him now than you were in your days of conscious delight and thrilling testimony. Faith by its very nature must be tried, and the real trial of faith is not that we find it difficult to trust God, but that God's character has to be cleared in our own minds…Faith in the Bible is faith in God against every thing that contradicts Him—"I will remain true to God's character whatever He may do." "Though He slay me, yet will I trust Him"—this is the most sublime utterance of faith in the whole of the Bible.[10]

OSWALD CHAMBERS IN MY UTMOST FOR HIS HIGHEST

Living in freedom means learning how to walk again—learning how to walk God's way for a change—because, listen, you can be 100 percent saved and still spend the majority of your time in Egypt. Unbelievers aren't the only ones who contribute to Egypt's overcrowding…"It was for freedom that Christ set us free." And His Word to you is to "keep standing firm and do not be subject again to a yoke of slavery" (Gal. 5:1), to "lay aside every encumbrance and the sin which so easily entangles us, and let us run with endurance the race that is set before us" (Heb. 12:1, italics mine). Yes, even the sin—that sin—the one that "so easily" entangles you, the one that works the hardest to keep you separated from complete freedom in Christ, even that one needs to be "laid aside." There's no other way. There's no kind of shortcut. There's no scenario that keeps your sin and your highest spiritual hopes in the same picture frame. It takes a deliberate separation—not once or twice or every now and then, but day after day, hour after hour, time after time.[11]

PRISCILLA SHIRER IN ONE IN A MILLION: JOURNEY TO YOUR PROMISED LAND

Afflictions, adversities, sufferings, sorrows, temptations, trials, doubts, disappointments roll in upon us. How can we go on in peace, patience and victory with such things in our life? Are they not enough to overwhelm us? No, not if faith spreads itself out over them and sends its roots deep down into the rich soil of God's great, eternal facts.[12]

RUTH PAXSON IN RIVERS OF LIVING WATER

ENJOY HIS PRESENCE

How was God the answer for the Red Sea place in the lives of His people? How is Jesus the answer for your Red Sea place today? How can you trust that He is enough for every impossible situation? And how is that a test of your faith? What do you need to believe in order to trust? Where do you need to trust God today? Always remember, dear friend, God keeps His promises, and He will never fail you or forsake you (Hebrews 13:5-6). Write your thoughts, then close with a prayer to your Lord.

REST IN HIS LOVE

"He died for all, so that they who live might no longer live for themselves, but for Him who died and rose again on their behalf" (2 Corinthians 5:15).

KNOWING THE TRUTH

Your word is truth. John 17:17
West Fork Trail, Sedona, Arizona, USA
Nikon D7000, ISO 100, f11, AEB, Adobe Photoshop, Nik Silver Efex Pro
MYPHOTOWALK.COM—CATHERINEMARTIN.SMUGMUG.COM

YOU WILL SEE AND BELIEVE

When Israel saw the great power which the LORD had used against the Egyptians, the people feared the LORD, and they believed in the LORD and in His servant Moses.

EXODUS 14:31

PREPARE YOUR HEART

Oh, what an amazing moment it is when one person chooses faith in God's Word and trust in Christ in the face of an impossibility. For the Red Sea place is no match for the One who spoke all of creation into existence. He is more powerful than any impossibility and has every answer for every question mark. There is no place for worry or fear in a life of faith. In fact, John Rice has said, "Worry is putting question marks where God has put periods." Don't you love that! Think about whatever you are facing and then ask, "Is God worried? Is He wondering what He is going to do? Was He caught off guard and is He now scrambling for answers?" The answer is "no" to all of the above. God has a plan. He knows everything. And maybe, just maybe, you are exactly where you are supposed to be, for God has led you there. And even if you made independent choices, you still have an amazing promise to trust. "And we know that God causes all things to work together for good to those who love God, to those who are called according to His purpose" (Romans 8:28). You can confess and repent of sin because Christ died on the cross for you and wants you to live free in newness of life (1 John 1:9). These are all truths from God's Word that you must remember, reason through, and believe. Jesus said, "And you will know the truth and the truth will set you free" (John 8:32 NLT). Oh dear friend, know the truth, and be set free today! Imagine that you are in the boat with the disciples out on the waters of the sea of Galilee. It is the fourth watch of the night. Jesus is walking on the water and all the disciples think He is a ghost. He cries out to them, "Take courage, it is I; do not be afraid" (Matthew 14:27). Then Peter said, "Lord if it is You, command me to come to You on the water." Jesus said, "Come." And Peter got out of that boat and walked on the water. And dear friend, that is what we must do at the Red Sea place. No more fear. No more worry. No more despair or discouragement. No more entangling sin or oppression weighing you down. Get out of the boat and walk on water with Jesus. That means instead of fear, you have faith in Christ. Instead of worry, you worship of God. Instead of despair, you depend on the Lord. And instead of discouragement, you delight in

God's Word. And instead of habitual sin, you live a sanctified life, holy to the Lord. When you trust the Lord at your Red Sea place, you are going to see God at work and experience Him firsthand for yourself. Draw near to the Lord and ask Him to teach you on this sacred journey in Exodus.

READ AND STUDY GOD'S WORD

1. And now, we're going into the Red Sea—yes we are. Just think, one person stepped out first into the water in response to God's word to go forward. There was courage and bravery in action. It always begins with one step. And what a step of faith for Moses to stretch out his hand in the face of possible doubts that anything would actually happen. Notice that Moses was no longer objecting or wrestling with God. No, not now. He had a trust in Yahweh great enough to stretch out his hand and believe. Read Exodus 14:19-30 and describe all that God did, what Moses did, and what the people of Israel did.

What God did

What Moses did

What the people of Israel did

2. Tests of faith always have the result of a greater faith in God and His Word. For ultimately, God wants to grow our faith. When our faith is tested in a trial, we are brought face to face with what we know is true in God's Word. And though we may doubt and worry, God's Spirit works in us to grow our faith. He is faithful to remind us of all that the Lord says— "But the Helper, the Holy Spirit, whom the Father will send in My name, He will teach you all things, and bring to your remembrance all that I said to you" (John 14:26). We learn that "faith comes from hearing,

and hearing by the word of Christ" (Romans 10:17). So when we hear the Lord's words, our faith will grow. We see this growth in the people of Israel when they saw God do a mighty miracle at the Red Sea. Read Exodus 14:31. What did the people see and what was the result?

3. How do you think Moses was an encouragement to the people of Israel?

4. So let us imagine finding ourselves at a Red Sea place, where we can't see a way out. There are three promises you can count on today: "For with God nothing is ever impossible and no word from God shall be without power or impossible of fulfillment" (Luke 1:37 AMP) and "Do not fear, for I am with you; Do not anxiously look about you, for I am your God. I will strengthen you, surely I will help you, surely I will uphold you with My righteous right hand" (Isaiah 41:10) and "Do not call to mind the former things, or ponder things of the past. Behold, I will do something new, now it will spring forth; will you not be aware of it? I will even make a roadway in the wilderness, rivers in the desert" (Isaiah 43:18-19). How do these promises along with what you have seen God do for His people in Exodus encourage you today? How do trusting God and believing Him set you free, in a sense, to serve and worship God?

5. The New Living Translation of Exodus 14:31 is "When the people of Israel saw the mighty power that the LORD had unleashed against the Egyptians, they were filled with awe before Him. They put their faith in the LORD and in his servant Moses." How have you seen God work in your own life and how did it fill you with awe and move you to put your faith in the Lord?

ADORE GOD IN PRAYER

Take some time now to pour out your heart to your Lord. Ask Him to work mightily at any Red Sea place you or a loved one might be facing. And then, ask Him to fill you with His power, show you His word, and give you faith to trust Him.

YIELD YOURSELF TO GOD

Dear believer, if you are in trouble, the voice of that trouble is designed to draw you nearer to God. God has favored you, favored you with an extraordinary means of growth in grace. To use Rutherford's simile, "He has put you down in the wine cellar in the dark. Now begin to try the well–refined wines on the lees (Is. 25:6). He has brought you to a sandy desert. Now begin to seek the treasures that are hid in the sand." Believe that the deepest afflictions are always neighbors to the highest joys. The greatest possible privileges lie close to the darkest trials. The more bitter your sorrow, the louder your song at the end. There is a reason, and that reason faith may discover and experience may live on. Our afflictions are the highway that leads us closer to God. Our troubles are a fiery chariot to bring us to God. Our afflictions, wave upon wave, will drive our souls nearer heaven. It is a blessed thing when God's judgments bring us closer to Him. May God bless you, my tested friend.

CHARLES SPURGEON IN BESIDE STILL WATERS

Whatever is the next grace for your soul, can you believe for its supply at once, straight out from the dry, bare need? Christ's process is very simple and very swift: "Whatsoever things ye desire, when ye pray, believe ye receive them, and ye shall have them." And not only with the barrenness of our souls can God deal with His quickening breath, but with our difficulties as well: with those things in our surroundings that seem the most unfavourable...Never mind if the trouble shows no sign of giving way: it is just when it seems most hopelessly unyielding, holding on through the spring days, alive and strong, it is then that the tiny buds appear that soon will clothe it with glory. Take the very hardest thing in your life—the place of difficulty, outward or inward, and expect God to triumph gloriously in that very spot. Just there He can bring your soul into blossom.

LILIAS TROTTER IN PARABLES OF THE CROSS

The real work of God for the children of Israel, was not when they awakened and found that they could get over the Red Sea; but it was "all that night" (Exodus 14:21). So there may be a great working in your life when it all seems dark and you cannot see or trace, but yet God is working. Just as truly did He work "all that night," as all the next day. The next day simply manifested what God had done during the night. Is there anyone reading these lines who may have gotten to a place where it seems dark? You believe to see, but you are not seeing. In your life-progress there is not constant victory; the daily, undisturbed communion is not there, and all seems dark. "The Lord caused the sea to go back…all that night." Do not forget that it was "all that night." God works all the night, until the light comes. You may not see it, but all that "night" in your life, as you believe God, He works.

Mrs. Charles Cowman in Streams in the Desert

There are times when the brightest–eyed Christians can hardly brush the tears away. Strong faith and joyous hope subside into a fear that is scarcely able to keep the spark of hope and faith alive. In times of gloom, when your soul is overwhelmed, grasp the promise and rejoice in the Lord. Although it is not always easy, cry with David, "Why are you cast down, O my soul? And why are you disquieted within me?" (Ps. 42:5). Question the cause of your tears. Reason until you come to the psalmist's conclusion, "Hope in God, for I shall yet praise Him" (Ps. 42:5). If you can believe God in the midnight of your soul, then you have ten times more cause to rejoice than to sorrow. If you can lie humbly at Jesus' feet, there are more flowers than thorns ready to spring up in your path. Joys lie in ambush. You will be surrounded with songs of deliverance.

Charles Spurgeon in Beside Still Waters

Enjoy His Presence

And now, the people of Israel are free indeed. They saw Yahweh perform a miracle as the walls of water appeared and they walked on dry land. Yahweh led them all the way. And Yahweh destroyed their enemies, the Egyptians. On the other side of the Red Sea, the people of Israel were in awe and believed. They were no longer enslaved by the Egyptians. They were experiencing what it means to be God's people, and He was their God. What a new place in their sacred journey following their God. Think deeply about these things, dear friend, for the same is true of you. God rescues you and sets you free. What is your most significant insight as you think through all you have learned today in your study? What does God want you to believe today? How do you see God's passion for His people in your quiet time today? Write your thoughts in the space provided.

Rest in His Love

"Faith comes from hearing, and hearing by the word of Christ" (Romans 10:17).

A New Day

Behold, I am doing something new. Isaiah 43:19
Bell Rock-Courthouse Butte, Sedona, Arizona, USA
Nikon D800E, ISO 100, f16, 1/40sec, Adobe Photoshop, Nik Silver Efex Pro
MYPHOTOWALK.COM—CATHERINEMARTIN.SMUGMUG.COM

YOU WILL WORSHIP

Then Moses and the sons of Israel sang this song to the LORD.

Exodus 15:1

PREPARE YOUR HEART

What do people do in the presence of God after witnessing a miracle and a dramatic rescue from their enemies? They worship God. Fanny J. Crosby was a woman of worship. Her Red Sea place began when she suffered blindness as an infant. Her trust in God and her love of writing verse began at a young age. At the age of eight, she wrote:

> Oh what a happy soul I am,
> Although I cannot see,
> I am resolved that in this world
> Contented I will be.
> How many blessings I enjoy
> That other people don't!
> To weep and sight because I'm blind
> I cannot and I won't.

Fanny Crosby had a faith resolved to live by God's word. She became one of the greatest hymnwriters of all time writing almost 9000 hymns. She wrote such beloved hymns as Blessed Assurance, Pass Me Not O Gentle Savior, All The Way My Savior Leads Me, and To God Be The Glory. She was blessed to work closely with D.L. Moody and Ira Sankey in the evangelistic campaigns. And Billy Graham and Cliff Barrows introduced To God Be The Glory into their evangelistic campaigns. As you draw near to God now, begin your time by meditating on and even singing the words of To God Be The Glory by Fanny Crosby.

> To God be the glory—great things He hath done!
> So loved He the world that He gave us His Son.
> Who yielded His life an atonement for sin,
> And opened the lifegate that all may go in.

Refrain:
Praise the Lord, praise the Lord,
Let the earth hear His voice!
Praise the Lord, praise the Lord,
Let the people rejoice!
O come to the Father thru Jesus the Son,
And give Him the glory—great things He has done!

READ AND STUDY GOD'S WORD

1. On the other side of the Red Sea place after watching their God in action, Exodus 15:1 tells us that Moses and the sons of Israel sang a song to the LORD. It is a beautiful day when God has delivered you through the Red Sea and moved you to a new place in your relationship with Him. The people of God were moved to a new place in their walk with Yahweh. They believed and that means they were moved to a new place of assurance and certainty about Yahweh. They experienced revival and that's what happens when people hear God's Word and respond in faith. The psalmist says, "Your word has revived me" (Psalm 119:50). Now the people sang in worship. Read Exodus 15:1-21 and write everything you learn about the Lord.

2. In Exodus 15:13 they sang, "In Your lovingkindness You have led the people whom You have redeemed; in Your strength You have guided them to Your holy habitation" (unfailing love NIV). These two truths were the outstanding characteristics of Yahweh that the people saw at the Red Sea place: Yahweh's lovingkindness and strength. Read the following verses and write what you learn about God's lovingkindness (unfailing love NIV) and strength. (Optional Verses: Psalm 23:6, 36:7-9, 37:39-40, 57:10, 62:5-8, 147:5, 10-11).

Psalm 32:10

Psalm 84:5-7

3. You see, dear friend, the people were taken out of Egypt and were now in the presence of perfect love and strength. What an incredible thing to now experience God's amazing love. And what a difference from their life in Egypt. Describe the differences they have already experienced between Egypt and their deliverance by God in and through the Red Sea.

ADORE GOD IN PRAYER

Talk with God today thanking Him for all He has taught you through the sacred journey of the Red Sea place.

YIELD YOURSELF TO GOD

> The spectacular victory wrought by God over the armies of Egypt not only guaranteed freedom, but confirmed the fact that Israel had indeed been the recipient of special favor. For the first time in over four hundred years the Israelites were able to call themselves free men…The chapters before us are an exquisite example of godly praise and thanksgiving. The song of Moses reflects the heart and mind of a true believer as he gives due recognition to the provisions of God. These chapters also give us marvelous portraits of Joshua, Moses, Jethro and Miriam… These narratives are not merely the dry rehearsal of national events passed on by tradition and preserved out of some religious necessity. They represent an infallible record of real experiences depicted with warm emotion and dedication.[13]
>
> JOHN J. DAVIS IN MOSES AND THE GODS OF EGYPT

ENJOY HIS PRESENCE

This week has been significant in the sacred journey in Exodus. There is no more earthly security and everything has changed for the people of Israel as they truly have launched out on the water by faith, led by Yahweh and encouraged by Moses, their leader. What is the most important truth you learned about your God from the song in Exodus 15? Close by writing your thoughts and a prayer to your Lord in your Journal.

REST IN HIS LOVE

"Blessed are those whose strength is in you, whose hearts are set on pilgrimage" (Psalm 84:5 NIV).

WELL WITH MY SOUL

I will see the goodness of the Lord. Psalm 27:13 NIV
Cathedral Rock, Sedona, Arizona, USA
Nikon D7000, ISO 100, f11, AEB, Adobe Photoshop, Nik Silver Efex Pro
MYPHOTOWALK.COM—CATHERINEMARTIN.SMUGMUG.COM

DEVOTIONAL READING
BY JAMES MCCONKEY

DEAR FRIEND,

This week you experienced the Red Sea place firsthand with Moses and the people of Israel. Look back over your week of study and summarize your favorite truths learned on this sacred journey.

What were your most meaningful discoveries this week as you spent time with the Lord?

Most meaningful insight:

Most meaningful devotional reading:

Most meaningful verse:

The Lord is my shepherd: therefore can I lack nothing (Psalm 23:1) If sheep could talk, and a wise and a foolish sheep were holding converse, I fancy the foolish sheep would speak after this fashion: "I know where the crystal brook babbles from the grotto, and I shall never want for drink. I know where the great oak spreads its leafy branches, and I shall not want for shade. I know the green pastures of tender grass, and I shall never want for food. I know where the door of the fold stands wide open, and I shall never want for refuge. I know these things and I shall never want." And then I hear the wise sheep answering thus: "Oh! Foolish sheep! Suppose the pastures of green and tender grass should dry up, what would you do for food? Suppose the woodman comes and cuts down the spreading oak tree, where would be your shade? Suppose the sun of summer dries up the babbling brook, how would you quench your thirst? Suppose the gaunt great wolf leaps into the fold, where would you go for protection? "Oh, foolish sheep! I have a better reason than yours for not wanting. I have the best shepherd in the world, therefore I shall not want. If the brook dries up, He will find another for me. If the tree is cut down by the woodman's ax, He will lead me to the shadow of a great rock in a weary land. If the pastures dry up in the summer's sun, He knows how to find others. And when the wolf comes, He will lay down His life, if need be, for His sheep. Oh, foolish sheep! I shall never want; not because I trust in things that may change, or men that prove false, but in the Shepherd who changeth not nor doth He ever fail."

JAMES MCCONKEY IN THE SURE SHEPHERD

It's a mark of maturity when we learn that freedom is a tool to build with, not a toy to play with, and that freedom involves accepting responsibility. Israel's exodus experience taught them that their future success lay in fulfilling three important responsibilities: following the Lord (13:17-22), trusting the Lord (14:1-31), and praising the Lord (15:12-21)…The person who trusts Jesus Christ is born again into the family of God, but that's just the beginning of an exciting new adventure that should lead to growth and conquest. God liberates us and then leads us through the varied experiences of life, a day at a time, so that we might get to know Him better and claim by faith all that He wants us to have.[14]

WARREN WIERSBE IN BE DELIVERED

Viewer Guide
﹌ WEEK FOUR ﹌

The Red Sea Place

In Week Four of *One Holy Passion*, you had the opportunity to journey with Moses and the children of Israel to the Red Sea where they saw God miraculously deliver them. Today we are going to talk about the Red Sea Place and what it means for you in your own life. So, grab your Bibles, and let's talk about the Red Sea place.

"God led the people around by the way of the wilderness to the Red Sea..." Exodus 13:18

What we learn about the Red Sea place in Exodus 13-14:

1. The Red Sea place is not an accident but by God's _____.
God leads you to the Red Sea place on _____ for His plan in your life.

Exodus 13:17-18, 21-22

God does what is best for us when He leads us, and anticipates all the possible scenarios. When He sets us free, He takes us on as His own, and leads us according to His will.

2. The Red Sea place is a very real _____ with no way back or out, but God is sovereign over the circumstances and works everything for His honor and glory.

Exodus 14:3-9, 1 Peter 4:12-13

3. The Red Sea place is a _____ of your faith and trust in God, and the place to cry out to God.

Exodus 14:10-12, 1 Peter 1:6-9

4. At the Red Sea place you will _____ to a greater faith and trust in God, as you listen to Him speak in His Word.

Exodus 14:13-16, Job 13:15

5. At the Red Sea place, you are going to see the God of the impossible do something only He can do. You will see that He is going to do the _____.

Exodus 14:19-23, Ephesians 3:20

6. At the Red Sea place, God will fight and defeat your _____ —those who are coming against you.

Exodus 14:24-28, 1 John 4:4, John 16:33, Ephesians 6:10-18

7. At the Red Sea place you will see God's _____ and you will _____ in the Lord.

Exodus 14:29-30

8. You will experience victory and make it _____ the Red Sea place to the other side in God's time and in God's way. God leads you through to lead you on.

Exodus 15:19, Isaiah 43:18-21

❧ *Video messages are available on DVDs or as Digital M4V Video. Audio messages are available as Digital MP3 Audio. Visit the Quiet Time Ministries Online Store at www.quiettime.org.*

INTO THE WILDERNESS

God can find places of refreshment for his people even in the wilderness of this world, wells in the valley of Baca, lest they should faint in their mind with perpetual fatigue: yet, whatever our delights may be in the land of our pilgrimage, we must remember that we do but encamp by them for a time, that here we have no continuing city.

MATTHEW HENRY

TO EXPERIENCE GOD'S HEALING

I, the LORD, am your healer.

EXODUS 15:26

PREPARE YOUR HEART

Lilias Trotter had the dream of being a missionary in Algeria. It was a surprising calling considering her gift of art and painting. John Ruskin, the leading art critic of the day had said that if her rare artistic talent was cultivated, she would become one of England's "greatest living artists." However, Lilias came to an important decision. She wrote, "I see clear as daylight now, I cannot give myself to painting…and continue to seek first the Kingdom of God and His Righteousness." Following that time, she applied to the North African Mission and was turned down because of her health. She was so determined to follow the Lord's leading to Algiers that she traveled with two friends to serve there. She spent the rest of her life, more than forty years, bringing the love of Christ to Arab people in North Africa.

Because she had a creative eye and a skilled gift of painting with watercolors, she also spent those forty years capturing the beauty in the desert. She was in the heart of the Sahara desert, a place many would call dry and barren. She painted in her journals and sketchbooks all that she saw—blossoms in the desert, the lines and curves of sand dunes, and the wonder of light and color all around her. And in that wilderness place, she learned the deep things of God and wrote those spiritual truths in her journals along with her watercolor artistry. All of this wondrous beauty was lost for many years following Trotter's death, until Miriam Rockness, a pastor's wife, became interested in the life and work of Lilias Trotter. She began researching her life and hunting down her journals, sketchbooks, and paintings. After five years of searching, Rockness traveled to England and the UK Headquarters of Arab World Ministries. And there she discovered Trotter's archives including her diaries and journals filled with beautiful watercolors and sketches. What she saw in them was a breathtaking picture of beauty in the desert places. And the message was clear throughout everything Lilias wrote and painted—that God is the One who paints the beauty into every landscape in life.

Going into the wilderness or desert place can be the greatest gift and leading by God any believer in Christ can ever experience. For there are lessons that can only be learned out in the wilderness. Seeing God is easier in the wilderness than in the world. Finding treasure in God's Word is more of a necessity for one who is out in the desert. Relying on God for every provision by faith is imperative. To Prepare Your Heart, ask God to teach you the lessons of the wilderness.

READ AND STUDY GOD'S WORD

1. The people of God had been delivered from the captivity of the Egyptians and are now following God's leading. If there was a sign at the next place of their journey, it might read like this: "Welcome to the wilderness. In this place you will have no visible means of support or security. You will have much to learn. You will learn to trust God for everything. You will depend on Him for every provision. You will see God as you have never seen Him before. And you will learn His ways and what it means to be His people. And though your faith will be stretched beyond the here and now, you will be led into one holy passion for your God and a passion for the impossible." The wilderness must have been quite a shock for the people of Israel. They were used to the fertile land of Egypt where they could see provision and had a sense of security, though they were slaves. Now, they have been set free, and they are out in the barren dry wilderness land being led by God, unable to see their destination. This newfound freedom would carry quite a learning curve, and the wilderness was the perfect place to grow. Read Exodus 15:22-27, their first wilderness experience only three days after they had seen God's miraculous power at the Red Sea. Describe what happened.

2. God made the bitter waters sweet there at Marah. This is a beautiful picture of how God is revealing Himself to His people as Yahweh Rophe, the LORD their healer. And He is the balm for their hearts wounded from suffering at the hands of the Egyptians. The wounds and scars of slavery and the world can go deep. The Lord is your healer and with time, He makes the bitter waters sweet. We learn in Exodus 15:25-26 that God is also testing His people. Read those verses and describe what God is teaching His people as a lesson in the wilderness.

3. There are a number of Psalms that speak of the wilderness experience in Exodus. (Psalms 78,80-81,105-106,114, and 135-136.) Read Psalm 78:14-24 and write your most significant insight about how the people acted in the wilderness.

4. Paul sheds light on the wilderness experience of the people in 1 Corinthians 10:1-13. Read these verses noting your most significant insight. What does God expect from His people when they are in the wilderness?

ADORE GOD IN PRAYER

Are you in a wilderness experience right now? Talk with God, pour out your heart, and ask Him to open your eyes to Him and also His Word in your wilderness.

YIELD YOURSELF TO GOD

For the Israelites, their experience in the wasteland was not meant to be a waste. The Land Between was to be pivotal in their formation as a people—it was where they were to be transformed from the people of slavery into the people of God. And they needed transformation. Let us consider that as they exit Egypt, the Israelites are more fully acclimated to the world of Egyptian idolatry than they are formed by the character and presence of the God of Abraham. As we watch them exit Egypt and enter the desert, we should not imagine a neatly ordered multitude of mature followers. The Israelites are an unruly mob of recently released slaves who are prone to complaining, frequently resentful of Moses' leadership, and longing to return to Egypt with every conceivable hardship. The Israelites desperately need the spiritual formation of the desert to become the people of God. In their current condition, they do not yet know their God and are unprepared to enter the Land of Promise. The desert experience is intended to shape, mold, and refine them into a community of trust.[1]

JEFF MANION IN THE LAND BETWEEN

Let us dare to test God's resources…Let us ask Him to kindle in us and keep aflame that passion for the impossible that shall make us delight in it with Him, till the day when we shall see it transformed into a fact.[2]

LILIAS TROTTER

ENJOY HIS PRESENCE

What is your most significant insight about this initial experience in the wilderness? What did God want the people to learn? What did they discover about God in that experience? How is living in the world like living in the wilderness at times? What is the value of possessing a passion for the impossible, as Lilias Trotter described? Write your thoughts in your Journal, then close by writing a prayer expressing all that is on your heart today.

REST IN HIS LOVE

"Now these things happened to them as an example, and they were written for our instruction, upon whom the ends of the ages have come" (1 Corinthians 10:11).

IN THE WILDERNESS

They went out into the wilderness. Exodus 15:22
Sedona, Arizona, USA
Nikon D810, ISO 64, f5.6, 1/1000sec, Adobe Photoshop, Nik Silver Efex Pro
MYPHOTOWALK.COM—CATHERINEMARTIN.SMUGMUG.COM

TO SEE GOD'S PROVISION

The LORD gives you meat to eat in the evening, and bread to the full in the morning.

EXODUS 16:8

PREPARE YOUR HEART

You know you've arrived in the wilderness experience when your life has encountered a bend in the road and you have no visible means of support. Things that were secure in your mind have now seemingly vanished into thin air. Provision for even basic needs no longer seems a given. Perhaps you lost your job or you are now on your own without any visible help. Or you may be suffering illness or experiencing a difficult relationship. You may have lost a loved one so very precious to you. Whatever the gateway into the wilderness, now you are there. What are you going to do? And what or who is going to help you make it through this desolate place?

There is good news to be found on this sacred journey in the book of Exodus, especially in the wilderness with the people of Israel. While they couldn't see God's provision, they had its promise because of God's presence. You can know the promise of God's provision because you are indwelt by the Holy Spirit and you hold God's Word in your hand. There are lessons to learn from the Lord that will help you respond in the wilderness. And you will discover the beauty of God that Lilias Trotter found there in the desert.

God always provides for His people. He promises. He can indeed prepare a table for His people in the wilderness (see Psalm 78:19). Paul discovered this same truth as a missionary completely dependent on God for his daily needs. He wrote, "I have received everything in full and have an abundance; I am amply supplied…And my God will supply all your needs according to His riches in glory in Christ Jesus" (Philippians 4:18-19). Have you discovered the God who provides for all your needs? Today ask God to open your eyes to His care and provision for you.

READ AND STUDY GOD'S WORD

1. Read Exodus 16:1-21 and write your most significant insight about God's provision for His people in the wilderness?

2. Read Exodus 16:6, 12 and look for the phrase "you will know" (verses 6 and 12). What did the Lord want His people to know and why was it important for them to know these truths?

3. Later in the Bible we learn what God was teaching His people out in the wilderness, especially in His provision for them. Read Deuteronomy 8:1-3 and write your most significant insight.

4. Read Exodus 16:22-30. What do you learn about the sabbath? What was its purpose?

5. In Exodus 17:1 (NASB) you discover that the people of God journeyed "by stages" through the wilderness. The lessons from the Lord don't come all at once, but little by little. God had rescued the people from Egypt, but He was working on maturing them and getting Egypt out of them. Read Exodus 17:1-7 and write your insights about the following:

What happened to the people at Rephidim (Exodus 17:1)

How did the people respond (Exodus 17:3-4)

What did the Lord do (Exodus 17:5-6)

What was the test of faith for the people (Exodus 17:6)

6. The people asked, "Is the LORD among us or not?" That question can come to us when we are in the wilderness. If we live only by sight, then we ask, "Where is the Lord?" But by faith we know what is true in God's Word. We are challenged in the time of need to either trust God's Word or rely on our feelings. In the wilderness where there is no visible means of support, God is teaching us to rely on His presence, power, and provision. God is so passionate for you to live freely in Him, walking by faith, unshaken by life's storms, knowing His amazing love, and able to experience intimacy with Him. The wilderness tests and instructs our faith. How has God been teaching you to rely on His provision in your own life?

ADORE GOD IN PRAYER

Turn to the Prayer pages in the back of this book and write out all your needs today on one page, then pray through each one, asking God to provide, thanking Him that He is your provider, and praising Him for His answer. Then, take some time to thank God for all He has given you.

YIELD YOURSELF TO GOD

> Independence is the characteristic of the new flood of resurrection life that comes to our souls as we learn this fresh lesson of dying—a grand independence of any earthly thing to satisfy our soul, the liberty of those who have nothing to lose, because they have nothing to keep. We can do without anything while we have God. Hallelujah!
>
> LILIAS TROTTER IN PARABLES OF THE CROSS

> Yesterday I looked at some birds in a cage. These poor little creatures are entirely dependent on those who feed them. They cannot help themselves. If seed and water is not supplied, they will die. Yet there they sit and sing with all their might. Their state of dependence never distresses them. They never think that their keeper will fail them. That is my position. I am God's singing bird. Perhaps I wonder where I shall get my bread or my next sermons, and a great many cares and troubles come to me. But why should I be troubled? Instead of mistrusting my keeper, who has fed me these many years, I had best sit and sing as loudly as I can. That is the best thing to do. The birds do it, so why not you and me?
>
> CHARLES SPURGEON IN BESIDE STILL WATERS

Enjoy His Presence

It is a red letter day when you depend on God alone, looking to Him as your sure provider. Then, you truly are living with a new freedom and experiencing an independence of soul, as Lilias Trotter describes. God wants you to rely on Him for everything. The people were beginning to learn this in the wilderness even as they tested the Lord asking, "Is the LORD among us or not?" What is God teaching you in this wilderness place found in Exodus? Write your thoughts in your Journal, then close with a prayer to the Lord expressing all that is on your heart.

Rest in His Love

"…man lives by everything that proceeds out of the mouth of the LORD" (Deuteronomy 8:3).

GOD PROVIDES

And my God will supply all your needs. Philippians 4:19
Sedona, Arizona, USA
Sony A6000, ISO 100 f4.5, 1/100sec, Adobe Photoshop, Nik Silver Efex Pro
MYPHOTOWALK.COM—CATHERINEMARTIN.SMUGMUG.COM

TO KNOW GOD'S POWER

Moses built an altar and named it The LORD is My Banner.

EXODUS 17:15

PREPARE YOUR HEART

Y
ou've heard the expression that when it rains it pours. Such was seemingly the case for the people of Israel. Their thirst and need for food became the least of their worries when they were attacked by Amalek, the chief of an Edomite tribe and a warrior descendant of Esau.

On this sacred journey have you noticed that God is never worried with any circumstance or need? And yet, the opposite is often true for us. Here is what we need to learn. God is Yahweh—everything we need for every circumstance of life. It's one thing to say it but quite another to know, believe, and live it out every day. Imagine what would happen if you lived a life trusting in God in such a way that nothing could shake you. God is passionate for your love and trust. As He becomes your one holy passion, more and more, you will discover a new trust and a deeper faith in everything He says. Your first question won't be "what's happening" or "what am I going to do?" It will be "what does God say, what is God going to do, and what does He want me to learn about Him?"

Meditate on the words of this Puritan prayer as you begin your quiet time:

Giver of all good,

Streams upon streams of love overflow my path.

Thou hast made me out of nothing,

hast recalled me from a far country,

hast translated me from ignorance to knowledge,

from darkness to light,

from death to life,

from misery to peace,

from folly to wisdom,

from error to truth,

from sin to victory.

Thanks be to thee for my high and holy calling.

I bless thee for ministering angels,
for the comfort of thy Word,
for the ordinances of thy church,
for the teaching of thy Spirit,
for thy holy sacraments,
for the communion of saints,
for Christian fellowship,
for the recorded annals of holy lives,
for examples sweet to allure,
for beacons sad to deter.
Thy will is in all thy provisions
to enable me to grow in grace,
and to be meet for thy eternal presence.
My heaven-born faith gives promise of eternal sight,
my new birth a pledge of never-ending life.
I draw near to thee, knowing thou wilt draw near to me.
I ask of thee, believing thou hast already given.
I entrust myself to thee, for thou hast redeemed me.
I bless and adore thee, the eternal God,
for the comfort of these thoughts,
the joy of these hopes.[3]

THE VALLEY OF VISION

READ AND STUDY GOD'S WORD

1. In the midst of learning to trust God to provide, now the people face a new area of trust. Where does victory in a battle come from? Now, they are going to learn that the Lord is the One who fights their battles. Read Exodus 17:8-16 and describe what happened.

2. In Exodus 17:15 you discover a new name for God, The Lord Is My Banner—Yahweh Nissi. God wanted His people to know that He is the one who gives victory in every circumstance. In this event, there is a reminder for us that we have an enemy, "the devil, who prowls around like a roaring lion, seeking someone to devour" (1 Peter 5:8). We will experience spiritual warfare (Ephesians 6:12). Be assured that your Lord, Yahweh Nissi, is all-powerful and victorious over all

enemies. Read the following verses and write what you learn about God's power and ability to fight your battles. (Optional Verses: Exodus 15:3, 1 Samuel 17:45-47, 50, Psalm 68:20, Isaiah 40:10-13).

2 Chronicles 20:15

Jeremiah 20:11

Ephesians 6:10-18

1 John 4:4

3. What a triumphant experience of victory for Moses and the people of Israel there in the wilderness. And now, God gave Moses a special blessing following the battle. Read Exodus 18:1-12 and write your most significant insight about how God blessed Moses.

4. As you have seen in your study over the last few days, there can be beauty, refreshment, renewal, and revival even in the most desolate wilderness. It comes in many forms—a provision from God, a promise in God's Word, a victory in a battle, or encouragement from a friend. Meditate on these verses and underline your favorite words or phrases and hold them as promises in your heart in the desert places of life.

"Even the wilderness and desert will be glad in those days. The wasteland will rejoice and blossom with spring crocuses. Yes, there will be an abundance of flowers and singing and joy! The deserts will become as green as the mountains of Lebanon, as lovely as Mount Carmel or the plain of Sharon. There the LORD will display his glory, the splendor of our God" (Isaiah 35:1-2 NLT).

"The afflicted and needy are seeking water, but there is none, and their tongue is parched with thirst; I, the LORD, will answer them Myself, as the God of Israel I will not forsake them. I will open rivers on the bare heights and springs in the midst of the valleys; I will make the wilderness a pool of water and the dry land fountains of water. I will put the cedar in the wilderness, the acacia and the myrtle and the olive tree; I will place the juniper in the desert together with the box tree and the cypress, that they may see and recognize, and consider and gain insight as well, that the hand of the LORD has done this, and the Holy One of Israel has created it" (Isaiah 41:17-20).

"For I am about to do something new. See, I have already begun! Do you not see it? I will make a pathway through the wilderness. I will create rivers in the dry wasteland" (Isaiah 43:19 NLT).

"And the LORD will continually guide you, and satisfy your desire in scorched places, and give strength to your bones; and you will be like a watered garden, and like a spring of water whose waters do not fail" (Isaiah 58:11).

"Therefore I am now going to allure her; I will lead her into the wilderness and speak tenderly to her" (Hosea 2:14).

ADORE GOD IN PRAYER

In what way do you need victory today? Realize that the LORD is your Banner and He is the One who can fight every one of your battles. Take your battles to the Lord today. Find hope in God's promises. "Thank You Lord, that You are Victor in my life."

YIELD YOURSELF TO GOD

Jesus is Victor. Calvary is the place of victory. Obedience is the pathway of victory. Bible study and prayer the preparation. Courage, faith, the spirit of victory—every temptation is a chance for victory, a signal to fly the flag of our Victor, a chance to make the tempter know anew that he is defeated. Roy Hession writes in Calvary Road: "Jesus is always victorious. We have only to keep the right relationship with Him and His victorious life will flow through us and touch other people."[4]

CORRIE TEN BOOM IN EACH NEW DAY

Who has not known men and women who, when they arrive at seasons of gloom and solitude, put on strength and hopefulness like a robe? You may imprison such folk where you please; but you shut up their treasure with them. You cannot shut it out. You may make their material lot a desert, but "the wilderness and the solitary place shall be glad, and the desert shall rejoice and blossom as the rose" (Isaiah 35:1-2).

JOHN HENRY JOWETT

ENJOY HIS PRESENCE

Think for a moment about what it must have been like for the people of Israel out in the wilderness. They were being provided for in every way by the Lord. And now, He has just won a great victory for them. And that victory came in the desert. What are they learning about God and His ways that will help them realize God's passion for them—His extravagant, unconditional, amazing love? How are they encouraged to grow in their own passion for Him? And how are they experiencing a time of revival and refreshing there in the desert? How are they realizing now that they are truly God's people? Then, what are you learning about God that is fanning the flame of your love for Him? Write out your most significant insights about what God is teaching you.

Rest in His Love

"But the LORD is with me like a dread champion; therefore my persecutors will stumble and not prevail. They will be utterly ashamed, because they have failed, with an everlasting disgrace that will not be forgotten" (Jeremiah 20:11).

Beauty In The Desert

Even the wilderness and the desert will be glad in those days. Isaiah 35:1
Sedona, Arizona, USA
Nikon D7000, ISO 110, f8, 1/250sec, Adobe Photoshop, Nik Silver Efex Pro
myPhotoWalk.com—catherinemartin.smugmug.com

TO MEET WITH GOD

Moses went up to God, and the LORD called to him from the mountain…

Exodus 19:3

PREPARE YOUR HEART

God made a promise to Moses on Mount Sinai when the bush was burning and he was standing on holy ground. God said, "Certainly I will be with you, and this shall be the sign to you that it is I who have sent you, when you have brought the people out of Egypt, you shall worship God at this mountain" (Exodus 3:12). What a journey it had been for Moses since that time. He surely knew more about Yahweh now than he did then. Moses was God's man for the hour and he was faithful to trust God. In Numbers 12:3 we learn that "Moses was very humble, more than any man who was on the face of the earth." And isn't it true that Moses is seemingly in the background and God has center stage in all that is happening in Egypt, at the Red Sea, and in the wilderness? Keep in mind that Exodus can be thought of in two divisions: 1-18 (God rescues and redeems His people, and delivers them out of Egypt) and 19-40 (God reveals Himself to His people, brings them near to Himself, and is intent on getting Egypt out of the people). Now we begin in earnest the journey to the heart of God. The wilderness is the place where you will meet with God and experience Him in deeper intimacy.

Begin your quiet time with the Lord meditating on these words by F.B. Meyer and ask God to give you the same kind of passion for God that Moses had: "Though Moses may have had commanding features of mind and body, and have been versed in all the learning of his time, yet the marvelous outcome of his life work was not due to any of these qualities, but to the faith that knit his soul to God…He was as thoroughly yielded to the purpose of God as the staff he held in his hand was to his own will. He fed daily on the promises of God, pleading them in prayer, and leaning his whole weight on them. And he often knew what it was to leave behind him the familiar and tried, for the strange and new. At the bidding of God he stepped out, though there seemed nothing to tread on…assured that God's faithfulness could not fail…are you willing to die to your own strength; to forsake your own plans for God's; to seek out and do His will absolutely; to take up the attitude of entire and absolute surrender to His purposes, to feed daily on the promises of God, as a girl on the pledge of her absent love, to step out in faith, reckoning, without emotion of any kind, on the faithfulness of God, only fully persuaded that He will perform what He has promised?"[5] Ask God to speak to you today as you draw near to Him in His Word.

READ AND STUDY GOD'S WORD

1. When Moses was at the burning bush, he heard God promise that after He delivered His people, He would bring Moses back to the same mountain to worship. Read Exodus 19:1-9 and write out what you learn about God and His passion for His people.

2. The people of Israel have now arrived at Sinai, brought there by God. And He has brought them there with great purpose—they will be His people and He will be their God. His people are set apart for Him. All the nations will be able to look at God's people and know they belong to God. God's nation will reflect the greatness of God. He is making them into a great and holy nation and a kingdom of priests. All of this is based on covenant, a solemn and binding agreement, with promises guaranteed by the faithfulness of God Himself, and a dynamic relationship entered into by the people of God. Read Exodus 19:4-8 again. In these words, you see that God is establishing His covenant with His people. What did God promise and how did the people respond?

3. In Exodus 19:6, God said He was making the people a holy nation and a kingdom of priests. The same is true for us. Read the following verses in the New Testament and underline those words and phrases that are most significant to you.

"As obedient children, do not be conformed to the former lusts which were yours in your ignorance, but like the Holy One who called you, be holy yourselves also in all your behavior; because it is written, 'YOU SHALL BE HOLY, FOR I AM HOLY'" (1 Peter 1:16).

"But you are A CHOSEN RACE, A royal PRIESTHOOD, A HOLY NATION, A PEOPLE FOR God's OWN POSSESSION, so that you may proclaim the excellencies of Him who has called you out of darkness into His marvelous light; for you once were NOT A PEOPLE, but now you are THE PEOPLE OF GOD; you had NOT RECEIVED MERCY, but now you have RECEIVED MERCY." (1 Peter 2:9-10).

"To him who loves us and has freed us from our sins by his blood, and has made us to be a kingdom and priests to serve his God and Father—to him be glory and power for ever and ever! Amen" (Revelation 1:5-6 NIV).

4. Read Exodus 19:9-25 about the preparation of the people to meet with God as He establishes the covenant. What impresses you the most about God and the preparation of the people?

5. God was inviting Moses and the people into His presence. Exodus 19:18 shows us just a glimpse of God's glory when it says that "Mount Sinai was all in smoke because the Lord descended upon it in fire; and its smoke ascended like the smoke of a furnace, and the whole mountain quaked violently." Can we know the glorious presence of God today in our own lives? Can we meet with God and experience Him? Read the following verses and write what you learn:

John 14:21-23

2 Corinthians 3:18

2 Corinthians 4:6

ADORE GOD IN PRAYER

Pray these words written by F.B. Meyer: "You are stirring up my nest, my Father; the old is changing and giving place to the new. Spread your wings beneath me and teach me to trust where I can see no earthly support to rest on." Then, write a one sentence prayer expressing your trust in the Lord today.

YIELD YOURSELF TO GOD

A spiritual kingdom lies all about us, enclosing us, embracing us, altogether within reach of our inner selves, waiting for us to recognize it. God Himself is here waiting our response to His presence. This eternal world will come alive to us the moment we begin to reckon upon its reality…God is real…More and more, as our faculties grow sharper and more sure, God will become to us the great All, and His presence the glory and wonder of our lives.[6]

A.W. TOZER IN THE PURSUIT OF GOD

Having interpreted the exodus for Israel in 19:4, 19:5-6 goes on to define what it will mean for Israel to be the Lord's people. Israel is spoken of as a treasured possession, a priestly kingdom and a holy nation, each addressing the purposes for which the Lord delivered her and shedding light upon the role of the law in Israel's life.[7]

W. ROSS BLACKBURN IN THE GOD WHO MAKES HIMSELF KNOWN

ENJOY HIS PRESENCE

What does it take for a man to get to the place where he will know and trust God? Just think about the journey Moses and the people of Israel have been on as they have traveled through the Red Sea and on into the wilderness. Many things carry us to the place where we will know and trust God including rejection, failure, suffering, pain, loss, brokenness and also great revelation from God Himself. When a man or woman get to the place where they see nothing in themselves and everything in God, they are on their way to a great trust in God and a life-changing, adventurous, exciting, deep, passionate relationship with Him. It is what life—eternal life—is all about. Knowing Him (John 17:3).

How is God bringing you to a new place of knowing and trusting Him? What Red Sea place or wilderness experience is God using in your life and how is He meeting you even now? What have you learned in your study today that fuels your passion for God? Write the one truth that impacted your life today. Then write a prayer to the Lord expressing your heart and passion for Him as a result of all you've learned of Him so far on this sacred journey in Exodus.

REST IN HIS LOVE

"If anyone really loves me, he will observe my teaching, and my Father will love him, and both of us will come in face-to-face fellowship with him; yes, we will make our special dwelling place within him" (John 14:23 wms).

SOLITUDE WITH JESUS

At daybreak, Jesus went out to a solitary place. Luke 4:42 NIV
Oak Creek Canyon, Sedona, Arizona, USA
Nikon D800E, ISO 100, f22, 0.3sec, Adobe Photoshop, Nik Silver Efex Pro
MYPHOTOWALK.COM—CATHERINEMARTIN.SMUGMUG.COM

TO LEARN GOD'S WAYS

*Then Moses came and recounted to the people all the words of the LORD
and all the ordinances; and all the people answered with one voice and
said, "All the words which the LORD has spoken we will do."*

EXODUS 24:3

PREPARE YOUR HEART

And now, Moses is on the mountain with God. God was ready to speak some words to Moses that would be significant not only for the people of Israel but also for all people in all times. He was going to give Moses what has become known as the Law including the Ten Commandments and the Book of the Covenant, also known as the Old Covenant. Dr. Ronald Youngblood, in his commentary on Exodus, describes the Ten Commandments as more than statues and regulations, but a "gracious gift from the Lord to insure the kind of community that would keep the Israelites healthy and happy."[8] John J. Davis, in his commentary, *Moses and the gods of Egypt*, writes that, according to both the Old and New Testaments, there are five purposes for the law: to reveal man's sin (Romans 3:19-20), to illustrate the hideous nature of sin (Romans 7:8-13), to reveal the holiness of God, to restrain and help a sinner come to Christ (Galatians 3:24), and restrain wrong behavior to protect the institutions of Israel. The law can't save a person, only Christ can. But the law is a tutor that leads us to Christ, so we can be justified by faith (Galatians 3:24).

Now the people of Israel are going to learn more about who God is, what God thinks, and what is important to God. This covenant God is making with His people is solemn and binding. Pray the prayer of David today as you begin your quiet time: "Make me know Your ways, O LORD; Teach me Your paths" (Psalm 25:4).

READ AND STUDY GOD'S WORD

1. Imagine now that you are with Moses on the mountain. Read Exodus 20:1-6, the first two of the ten great commandments. What do you learn about God?

2. Read Exodus 20:7-17 and write the next eight of the ten commandments.

3. This is a great moment in the history of Israel as God is speaking to Moses and the people of Israel are watching from afar. Read Exodus 20:18-26 and describe what the people learned about God.

4. In Exodus 21-23 we find an elaboration of the Ten Commandments in what is known as the book of the covenant. In Exodus 23:31-33, God speaks about the inhabitants in the land He is going to give His people. He commands His people not to make a covenant with the inhabitants and not to allow them to stay in the land because it will cause His people to sin and will be a snare to them. With Exodus 23:31-33 in mind, think about your own walk with God as you live in the world. Remember this world is passing away and is temporal. Your future is eternal life and a kingdom that never passes away. How friendly are you with the ways of the current culture and the things of the world? Read Romans 12:1-2 and 1 John 2:15-17 and write what you learn.

5. The Old Covenant could not save people and ultimately shows that "all have sinned and fall short of the glory of God" (Romans 3:23). Therefore, it really is "a tutor to lead us to Christ, so we may be justified by faith" (Galatians 3:24). There is another covenant, the New Covenant, and a better one, enacted by Jesus Christ Himself that is ratified by His blood. Read Jeremiah 31:31-34, and Hebrews 8:1-13, 9:15 and write your most significant insight about the New Covenant.

ADORE GOD IN PRAYER

Pray the words of the prayer in Psalm 119:129-135—"Your testimonies are wonderful; therefore my soul observes them. The unfolding of Your words gives light; It gives understanding to the simple. I opened my mouth wide and panted, for I longed for Your commandments. Turn to me and be gracious to me, after Your manner with those who love Your name. Establish my footsteps in Your word, and do not let any iniquity have dominion over me. Redeem me from the oppression of man, that I may keep Your precepts. Make Your face shine upon Your servant, and teach me Your statutes."

YIELD YOURSELF TO GOD

That God proclaimed the ten commandments to the Israelites Himself and in such dramatic fashion emphasizes the primary position of the ten commandments among all the statues given Israel. The primary position of the ten commandments is also emphasized in that they were later inscribed by the finger of God upon two stone tablets (Exodus 31:18; 32:15-16).[9]

JOHN G. BUTLER IN MOSES THE EMANCIPATOR OF ISRAEL

Let our love to God go into the minutest details. Let us be earnest in all essentials but never indifferent to the non–essentials. God's lovingkindness goes into detail, and so should my obedience. May gratitude to God permeate my entire life; may it flood all my faculties, and may it saturate me through and through. Great God, Your love surrounds me. I breathe it. I live on it. I shall die in it. I shall live forever in it. It will make my bliss eternal. I give my soul to You in obedience. I give up my thoughts, work, desires, judgments, tastes, and everything else to Your sweet love, which so wonderfully embraces and surrounds me. Amen.

CHARLES HADDON SPURGEON IN BESIDE STILL WATERS

ENJOY HIS PRESENCE

When the people heard the words of the LORD from Moses, they answered with one voice, "All the words which the LORD has spoken, we will do" (Exodus 24:3). Hearing God's commands inspired the people to a great obedience. And they should do the same for you as well. You are called out of the world to belong to God as His beloved child. Oh, what a privilege to be recipients of the New Covenant, set in place by Jesus Christ, with the promises of forgiveness of sins and eternal life, reconciled to God through the blood of Christ, and being given God's love, a love that can never be taken from us. We now have the opportunity to love and serve Him during our brief stay on earth (2 Corinthians 5:11-21). What did you learn today that fills you with one holy passion and encourages you to love and serve your God? Write your thoughts in your Journal.

REST IN HIS LOVE

"Don't copy the behavior and customs of this world, but let God transform you into a new person by changing the way you think. Then you will learn to know God's will for you, which is good and pleasing and perfect" (Romans 12:2 NLT).

TEACH ME YOUR WAYS

Teach me Your ways, O LORD, that I may live according to Your truth. Psalm 86:11 NLT
Sedona, Arizona, USA
Nikon D810, ISO 400, f5.6, 1/500sec, Adobe Photoshop, Nik Silver Efex Pro
MYPHOTOWALK.COM—CATHERINEMARTIN.SMUGMUG.COM

DEVOTIONAL READING
BY JEFF MANION

Dear Friend,

You have walked in the wilderness on this sacred journey in Exodus with Moses and the people of Israel. Oh there is so much to be learned in the wilderness. Take some time to think about all you have learned and write a prayer to the Lord expressing all that is on your heart.

What were your most meaningful discoveries this week as you spent time with the Lord?

Most meaningful insight:

Most meaningful devotional reading:

Most meaningful verse:

Moses experienced God's tender care in the wilderness. There he was breaking under a load too heavy to carry, and God called him to approach the tabernacle, the tent representing God's presence, to draw near and receive help from God, the grace of additional shoulders to carry the load. God calls us to draw near, as well. "Come unto me. Cry out. Share your heart. Draw near and let me take care of you. Come and receive." That invitation to draw near to God is our hope—he is our hope. We draw near to experience his comfort when we are crushed by loss, his closeness when we feel abandoned, and his slow, sure healing when crippled by grief. He is the God who provides. He knows what we need even when we do not. And he knows how he will provide it.[10]

JEFF MANION IN THE LAND BETWEEN

God is in the darkness and God is in the wilderness…maybe life has just crashed in on you. Wounds and rejection can pile up. Perhaps you feel you have no one to turn to, no one to talk to, no one to help you. If you and I are not careful, that aloneness can cause us to wander in our spirits also. We want to get away from the darkness, to get out of the wilderness, but in our frantic effort we stumble from remorse to resentment, from self-pity to self-flagellation, from self-deception to depression, from brokenness to bitterness, from faith to agnosticism, from frustration to anger, from hurt to hardness, from hardness to helplessness. May I ask you something I have asked myself? Deep down in the hidden chambers of your soul, are you offended by God? Angry with Him even? Are you wandering *from* God? You thought you knew Him, but now He seems remote at best. The solemn conclusion I've come to is that if He is everywhere, that means He is also in the wilderness.[11]

ANNE GRAHAM LOTZ IN WOUNDED BY GOD'S PEOPLE

Viewer Guide
WEEK FIVE

Lessons In The Wilderness

In Week Five of *One Holy Passion,* you had the opportunity to continue your sacred journey and travel with God, Moses, and the people of Israel into the wilderness. Today we are going to learn lessons in the wilderness to encourage us when we find ourselves in a dry, barren, challenging, lonely place. So, grab your Bibles, and let's discover lessons in the wilderness.

"Then Moses led Israel from the Red Sea, and they went out into the wilderness of Shur; and they went three days in the wilderness and found no water" (Exodus 15:22).

The wilderness is the place where your soul can _____.

Lessons In The Wilderness

1. A time in the wilderness often follows a great time of _____.
Exodus 15:22

2. God is the One _____us into the wilderness. It is by His design. Exodus 15:22

3. In the wilderness, there is no visible means of _____ and no sense of _____, so that you can learn God is your support, provision, and security. Exodus 15:22

4. God is _____ in the wilderness and He is everything you need for every circumstance of life. Exodus 15:24-26

He is the LORD, your healer and makes the bitter waters sweet. (see Exodus 15:26).

5. In the wilderness, we learn the lesson of _____.
Exodus 15:25

6. In the wilderness, we learn the lesson of _____ carefully to God speak in His Word and doing what He says. This is the wilderness lesson of _____—taking God at His Word.

7. God can bring you to an _____in the desert, a place where you are renewed and revived. Exodus 15:27

8. The wilderness is a _____in stages. Exodus 17:1

9. The wilderness is a place where you will _____ with God. Exodus 19:2-4, 17, Hosea 2:14

10. The wilderness is the perfect setting for spiritual _____ in your life. God is going to transform you in the wilderness. The wilderness becomes a place of great blessings.

Video messages are available on DVDs or as Digital M4V Video. Audio messages are available as Digital MP3 Audio. Visit the Quiet Time Ministries Online Store at www.quiettime.org.

EXPERIENCING GOD

To know God we must have perceived him, we must have spoken to him, we must have been made at peace with him, we must have lifted up our heart to him, and received communications from him. If you know the Lord your secret is with him, and his secret is with you, he has manifested himself unto you as he does not unto the world. He must have made himself known unto you by the mysterious influences of his Spirit, and because of this you know him... A sight of God is the most wonderfully sanctifying influence that can be conceived of. Know God, and you will grow to be like him.[1]

CHARLES SPURGEON

THROUGH WORSHIP

Then He said to Moses, "Come up to the LORD, you and Aaron, Nadab and Abihu and seventy of the elders of Israel, and you shall worship at a distance."

EXODUS 24:1

PREPARE YOUR HEART

Knowing God always begins with an invitation from God to draw near to Him. If He did not reveal Himself and invite us in, we could not experience Him in an intimate, ongoing, vibrant, dynamic relationship. The Bible, which is the word of God, is filled with invitations from God to draw near and know Him. Stop and think about this fact for a moment. The one true God, Creator of the universe, all-powerful, all-knowing, eternal, holy, gracious, kind, compassionate, loving, merciful is inviting you, dear friend, to come near and know Him. Just to receive His invitation puts you in a choice, inner circle of His beloved servants.

In this new week of study, the journey in Exodus becomes more sacred now as God's people are at Mount Sinai, the place where they will meet with God. God, who has proven His passion for His people, is now enacting a covenant with them whereby they can experience a relationship as His people for His own possession. In this relationship, He will be their God. The covenant is a solemn and binding agreement, and establishes this relationship with promises guaranteed by a God who is faithful, gracious and loving. And we see now that the wilderness, the place of dryness and desolation, is transformed into the holy place of worship, where God reveals Himself to His people. Always remember that your wilderness experience can turn into a place of worship with your God. For in that wilderness, in His time, He is going to show Himself to you in a new way.

As you begin your quiet time today, ask the Lord to give you a heart to draw near to Him in love and worship.

READ AND STUDY GOD'S WORD

1. This week you are going to have the privilege to spend time in your sacred journey at Mount Sinai where God is going to meet with Moses and His people. Read Exodus 24:1 and write what God is asking of His people.

2. The two words that stand out in Exodus 24:1 are "Come up" and "worship." Whenever you draw near to God, you are looking up, so to speak, for God is always greater and higher than any place, person, or circumstance. To "come up" means to ascend. It is always an ascent to go to God. So as Moses and others came near to God, they were to worship. The Hebrew word for "worship" is "shacah" and means to bow down in reverence. Worship is the natural response when you are in the presence of God. Worship is an important part of our relationship with God, for then we are humble and reverent before our God. Read the following verses and write out your most significant insights about worship.

Genesis 24:26-27 the servant of Abraham

Exodus 34:5-8 Moses

Job 1:20-22 Job

Psalm 29:2-4 David

Romans 12:1 Us

Revelation 1:10-18 John

3. As you think about all the different examples of worship in the Bible, what is it that led each to fall on their face before God?

4. Have you ever experienced a time where you drew near to God and worshipped? Describe your time alone with God.

5. How can the Word of God help you in worshipping God?

ADORE GOD IN PRAYER

Sing the Doxology to the Lord: Praise God from whom all blessings flow; praise Him, all creatures here below; praise Him above, ye heavenly host. Praise Father, Son, and Holy Ghost.

YIELD YOURSELF TO GOD

Being in the dazzling presence of God is a wondrous experience; realizing God's majestic, just, and compassionate action in the world and in our lives urges us to let all thanks break loose! We come so often to God, if we come at all, as beggars. We ask and beg: give me; bless me; help me; guide me; grant me. And that's one necessary level of our existence. But in thanksgiving and adoration we come to God not to ask but to give! We come not whimpering but shouting praise; not in guilt but in gratitude. We feel not distant from God but close to God. We are like a traveler who is home again at last, the prodigal at a banquet. Those moments may be seldom, but when they happen we know that we were created *for God*…For a moment, for eternity, we forget tears and struggles and all is joy! We know we are created for God! We know that with certainty in those precious moments where we sing the Doxology with so much inner strength and conviction that we become the choir directors of the universe.[2]

DON POSTEMA IN SPACE FOR GOD?

ENJOY HIS PRESENCE

How does worship help you in experiencing a deeper, more intimate relationship with God? How can you include worship in your daily quiet time with the Lord? Close by writing a prayer to the Lord.

REST IN HIS LOVE

"Honor the LORD for the glory of his name. Worship the LORD in the splendor of his holiness." (Psalm 29:2 NLT).

THE SPLENDOR OF HIS HOLINESS

Worship the LORD in the splendor of His holiness. Psalm 29:2 NLT
Sedona, Arizona, USA
Nikon D810, ISO 1000, f5.6, 1/8000sec, Adobe Photoshop, Nik Silver Efex Pro
MYPHOTOWALK.COM—CATHERINEMARTIN.SMUGMUG.COM

WITH COVENANT

...and they saw the God of Israel; and under His feet there appeared to be a pavement of sapphire, as clear as the sky itself."

EXODUS 24:10

PREPARE YOUR HEART

The best day of your life is the day you enter into a relationship with God through the Lord Jesus Christ. According to Paul, God has "blessed us with every spiritual blessing in the heavenly places in Christ, just as He chose us in Him before the foundation of the world, that we would be holy and blameless before Him. In love He predestined us to adoption as sons through Jesus Christ to Himself, according to the kind intention of His will, to the praise of the glory of His grace, which He freely bestowed on us in the Beloved. In Him we have redemption through His blood, the forgiveness of our trespasses, according to the riches of His grace which He lavished on us" (Ephesians 1:3-8). Experiencing God in an intimate relationship is not something unplanned or haphazard. These words clearly show that God had you in mind for Himself before the foundation of the world. In fact, all that we see in Exodus leads to all that we see in the New Testament. The Old Covenant, ratified by blood, led to the New Covenant, ratified by the very life and blood of your Savior, Jesus Christ. The temporal has given way to the eternal.

Today in your quiet time you will see the passionate intention of your Lord to have a relationship with His people as He ratifies the covenant. Ask the Lord to open your eyes that you might behold wonderful things in His Word.

READ AND STUDY GOD'S WORD

1. Now God is going to ratify and establish the covenant with His people. We are going to see the solemn and binding nature of the covenant God is establishing with His people. Read Exodus 24:4-11 and summarize each event that took place.

Verse 4

Verse 5

Verse 6

Verse 7

Verse 8

Verses 9-10

Verse 11

2. Sealing a covenant with blood was common. When Moses first sprinkled blood on the altar, this signified that God was the divine sovereign or suzerain initiating the covenant.[3] Then, once the people agreed to obey all that was written in the Book of the Covenant, then they were sprinkled with the other half of the blood, showing their commitment. A fellowship meal followed the ratification of the covenant. This is such a beautiful picture for God's people as it points to the New Covenant ratified with the blood of Jesus Christ. Read the following verses and write out what you learn:

Romans 3:21-26 Sacrifice

Hebrews 7:22-27 Priest, Mediator of Covenant, Intercessor

Hebrews 9:11-22 Blood

Matthew 26:26-29 The covenant meal

Revelation 1:5-6 Redemption and purpose

3. God gave a glimpse of His glory as the covenant was ratified. Sometimes God will give you an experience of His presence in your sacred journey with Him. In Exodus 24:10 we see that they saw "the God of Israel; and under His feet there appeared to be a pavement of sapphire, as clear as the sky itself." Read the following verses and note what is most impressive to you about these visions of God.

Ezekiel 1:26-28

Revelation 4:3

ADORE GOD IN PRAYER

Talk with God about all you have seen of Him today. Worship Him as you think about the vision of Him in glory.

YIELD YOURSELF TO GOD

The portrayal of the Son of God as our priest in Hebrews 7:1-28 is complemented in Hebrews 8:1-9:18 by the teaching that he is also our sacrifice. Christ is both priest and victim. His death is to be understood as a covenant sacrifice which enabled him to ratify the new covenant and to activate its provisions. By the presentation of his life to God as an unblemished offering he overcame the two most serious weaknesses in the old covenantal arrangement; namely severely restricted access to God and the inadequacy of the sacrifice offered to provide decisive cleansing. His fully sufficient sacrifices achieved a decisive removal of sin and won for his people unlimited access to God.[4]

WILLIAM LANE IN HEBREWS, A CALL TO COMMITMENT

When God makes his covenant with his people, he promises to be their God, and he binds himself to that promise…God's covenant is his marriage bond with his people. He commits himself to us in unconditional love. Just as in a marriage covenant we do not say, "I promise to love you and cherish you, *but only if* you will…" but rather, "I promise to love you and cherish you till death parts us," so it is with God. He does not love us *if* we love him. He loves us with an unconditional love; *therefore* we should love him. The message of the covenant is one of God's totally free grace to his people. Of course, it calls for a response of total commitment. But notice the order: God's covenant love is not the *result* of our commitment; it is the *cause* of it. The pattern is, "I will, *therefore* you should;" *not* "I will, but *only* if you will first." The whole message of the Bible is shaped around God's coming to us in this covenant love. The history of God's purposes of salvation centers on the covenants he made with several individuals, and with their families and posterity. We find God making his covenant with Noah, Abraham, Moses, David, and finally in Jesus Christ. In each of these covenants we discover who God is, and how fully and completely we can trust him. In fact the message we are meant to hear is this: Down through the centuries God was absolutely faithful to his promises. If he has kept his word all these years, can you not trust him fully and completely too? *He has proved his trustworthiness and faithfulness.*[5]

SINCLAIR FERGUSON IN A HEART FOR GOD

ENJOY HIS PRESENCE

Think about God's covenant with His people and what it means for their relationship with Him. God wanted a relationship with His people in the context of a solemn, binding covenant with promises guaranteed by God Himself. Just as in a marriage, there is a commitment and the security that the covenant guarantees. God took the relationship with His people seriously and went to great lengths to establish His covenant with them. How do you see God's amazing love in His covenant and all He has done for you, and how does it inspire you to love Him with all your heart? Take this opportunity to renew your commitment to the Lord, making it a sacred moment alone with Him. What is the most important truth you learned today and how will you apply it to your life? Close by writing a prayer to your Lord

REST IN HIS LOVE

"Jesus Christ, the faithful witness, the firstborn of the dead, and the ruler of the kings of the earth. To Him who loves us and released us from our sins by His blood" (Revelation 1:5).

GOD'S AMAZING LOVE

To Him who loves us and released us from our sins by His blood. Revelation 1:5
Bell Rock, Sedona, Arizona, USA
Sony A6000, ISO 100, f7.1, 1/80sec, Adobe Photoshop, Nik Silver Efex Pro
MYPHOTOWALK.COM—CATHERINEMARTIN.SMUGMUG.COM

ON MOUNT SINAI

The glory of the LORD rested on Mount Sinai, and the cloud covered it for six days; and on the seventh day He called to Moses from the midst of the cloud."

EXODUS 24:16

PREPARE YOUR HEART

Have you learned to go to the mountain to draw near to God and gain a fresh perspective of who He is, what He does, and what He says? Going to the mountain is a metaphor for getting alone with God in quiet time. It's a time where you sit with God, talk with God, open His Word, meditate on what He says, and see Him in a new way. There is always something new to learn about God, for He is infinite, eternal, and glorious.

Today, as you begin your quiet time, pray the words of this beautiful hymn written by Walter Chalmers Smith, a pastor of the Free High Church of Edinburgh in 1874. He based the words of Immortal, Invisible, God Only Wise on 1 Timothy 1:17.

> Immortal, invisible, God only wise,
> In light inaccessible hid from our eyes;
> Most blessed, most glorious, the Ancient of Days;
> Almighty, victorious, Thy great name we praise.
>
> Unresting, unhasting, and silent as light;
> Nor wanting, nor wasting, Thou rulest in might.
> Thy justice, like mountains, high soaring above
> Thy clouds, which are fountains of goodness and love.
>
> To all, life Thou givest, to both great and small,
> In all life Thou livest, the true life of all;
> We blossom and flourish as leaves on the tree,
> And wither and perish, but naught changeth Thee.

Great Father of glory, pure Father of light;
Thine angels adore Thee, all veiling their sight;
All praise we would render: O help us to see
'Tis only the splendor of light hideth Thee.

READ AND STUDY GOD'S WORD

1. Mount Sinai was a significant place for Moses. It was where he first experienced God in the burning bush (Exodus 3). And it was where God brought him and the people of Israel after He rescued and redeemed them out of the hands of the Egyptians. And now, it is the place where God is going to meet with him for forty days and nights to give him further instructions about the tabernacle (the tent of meeting with God), the priests, and the writing of the testimony on both sides of the tablets. Read Exodus 24:12-18 and describe Mount Sinai and everything you learn about God.

2. In the Bible, going to the mountain was often the place to meet with God. Jesus made it a habit to go to the mountains to pray (Matthew 14:23, Luke 6:12). One day He took some of His disciples to a mountain and they experienced God in a new way. Read Matthew 17:1-8 and describe what happened.

3. How is your quiet time with the Lord? How is your time in God's Word? How is your prayer life these days? What will help you to spend more time alone with Him? How has your sacred journey in Exodus drawn you closer to God?

ADORE GOD IN PRAYER

Pray through the words of this prayer by F.B. Meyer: "May I love you, my God and Father, with a holy, absorbing, and increasing love, not for what you give, but for who you are."

YIELD YOURSELF TO GOD

What is the chief thing, the greatest and most glorious, that man can see or find upon earth? Nothing less than God Himself. And what is the chief, the best, the most glorious thing that a man can and needs to do every day? Nothing less than to seek, to know, to love, and to praise this glorious God. As glorious as God is, so is the glory that begins to work in the heart and life of the man who gives himself to live for God. My brother and sister in Christ, have you learned the first and greatest thing you have to do every day? Nothing less and nothing greater than to seek this God, to meet Him, to worship Him, to live for Him and for His glory. It is a great step in the life of a Christian when he truly sees this truth and yields himself to consider fellowship with God every day as the chief purpose of his life.[6]

ANDREW MURRAY IN GOD'S BEST SECRETS

To compel the mind to dwell long on the great truths of God, until from every angle we get a glimpse of their majesty, will produce in the mind a positiveness of conviction that will give steadiness of faith and set our feet upon a rock.

JOHN WILMOT MAHOOD IN THE LOST ART OF MEDITATION

ENJOY HIS PRESENCE

God has a Mount Sinai for you even in the wilderness where you can draw near to Him. In fact, the wilderness is the very best place to find a quiet place to draw near to God. In the wilderness, when you open the pages of God's Word, you will see God's truth more clearly and apply it to your life. In the wilderness, you can pour out your heart in prayer unhindered by distraction. Think about all the time Moses spent with God and the difference his knowledge of God made in his ability to trust. What have you learned that encourages you to go to the mountain, so to speak, and spend time alone with God? Write out your thoughts, then talk with God about your desire to know Him. Also, take some time to meditate on the photography and promise on the next page as you close your quiet time.

REST IN HIS LOVE

"It was at this time that He went off to the mountain to pray, and He spent the whole night in prayer to God." (Luke 6:12).

SEEING JESUS

We saw Him with our own eyes and touched Him with our own hands. 1 John 1:1 NLT
Bell Rock-Courthouse Butte, Sedona, Arizona, USA
Nikon D7000, ISO 100, f11, AEB, Adobe Photoshop, Nik Silver Efex Pro
MYPHOTOWALK.COM—CATHERINEMARTIN.SMUGMUG.COM

IN THE SANCTUARY

"Let them construct a sanctuary for Me, that I may dwell among them.""

EXODUS 25:8

PREPARE YOUR HEART

On this sacred journey in Exodus, God rescued and redeemed His people, taking them out of Egypt and bringing them to Himself. Then He established and ratified a covenant with them committing Himself to be their God so they could be His people. And now, God is going to give instructions for them to build a tabernacle where He can meet and dwell with His people. This is such a powerful instruction to the people of God to build a tabernacle, when you think about it. Just imagine, God, the Creator of the universe, loves His people so much that He desires to dwell with His people.

This thought gives way to something relevant and profound for you. God loves you and wants to dwell with you. He has made the way clear for you to be with Him forever. This life is not all there is nor is it the best there is. Eternal life, face to face with the Lord is your future. And what an exciting future it is. Your experience of intimate communion with your Lord is available now, for if you know Him personally, you have the blessed reality of Christ living in you through the indwelling Holy Spirit.

Meditate on these words by Gerhard Tersteegen, then ask God to quiet your heart and speak to you in His Word today.

> God reveals His presence: Let us now adore Him,
> And with awe appear before Him.
> God is in His temple: All within keep silence,
> Prostrate lie with deepest reverence.
> Him alone God we own,
> Him our God and Saviour; Praise His name for ever.

READ AND STUDY GOD'S WORD

1. In your study today, the goal is to see the passion God has to be with you. God is now going to give instructions to build the tabernacle, a movable place where God would dwell and meet

with His people as they lived in the wilderness. It was basically in the shape of a rectangular box with two sections, the Holy Place and the Most Holy Place (half the size of the Holy Place and separated by a veil). The Most Holy Place was the residence for God's shekinah glory. Only the High Priest could enter the Most Holy Place once a year on the Day of Atonement to sprinkle blood on the mercy seat to atone for his and the people's sins.

Read Exodus 25:1-9 and write your insights about who wanted a sanctuary built, who was going to build it, and why it was to be built.

2. The construction of the tabernacle is such a beautiful picture that points to a fulfillment in the Lord Jesus Christ. What we discover is that God is a God of detail and there is meaning and purpose in everything He does. Read about the following parts of the tabernacle in the verses listed in Exodus, write your most significant insights, and note how they are fulfilled in Christ. You may want to look at the tabernacle diagram under Yield Yourself To God on page 209.

The Bronze Altar—Exodus 27:1—located outside the tabernacle in the court (Exodus 27:9), Jesus' death on the cross paid for our sins (Romans 5:8).

The Bronze Laver—Exodus 30:17-21—located near the bronze altar for ceremonial washing for purity before approaching God, Jesus makes us a brand new person, holy and acceptable to God (2 Corinthians 5:17).

The Holy Place—The first room in the tabernacle housing the table of showbread, the golden lampstand, and the altar of incense

The Table of Showbread (Bread of Presence)—Exodus 25:23-30, Jesus is the bread of life (John 6:35).

The Golden Lampstand—Exodus 25:31-40, Jesus is the light of the world (John 8:12).

The Altar Of Incense—Exodus 30:1-10, a symbol of the fragrant prayers of God's people rising to the Father, Jesus is our intercessor before God the Father (Romans 8:34) and we may now come boldly in prayer in Jesus' name (John 14:13-14).

The Veil between the Holy Place and the Most Holy Place—Exodus 26:31-33— shielded sinful man from a holy God, When Jesus died on the cross, the temple veil was split in two from top to bottom, showing that He has made the way clear that we can know God (Matthew 27:50-51, see also Hebrews 10:19-22).

The Ark Of The Covenant and the Mercy Seat in the Most Holy Place—Exodus 25:10-22 the place where God would dwell with His people. Jesus now lives in us (Galatians 2:20).

3. The Lord Jesus shows us the heart of our God. John tells us that "the word became flesh, and dwelt among us, and we saw His glory, glory as of the only begotten from the Father, full of grace and truth" (John 1:14). That word for "dwelt" literally means "tabernacled." Jesus tabernacled among us! The Lord wants to "tabernacle" with us. We see this in the story of Zaccheus. Read Luke 19:1-10 and note the desire of the Lord and what happened when He went to Zaccheus' house.

4. The beautiful fact is that today the Lord still desires to dwell with His people. However, through the Holy Spirit, He doesn't just dwell with His people, but He lives *in* His people. Think about the intimacy of that kind of relationship with your Lord. Paul teaches in Galatians 2:20 that "Christ lives in me, and the life which I now live in the flesh I live by faith in the Son of God, who loved me and gave Himself up for me." We are called a temple of the Holy Spirit (1 Corinthians 6:19). Read Revelation 3:20 and write your favorite part of this expressed heartfelt desire of Jesus.

5. Read Revelation 21:3-6. What is the ultimate fulfilment of God's desire to tabernacle with His people?

ADORE GOD IN PRAYER

Talk with God now about all you have learned and commune with your Lord, knowing He is right there with you, now living in you.

YIELD YOURSELF TO GOD

The Exodus passages that discuss the materials for the Tabernacle refer to the structure itself by several different names, each of which symbolizes a particular function or purpose that it served. The best known and most common term is "tabernacle" (25:9), which means literally "dwelling place" and signifies the Lord's desire and intention to "dwell among" His people (29:45-46)...A second name for the Tabernacle that stresses the immanence—the nearness—of God is "Tent of Meeting" (35:21)...third, the "tabernacle of the Testimony (38:21) or "Tent of the Testimony" (Numbers 9:15). It served as the repository for the "ark of the Testimony (25:22), which held the "two tablets of the Testimony" (31:18) on which the Ten Commandments were inscribed...its fourth name—which appears earliest in the text of Exodus—is "sanctuary" (25:8). Meaning literally "place of holiness," it stresses the transcendence, the otherness, the aloofness of God. Not only immanent (right here), God is also transcendent (out there). But though the Tabernacle is a sanctuary, the same verse that calls it that goes on immediately to say that the Lord will "dwell among" His people (25:8). God lives not only "in a high and holy place, but also with him who is contrite and lowly in spirit" (Is. 57:15).[7]

DR. RONALD YOUNGBLOOD IN EXODUS

While I was studying the organization of the tribes of Israel camped around the tabernacle, I noticed a design in Numbers 2 that God Himself specifically directed, outlined, and engineered. Look at the organization of the camps around the tabernacle (see next page). Imagine that you are in an airplane looking down on the people of Israel and the tabernacle. What shape do you see? It's clear, isn't it! You see the cross...these people, without even realizing it, were witnesses of redemption. Then I thought about God looking at the earth and seeing His people in the wilderness, camped in the shape of the cross. I wondered what He must have thought, knowing about the sacrifice of Jesus on the cross for the sins of man. Then I thought about how we are now the temple of God, living tabernacles housing the person of God through the Holy Spirit....Did you know the human body is formed in the shape of a cross? You and I, living tabernacles where the Lord is living through the power of the Holy Spirit bear the shape of a cross. We are walking through life on earth now as living witnesses of redemption.[7]

CATHERINE MARTIN IN SET MY HEART ON FIRE

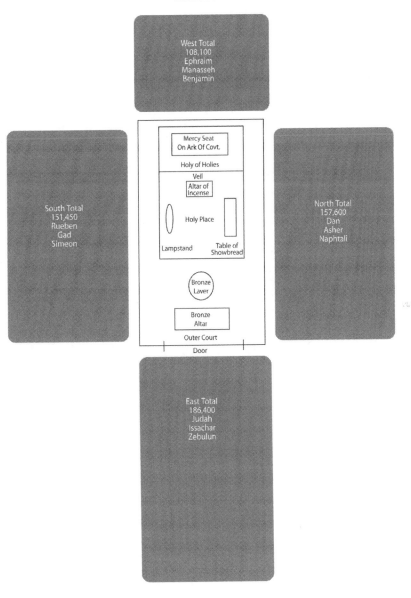

ENJOY HIS PRESENCE

Think about this. If God cared so much about the place where He dwells to spell out in intricate detail the entire layout of the tabernacle, imagine how important you are as the temple of His Holy Spirit, the one in whom He dwells now. You are a witness of redemption in this world. Let His light shine in you today, dear friend. What is the most important truth you have learned from your quiet time today? Write your thoughts in your Journal, then close by writing a prayer.

REST IN HIS LOVE

"Behold, I stand at the door and knock; if anyone hears My voice and opens the door, I will come in to him and will dine with him, and he with Me" (Revelation 3:20).

FELLOWSHIP WITH JESUS

I will come in to him and will dine with him, and he with Me. Revelation 3:20
Courthouse Butte, Sedona, Arizona, Utah, USA
Nikon D810, ISO 400, f22, 1/50sec, Adobe Photoshop, Nik Silver Efex Pro
MYPHOTOWALK.COM—CATHERINEMARTIN.SMUGMUG.COM

WITH OFFERINGS

*It shall be a continual burn offering throughout your generations at the doorway of the
tent of meeting before the LORD, where I will meet with you, to speak to you there."*

Exodus 29:42

PREPARE YOUR HEART

Oh what a week of study we have had as we have looked at Moses and the people of God as they are drawn into a relationship with Yahweh where they are experiencing Him. They heard the words "Come up" as God invited the people to Himself. Then, He established the covenant and ratified it for a solemn and binding agreement with these people who became the nation with the one true God—He was their God and they were His people, His treasured possession, a holy nation, and a kingdom of priests. No longer enslaved to Egyptian slavemasters, the people of Israel are now in covenant with their God who loves them as the apple of His eye. Then, God called Moses to come up to Mount Sinai to receive instructions that would lead to God dwelling with His people. The instructions included the building of a tabernacle with a Most Holy Place that would be great and glorious with the presence of God. Now just imagine what it would mean to have God dwelling with His people. Think back to the appearance of Mount Sinai as viewed by the people with a cloud of consuming fire (Exodus 24:17). How then, can anyone approach God? Now God is going to establish the formal priesthood with the tribe of Levi and the line of Aaron to serve Him in a special way. They would be set apart in a special way, wear special garments consecrated by God, and would be the ones to present offerings and sacrifices on behalf of the people as God dwelt with His people.

Think about that word "offering." A sacred holy word that includes the idea of sacrifice and death. Ask God now to prepare your heart as you bring yourself to the Lord offering a surrendered heart to draw near to Him and study His Word.

READ AND STUDY GOD'S WORD

1. Today in your study you are going to look at select verses about the priesthood and the function of the priests as they served on behalf of God and the people. A priest goes to God on

behalf of the people and to the people on behalf of God. Read the following verses and write what you learn.

Exodus 28:1-4, 43 The priests and their garments

Exodus 28:21, 30 The breastplate

Exodus 29:1-2, 35-37 Consecration of priests

Exodus 29:11-12 Slaughter of bull before the LORD at the doorway of tent of meeting

Exodus 29:38-46 Offering

Exodus 30:1, 10 Sin offering of atonement

2. Do you see how serious it is to come near to God? Sacrifice and shedding of blood are necessary to pay for sins. God is holy. As we learn in Romans 3:23 "All have sinned and fall short of the glory of God." God so loves us that He knew we needed a permanent sacrifice, one that would pay for all sins and allow our entrance in the greater, more perfect tabernacle of heaven. So we have a great high priest who is the perfect Lamb sacrificed on our behalf and He entered heaven where He ever lives to make intercession for us. Dear friend, you must see this for yourself.

Even if you've read these verses a thousand times, they are still powerful truths to impress your heart and mind.

Hebrews 4:14-16

Hebrews 9:6-15, 24-28

3. Following these instructions, God established the sign of this covenant with His people. The sign of the covenant with Noah was the rainbow, the sign of the covenant with Abraham was circumcision, and now, the sign of the covenant with Moses was the Sabbath. Read Exodus 31:12-18 and write what you learn about the Sabbath.

4. Continually we have seen how the Old Testament sees a fulfillment in the New Testament through Christ. In Hebrews 4:9-10 we learn "So there remains a Sabbath rest for the people of God. For the one who has entered His rest has himself also rested from his works, as God did from His." Think about this for a moment. It's the kind of rest you can experience in Christ and based on His merits, not your own. Read Matthew 11:28-30 and respond to Christ's invitation.

5. Think now about all you have learned today. How does God's establishment of the priesthood, the instructions about offerings for sin, and the sign of the covenant, the Sabbath help you see God's passion for His people?

6. Think about your own nearness to God. We have an offering we can make even now. Paul wrote a treatise in his letter to the Romans on all that Christ has done for us. Then he made the great conclusion and application for our lives as he expressed what we should do in light of all these mercies. He wrote, "Therefore I urge you, brethren, by the mercies of God, to present your bodies a living and holy sacrifice, acceptable to God, which is your spiritual service of worship" (Romans 12:1). This is a blessed and holy surrender to God of all that you are. Think about these words and write your thoughts about your own surrender to God and what that means.

ADORE GOD IN PRAYER

Pray this prayer of surrender Betty Scott Stam:

> Lord, I give up all my own plans and purposes,
> all my own desires and hopes
> and accept Thy will for my life.
> I give myself, my life, my all
> Utterly to Thee to be Thine forever.
> Fill me and seal me with Thy Holy Spirit.
> Use me as Thou wilt, send me where Thou wilt
> and work out Thy whole will in my life
> at any cost now and forever.

YIELD YOURSELF TO GOD

The idea of a priesthood naturally implies a consciousness of sin and the need for mediatorial representation. The building of the tabernacle was only the first step in the restitution of complete fellowship with God. While Moses was the mediator of the law and the covenant, Aaron and his sons were the mediators of the blood sacrifice.[8]

JOHN J. DAVIS IN MOSES AND THE GODS OF EGYPT

We have a champion who fights for us—his name is Jesus! We have a high priest who shares our vulnerability. He resembles us, just like one brother resembles another. What set him apart from others who might approach us is that he proved to be both merciful and faithful in the service of God. Moreover, he made atonement for the sins which had separated us from God...The incarnation of the Son of God made possible a penetration of our situation. God knew that this was imperative...It permitted the Son of God to share our humanity and to experience death on our behalf. Because he identified himself with us, he arrested ability of death to humiliate us. No longer are we paralyzed by the fear of death... Through our identification with him we shall discover that death is unable to hold us. Through Jesus, we shall experience the glory and splendor God intended for the whole human family.[9]

WILLIAM LANE IN HEBREWS, A CALL TO COMMITMENT

ENJOY HIS PRESENCE

Will you lay yourself at the feet of Jesus today to be His, wholly His, with a heart of surrender? The offering you can make to your Lord is yourself. Share a time when you surrendered yourself to the Lord and what it meant for your relationship with Him. Think about what you learned about the Sabbath and step away from the busyness of life and carve out time to be still and know that He is God. What is the most important truth you have learned in your study today? Close by writing a prayer expressing all that is on your heart.

REST IN HIS LOVE

"Therefore I urge you, brethren, by the mercies of God, to present your bodies a living and holy sacrifice, acceptable to God, which is your spiritual service of worship" (Romans 12:1).

SURRENDER TO GOD

Present your bodies a living and holy sacrifice. Romans 12:1
Sedona, Arizona, USA
Sony A 6000, ISO 100, f9, 1/320sec, Adobe Photoshop, Nik Silver Efex Pro
MYPHOTOWALK.COM—CATHERINEMARTIN.SMUGMUG.COM

DEVOTIONAL READING
BY F.B. MEYER

DEAR FRIEND,

Think about all you have learned this week on this sacred journey in Exodus as we experienced God at Mount Sinai. Write a prayer to the Lord thanking Him for all that He is teaching you.

What were your most meaningful discoveries this week as you spent time with the Lord?

Most meaningful insight:

Most meaningful devotional reading:

Most meaningful verse:

I f the people had only seen the devouring fire on the top of Sinai, the pavilion of God's presence, they would never have dared to think that there was any community of interest between Him and them. To their minds, He would always have seemed distant and unapproachable. So God said, "Let them make me a sanctuary (Exodus 25:8). Thus was ordained that this larger tent should be pitched among them, only differing from their own in its proportions and materials; but standing on the same level sand, struck and pitched at the same hour with theirs and enduring the same vicissitudes of weather and travel. Did not this say, as plainly as words could, that the tabernacle of God was with men and that He was willing to dwell with them and become their God? Did it not teach that Jehovah [Yahweh] had become a pilgrim with the pilgrim host; no longer a God afar off, but a sharer in their national fortunes? And is not this the very lessons of the Incarnation?

F.B. MEYER

Viewer Guide

Intimacy With God

In Week Six of *One Holy Passion*, you had the opportunity to study the ways God was drawing His people into a relationship with Himself. Today I want to look at intimacy with God and three main truths we see in Exodus about -our intimate relationship . Grab your Bibles, and let's dig in more deeply together as we study intimacy with God.

"Let them construct a sanctuary for Me, that I may dwell among them" (Exodus 25:8).

What can we learn in Exodus about our intimate relationship with God?

1. Our intimate relationship with God is _____
and _____.

The Covenant — Exodus 24:4-11, Hebrews 7:22, 8:6, 1 John 3:1

2. Our intimate relationship with God is _____.

The Tabernacle — Exodus 25:8-9, John 1:14, 2 Corinthians 1:9, Galatians 2:20, Revelation 21:3-6

3. Our intimate relationship with God is _____.

Priests and Offerings — Exodus 29:42, Romans 3:23, 6:23, John 3:15-17, Revelation 5, Philippians 2:8-11, Ephesians 2:7-9, John 1:12,

Ways to grow in your intimate relationship with God

1. Find a Bible that you love and live in it.

2. Write God's Word and your words to God in prayer in your Quiet Time Journal.

3. Choose good devotional reading.

4. Talk with God throughout the day.

Video messages are available on DVDs or as Digital M4V Video. Audio messages are available as Digital MP3 Audio. Visit the Quiet Time Ministries Online Store at www.quiettime.org.

JOURNEY TO THE HEART OF GOD

Exodus 32-40

There are two notable effects of light in this part of Southern India. One is seen on a clear evening… The other is still more fugitive. It is never seen except in thundery weather… The sun's rays striking up from the sea in sunrise are flung back by the thunder-cloud, and falling on mountain and forest turn the whole world to rose. The loveliness of such moments is unearthly. You stand speechless on some rock in the heart of that celestial rose. You can only worship. Worthy, worthy to be worshipped is the God who can imagine such beauty and command it. All your soul worships. Be still and know that I am God.[1]

AMY CARMICHAEL

HE IS ALL GRACE

Then the LORD relented and did not bring on his people the disaster he had threatened.

Exodus 32:14

PREPARE YOUR HEART

Who is this God who spoke to Moses in a burning bush, fought battles with Pharaoh and the Egyptians, and led a group of people out into the wilderness? Who is this One who has now established a covenant with the group of people He rescued, the One who now wants to dwell with them? There comes a point in every person's life when they ask, "Who are You, God? What are You like? Teach me Your ways. I want to know You."

God is so much more than we imagine Him to be. So often, we equate His character with what we see in man. He is wholly other, uncreated, infinite, and eternal. But He is also intimate and personal. When you read the Bible, as you see God in action, you discover that He has emotion and deep lovingkindness. God reveals Himself throughout Scripture, and desires that we know and love Him. A. W. Tozer, author of *The Pursuit of God*, writes: "God is a Person, and in the deep of His mighty nature He thinks, wills, enjoys, feels, loves, desires and suffers as any person may…The continuous and unembarrassed interchange of love and thought between God and the soul of the redeemed man is the throbbing heart of New Testament religion."[2]

In Exodus, the outstanding feature throughout is Yahweh and His passion for His people. He reached out of the heavens and carried His people from Egypt to Himself. Oh how He loves His people! And now, in this week's study, we are going to see more deeply into the heart of God. How does our sin impact Him? What does our humble confession and repentance mean to Him? How does He feel when we wear our heart on our sleeve and cry out to know Him? And how does He express His passionate heart for His people? And finally, what kind of service pleases Him? Now we take a journey to the heart of God and know Him more intimately that we may love Him with one holy passion.

As you begin your quiet time, write a simple prayer to the Lord, expressing your desire to know Him.

READ AND STUDY GOD'S WORD

1. Moses was on Mount Sinai for forty days and forty nights meeting with God and receiving instructions for the tabernacle and the priesthood. And then, God gave Moses the two tablets of the testimony, "tablets of stone, written by the finger of God" (Exodus 31:18). It was a high moment for Moses. He had met personally with Yahweh. Moses undoubtedly realized the greatness of that time with God and saw in a new way just how much the people meant to their God. Now He intended to dwell with them and gave instructions for the place where He would meet with His people.

God saw what Moses could not see. He saw the impatience of the people during those forty days, their disobedience, and tendency to quickly turn away from all that God commanded. Read Exodus 32:1-14 and write your most significant insights about the following questions:

How did the people sin against God?

What did God say about their sin?

What did Moses want God to do and what was the basis of his entreaty with God?

How did God respond to all that Moses said?

2. Read Exodus 32:15-35 and describe what happened when Moses and Joshua came down from Mount Sinai into the camp. Note how Moses responded in verse 19.

3. We see in Exodus 32 that Moses interceded on behalf of the people, and God honored His servant's prayer and relented concerning the complete disaster that could have befallen His people who had sinned. They had broken the covenant by violating the first two commandments, "You shall have no other gods before Me," and "You shall not make for yourself an idol…" (Exodus 20:3-4). There were still consequences for the sin of the people, but not what could have come their way in violation of the covenant. God originally expressed that all the people would be destroyed and He would make Moses a great nation (Exodus 32:10).

When God relented and did not bring on His people the disaster He had threatened (Exodus 32:14), He was revealing His character of grace. Joseph Cooke, in his book *Celebration of Grace*, describes grace as "nothing more or less than the face that love wears when it meets imperfection, weakness, failure, sin. Grace is what love is and does when it meets the sinful and the undeserving."[3] Grace is God's love in action.[4] Read the following verses and write out what you learn about grace and those who are under grace?

Romans 6:12-18

Romans 8:1-2

Ephesians 2:8-9

Hebrews 4:14-16

1 Peter 5:10

4. What does knowing God is a God of all grace mean to you today?

ADORE GOD IN PRAYER

Pour out your heart to the Lord about your need for His grace and thank Him for being a God of all grace.

YIELD YOURSELF TO GOD

God deals with impossibilities. It is never too late for Him to do so, when the impossible is brought to Him, in full faith, by the one in whose life and circumstances the impossible must be accomplished if God is to be glorified. If in our own life there have been rebellion, unbelief, sin, and disaster, it is never too late for God to deal triumphantly with these tragic facts if brought to Him in full surrender and trust. It has often been said, and with truth, that Christianity is the only religion that can deal with man's past. God can "restore … the years that the locust hath eaten" (Joel 2:25); and He will do this when we put the whole situation and ourselves unreservedly and believingly into His hands. Not because of what we are but because of what He is. God forgives and heals and restores. He is "the God of all grace." Let us praise Him and trust Him.

MRS. CHARLES COWMAN IN STREAMS IN THE DESERT

ENJOY HIS PRESENCE

Oh how quickly the people of God broke covenant with God. Making a golden calf and then worshipping it was a serious affront to a holy God and in direct violation of the covenant. Moses interceded for the people and God relented. However there was a consequence in the camp and some people lost their lives for sin. This gives us a glimpse into the powerful truth that Christ died for our sins and, according to Isaiah 53:6, the iniquity of us all fell on Him. We are now under grace. The Word of God has shown us that "there is, therefore, now no condemnation to those who are in Christ Jesus" (Romans 8:1). However, we also learn that grace is not a license to sin. And there are consequences for sin. How does God's grace encourage you today? And how does God's grace become an encouragement not to sin? What are forms of idolatry in our culture today and what should be our attitude toward sin? Always remember that "if we confess our sins, He is faithful and righteous to forgive us our sins and to cleanse us from all unrighteousness" (1 John 1:9).

Also, how quickly our vision becomes clouded and we forget God's Word. Hold on to what God says and allow it to lead you to the very Person of God Himself. A.W. Tozer writes: "The Bible is not an end in itself, but a means to bring men to an intimate and satisfying knowledge of God, that they may enter into Him, that they may delight in His Presence, may taste and know the inner sweetness of the very God Himself in the core and center of their hearts."[5] How has your study today encouraged to hold on to God's Word and delight in God's presence?

Draw near to God and ask Him for His mercy and grace in your time of need. Close by writing a prayer to the Lord, expressing all that is on your heart.

REST IN HIS LOVE

"Therefore let us draw near with confidence to the throne of grace, so that we may receive mercy and find grace to help in time of need." (Hebrews 4:16).

THE MERCY OF JESUS

Blessed are the merciful for they shall receive mercy. Matthew 5:7
Sedona, Arizona, USA
Nikon D7000, ISO 100, f5, 1/1000sec, Adobe Photoshop, Nik Silver Efex Pro
MYPHOTOWALK.COM—CATHERINEMARTIN.SMUGMUG.COM

HE DISCIPLINES HIS PEOPLE

When the people heard this sad word, they went into mourning, and none of them put on his ornaments.

EXODUS 33:4

PREPARE YOUR HEART

Oh, how God loves His people. How is God going to bring His people to the place where they honor, reverence and love Him? He desires faithfulness, love and commitment. And He feels deeply with genuine emotion regarding our actions toward Him. Hear the feelings in His statement about His people when they built the golden calf. He said that the people "have corrupted themselves. They have quickly turned aside from the way which I commanded them…I have seen this people, and behold, they are an obstinate people" (Exodus 32:7-9). God sees our ways and is not silent nor unaffected.

In speaking of the sins of the people through Isaiah, God said, "I permitted Myself to be sought by those who did not ask for Me; I permitted Myself to be found by those who did not seek Me. I said, 'Here am I, here am I,' to a nation which did not call on My name. I have spread out My hands all day long to a rebellious people, who walk in the way which is not good, following their own thoughts, a people who continually provoke Me to My face, offering sacrifices in gardens and burning incense on bricks; who sit among graves and spend the night in secret places; who eat swine's flesh, And the broth of unclean meat is in their pots. Who say, 'Keep to yourself, do not come near me, for I am holier than you!' These are smoke in My nostrils, a fire that burns all the day" (Isaiah 65:1-5).

These words from God in both Exodus and Isaiah give a glimpse into Yahweh's heart. What does God do with a rebellious people? What does He do when we ignore Him, reject Him, or refuse to love and honor Him and go about our own way? Remember God is passionate for you and loves you so much that He gave His only begotten Son to die in your place that you might be forgiven and receive eternal life. So there comes a time, according to God's Word, when He disciplines His people. In Hebrews 12:11, we see that God disciplines with the purpose of yielding the peaceful fruit of righteousness. So today, as you draw near to God, ask Him to speak to you in

His Word as you look at how He related with His people when they sinned and broke covenant. Ask Him to grow you deeper in your own intimate relationship with Him.

READ AND STUDY GOD'S WORD

1. In the aftermath of the idolatry of His people, God spoke to Moses. Read Exodus 33:1-6 and write in 2-3 sentences what God said.

2. In these words, God is saying it will now be a distant relationship, not like what He really wanted with the people. How did the people respond to this sad word (see Exodus 33:4)? Note: Ornaments might be thought of as jewelry and other adornment, and not worn when a person is in mourning.

3. You are going to see as we go on in Exodus, that Moses intercedes, and once again experiences a beautiful answer of heavenly grace from Yahweh. When you think about the response of the people as they mourned, how was this a matter of discipline, and how do you think it could impact their relationship with God for their good and well-being? How does their response indicate that a passion for God was growing in their hearts?

4. Read Hebrews 12:4-13 and write everything you learn about the discipline of the Lord.

5. How does God's discipline reveal His passion for His people? Always remember how much He loves you, that there is no condemnation to those who are in Christ Jesus (Romans 8:1). You are accepted in the beloved (Ephesians 1:6).

6. How have you experienced the discipline of the Lord and what was the result in your relationship with Him? How did it lead you to love, maturity, and commitment to the Lord?

ADORE GOD IN PRAYER

Pray the words of Brennan Manning from *The Ragamuffin Gospel*: "Lord Jesus, we are silly sheep who have dared to stand before you and try to bribe you with our preposterous portfolios. Suddenly we have come to our senses. We are sorry and ask you to forgive us. Give us the grace to admit we are ragamuffins, to embrace our brokenness, to celebrate your mercy when we are at our weakest, to rely on your mercy no matter what we may do. Dear Jesus, gift us to stop grandstanding and trying to get attention, to do the truth quietly without display, to let the dishonesties in our lives fade away, to accept our limitations, to cling to the gospel of grace, and to delight in your love."[6]

YIELD YOURSELF TO GOD

"After you have suffered for a little while, the God of all grace, who called you to His eternal glory in Christ, will Himself perfect, confirm, strengthen and establish you" (1 Peter 5:10). The graces of the Christian character must not resemble the rainbow in its transitory beauty, but, on the contrary, must be established, settled, abiding. Seek, O believer, that every good thing you have may be an abiding thing. May your character not be a writing upon the sand, but an inscription upon the rock! May your faith be no "baseless fabric of a vision," but may it be built of material able to endure that awful fire which shall consume the wood, hay, and stubble of the hypocrite. May you be rooted and grounded in love. May your convictions be deep, your love real, your desires earnest. May your whole life be so settled and established, that all the blasts of hell, and all the storms of earth shall never be able to remove you. But notice how this blessing of being "established in the faith" is gained. The apostle's words point us to suffering as the means employed—"After you have suffered for a little while." It is of no use to hope that we shall be well rooted if no rough winds pass over us. Those old gnarlings on the root of the oak tree, and those strange twistings of the branches, all tell of the many storms that have swept over it, and they are also indicators of the depth into which the roots have forced their way. So the Christian is made strong, and firmly rooted by all the trials and storms of life. Shrink not then from the tempestuous winds of trial, but take comfort, believing that by their rough discipline God is fulfilling this benediction to you.

CHARLES SPURGEON IN MORNING AND EVENING

ENJOY HIS PRESENCE

Think now about the beautiful side of discipline and the good it accomplishes in your life. Talk with God as you close your quiet time about His discipline in your own life and how He has led you closer to Himself. Then, meditate on these words by Ken Gire[7]:

> The soul is like a bird,
>   shaken from its peaceful roost by the inclement
> circumstances of life,
>   where windblown branches
>   and sudden gusts from darkening horizons
>   thrust it into weather that is wild and uncertain.
> And sometimes, however hard we beat our wings,
>   we can't seem to overcome the elements galing against us.
> We are thrashed about in the air,
>   windsheered and weary,
>   wondering if our cries for help are reaching God.
> But then the tempest subsides,
>   for awhile anyway,
>   and the updrafts of God's Spirit lift us to new heights,
>   above the wind, above the rain, above the earth.
> And, for a moment,
>   we soar.

KEN GIRE IN BETWEEN HEAVEN AND EARTH

REST IN HIS LOVE

After you have suffered for a little while, the God of all grace, who called you to His eternal glory in Christ, will Himself perfect, confirm, strengthen and establish you" (1 Peter 5:10).

THE DISCIPLINE OF THE LORD

He disciplines us for our good, so that we may share His holiness. Hebrews 12:10
Sedona, Arizona, USA
Nikon D810, ISO 64, f2.8, 1/320sec, Adobe Photoshop, Nik Silver Efex Pro
MYPHOTOWALK.COM—CATHERINEMARTIN.SMUGMUG.COM

FACE TO FACE WITH GOD

Thus the LORD used to speak to Moses face to face, just as a man speaks to his friend.

EXODUS 33:11

PREPARE YOUR HEART

She walked into the room where there were about thirty young people waiting for the guest speaker. He was an astronomer who was going to show slides of the stars and planets. "How boring," she thought. "Why did I even come tonight?" She was hoping for a rousing message from a passage in the Bible. Since she had given her life to the Lord earlier that year, she had heard messages like that at church, and was growing in her faith. So now she was going to hear a scientific lecture. The astronomer began by talking about the size of the universe and spoke of galaxies and planets. Then, he showed slides, one after another, of countless stars. Soon, this young Christian girl was drawn into the message. He spoke of God as Creator of the universe. And God's greatness and glory began to dawn on this girl as she saw the infinite nature of His person and character. She was so overwhelmed she could hardly speak. She slipped out at the end of the presentation, and drove home, deep in thought. She got out of the car and stood outside, looking up at the dark sky filled with stars and planets too numerous to count. Suddenly, she was aware that she was not alone. She sensed, in that moment, the presence of God Himself. She was utterly undone by His greatness, and ran into the house, dove into bed, and covered her head with a pillow to try and escape the awesome glory because it was more than she could comprehend. And still, God was there. She sensed the truth of the words in Jeremiah 31:3 "I have loved you with an everlasting love." She never forgot that experience of God and it helped her realize that God is more than we know or understand Him to be. And someday, we shall see Him face to face in glory.

Today, as you continue your sacred journey in Exodus, you are going to walk with Moses to the top of Mount Sinai, where you will be given a great and glorious vision of God. Draw near to God now, and ask Him to prepare your heart to meet with Him today.

READ AND STUDY GOD'S WORD

1. Moses was given a most intimate relationship of communion with Yahweh. Read Exodus 33:7-11 and describe his relationship with God.

2. Sometimes the greatest moments with God follow difficult times of suffering. Just imagine the disappointment in the heart of Moses because of the sin of God's people. Just imagine, then, how he must have felt upon hearing God say He would not be going with the people. Moses enjoyed a "face to face" relationship with God, meaning heart to heart. Moses was invited to share God's heart and to pour out his heart in communion with the LORD. And now, Moses does indeed pour out his heart to God and God responds with grace and mercy to His beloved servant. Read each of the verses below and write out Moses' requests and God's response.

Exodus 33:12-14

Exodus 33:15-17

Exodus 33:18-34:8

Exodus 34:9-10

3. Moses was with God for forty days and forty nights on Mount Sinai. Read Exodus 34:28-35 and write your most significant insight about what happened to Moses as a result of being in God's presence (see 2 Corinthians 3:12-18).

4. We are given the opportunity for a face to face relationship with our Lord now, and with a promise of something even better in heaven. Read the following verses and underline your favorite words and phrases.

> "If anyone really loves me, he will observe my teaching, and my Father will love him, and both of us will come in face-to-face fellowship with him; yes, we will make our special dwelling place within him" (John 14:23 WMS).

> "For now we see only a reflection as in a mirror; then we shall see face to face. Now I know in part; then I shall know fully, even as I am fully known" (1 Corinthians 13:12 NIV).

> And we all, who with unveiled faces contemplate the Lord's glory, are being transformed into his image with ever-increasing glory, which comes from the Lord, who is the Spirit (2 Corinthians 3:18 NIV).

> "Beloved, now we are children of God, and it has not appeared as yet what we will be. We know that when He appears, we will be like Him, because we will see Him just as He is" (1 John 3:2).

ADORE GOD IN PRAYER

Spend some time now alone with God talking with Him about all you have learned. Worship and thank Him for what He is showing you in His Word as you go on this sacred journey in Exodus.

YIELD YOURSELF TO GOD

Moses, high on a mountain, actually saw God. God spoke to him. We do well to stand in reverent awe of this. Nothing in our experience can compare even remotely. Moses himself was dramatically affected. This was the man who had seen the burning bush in the wilderness, who had received the Law on the mountaintop, who had talked to God "as with a friend." But this experience so surpassed all those in its glory and power that it had a physical effect on Moses: his face began to radiate reflected light. Yet it was incomplete; it did not fulfill all Moses' human longing. He was not allowed to see God's face. Thus, though the glory Moses saw transformed him, the effect was temporary. The radiance faded, and he put a veil over his face to hide the sadly fading glory, as Paul explains in 2 Corinthians 3:13. Like the Law, Moses' climactic experience with God pointed toward the future.[8]

TIM STAFFORD IN KNOWING THE FACE OF GOD

If every fraction of a second tells in the film in the camera, while "unveiled" it faces the light, must not something of the same unseen work go on upon our spirits in every moment of unveiling before the Lord? When Moses went in before the Lord to speak with Him, he took the veil off. Bare absolute contact with God's Presence—if our times alone with Him were but that all the time, they would be mighty in their outcome.[9]

LILIAS TROTTER IN BLOSSOM IN THE DESERT

As we look unto Jesus we come to look like Jesus. Those that wait upon Him shine with His glory. When Moses came out of the mountain, his face was shining with the glory of God. Why? Because he had gazed into the face of God for forty days. And when he came down, he stood a transfigured man before the people, with the image of God in his face, so that he had to cover it, for they could not bear looking upon it. How beautiful then is it that as we look unto Jesus, we are transformed into the image of Jesus. That even down here in the dark night of faith, somehow or other, we grow like Him. The moment a man perfectly sees Jesus, that moment a man is going to be perfectly like Jesus. "When He shall appear, we shall be like Him, *for* we shall *see* Him as He is" (1 John 3:2)—"we shall be like Him, *for* we shall see Him." Through the imperfect glass of faith, the likeness is imperfect. With the perfect face-to-face vision, the image shall be perfect. Here the picture is being taken in a cloudy day, "through a glass darkly" (1 Corinthians 13:12). It takes long time-exposures, and the work seems to be slow. Then it will be an instantaneous flash, and "we shall be like Him." In an instant, "in a moment, in the twinkling of an eye"—the Lord, the glory, the likeness! Thanks be unto God. We are waiting for that glad moment. The instant we see Jesus Christ face to face, that instant we will be changed into the glory of Jesus Christ. And just so far as we see Him now in communion, so far are we made like Him, even down here.[10]

JAMES McCONKEY IN PREVAILING PRAYER

From the beginning, God has desired to dwell among us. In the wilderness, God dwelt among the people of Israel, and they saw His glory daily. Today, God desires to live even closer than that to us, but not in a tent made with human hands. He desires to dwell within us, upon His rightful throne within our hearts. He desires for us to be His living tabernacles, so that we may personally experience His glory. God's spirit longs to fill us…Draw near to God, and he will draw near to you.[11]

J. STEVEN BABBIT IN THE PRESENCE OF GOD

When we realize this truth of God's presence with us, certain things should follow in our lives, as they did in Moses' life. We should be filled with a new humility, because we have met God. We should be encouraged by a fresh sense of security— we have met God and lived; what else is there to fear? We should be filled with undying gratitude, that God the Lord has worked on our behalf. Is this the God you know? And is this the way you know him? When you do, nothing else matters. Or better, everything else begins to fit into its proper place in the service of God.[12]

SINCLAIR FERGUSON IN A HEART FOR GOD

ENJOY HIS PRESENCE

Oh how important your time alone with God is in your relationship with Him. Do you long to know Him more? Do you desire to discover His passion for you and grow in your passion for Him? Close your time today by writing a prayer to the Lord.

REST IN HIS LOVE

"Beloved, now we are children of God, and it has not appeared as yet what we will be. We know that when He appears, we will be like Him, because we will see Him just as He is" (1 John 3:2).

FACE TO FACE WITH JESUS

Now we see in a mirror dimly, but then face to face. 1 Corinthians 13:12
Oak Creek Canyon, Sedona, Arizona, USA
Nikon D7000, ISO 400, f9, 1/80sec, Adobe Photoshop, Nik Silver Efex Pro
MYPHOTOWALK.COM—CATHERINEMARTIN.SMUGMUG.COM

NO RIVAL LOVE

You shall not worship any other god, for the Lord, whose name is Jealous, is a jealous God.

EXODUS 34:14

PREPARE YOUR HEART

Marriage ceremonies are beautiful declarations of love. A special moment occurs when the organist plays the bridal processional music, everyone stands, and the bride appears in her beautiful gown and walks down the aisle and into the arms of the man she is going to marry. If you've ever looked into the eyes of that man, there is an unabashed love for his beloved. There is a belongingness between the two, a love that cherishes each other, and a commitment that is made "until death do us part."

God cherishes and loves you with a much greater kind of love. He gave what was most precious to Him so He could live with you forever. Today, you are going to have the opportunity to journey even deeper into God's heart to see His love for you—an eternal love that nothing and no one can touch.

Begin your quiet time by praying through Paul's prayer in Ephesians 3:14-21, personalizing the words and asking God to show you how wide, long, high, and deep His love is. "When I think of all this, I fall to my knees and pray to the Father, the Creator of everything in heaven and on earth. I pray that from His glorious, unlimited resources He will empower you with inner strength through His Spirit. Then Christ will make His home in your hearts as you trust in Him. Your roots will grow down into God's love and keep you strong. And may you have the power to understand, as all God's people should, how wide, how long, how high, and how deep His love is. May you experience the love of Christ, though it is too great to understand fully. Then you will be made complete with all the fullness of life and power that comes from God. Now all glory to God, who is able, through his mighty power at work within us, to accomplish infinitely more than we might ask or think. Glory to Him in the church and in Christ Jesus through all generations forever and ever! Amen" (Ephesians 3:14-21 NLT).

READ AND STUDY GOD'S WORD

1. God again promised Moses that He was making a covenant with His people. And in His beginning words, He declared to Moses a deep truth about who He is. Read Exodus 34:10-16 and write what impresses you the most about God.

2. What a powerful truth about God. His name is "Jealous" and He is a jealous God (Exodus 34:14. In looking at this name, we cannot define Jealous with what we see in the world. No, we must look at what Yahweh means in communicating this name to Moses and His people. The New Jewish Version translates this to read, "His name is Impassioned." Dr. Ronald Youngblood, in his Exodus commentary, writes that "Jealous" means "He brooks no rivals and is zealous for His uniqueness and holiness."[13] According to the United Bible Society Handbook on Exodus, the meaning is "I want you to be completely loyal to me," or "because I, the Lord, tolerate no rivals."[14] In this revelation from God, Yahweh is opening up His heart and revealing His amazing, passionate love for His people. They are His and He has taken them for His very own treasured possession to love and care for them always. With that in mind, look at the following verses and write what you learn about the Lord's love for you.

Isaiah 54:4-12

Jeremiah 31:3

John 3:16

Ephesians 5:22-27

1 John 3:1-2

Revelation 21:1-3

3. The Lord Jesus is the lover of your soul. He has loved you with an everlasting love. And He is looking forward to the day when you will be together with Him in heaven forever. He wants no rival love. Jesus told the church at Ephesus that He had this against them: "You have left your first love" (Revelation 2:4). You see, the Lord Jesus is your One and Only. Everything falls into place including your love for others when He is your first love. After Jesus rose from the dead, He met with Peter at the Sea of Galilee for a personal conversation. Peter had denied Him three times during Jesus' arrest. And now, Jesus is going to ask him a question three times. Read John 21:15-17 and write your insights about this encounter with Jesus and what you see about the heart of God in this passage.

ADORE GOD IN PRAYER

> Jesus, lover of my soul, let me to Thy bosom fly,
> While the nearer waters roll, while the tempest still is high.
> Hide me, O my Savior, hide, 'til the storm is past;
> safe into the haven guide, O receive my soul at last!

Other refuge have I none, hangs my helpless soul on Thee,
Leave, O leave me not alone, still support and comfort me.
All my trust on Thee is stayed, all my help from Thee I bring;
Cover my defenseless head with the shadow of Thy wing.

Plenteous grace with Thee is found, grace to cover all my sin;
Let the healing streams abound, make and keep me pure within.
Thou of life the fountain art, freely let me take of Thee;
Spring Thou up within my heart, rise to all eternity. Amen.

CHARLES WESLEY

YIELD YOURSELF TO GOD

What then, is our own answer to Jesus' question, "Do you love me more than these?" Our answer means more to Him than any other aspect of our relationship! It means more to Him than our service or our time or our money. He wants the full worship of our hearts, our overflowing adoration, our highest delight in His presence. He wants the Only true gift we can offer Him—the gift of ourselves! And when we give Him our hearts, we give ourselves. As J. Sidlow Baxter points out, when we earnestly love Him, then everything else falls into its proper place, and our Lord suffuses us with His sanctifying Spirit. When we truly know and love Him, He becomes the most real person in our lives…Yet our love for Him, transcendent above all other loves, does not preclude those other loves. Rather, when we love God most dearly, the reciprocal interplay of His love and our returning love actually enriches every other love. His love flows through us to others. Our love for Him opens up our heart so that we find it natural to love others. The danger of other loves lies in the possibility of their becoming rival loves, taking first place in our life, diminishing our love for God, or obscuring Him as the central object of our heart's deepest love…The real, authentic mark of the truly Christian life is love—supreme, transcendent love for the Lord Jesus Christ, and selfless, caring, nurturing love for others. This supreme love for Jesus sets us free from the persistent claims of a self-focused love, and provides the solution to many of the problems in our lives.[15]

DWIGHT HERVEY SMALL IN NO RIVAL LOVE

ENJOY HIS PRESENCE

The words of William R. Featherstone's hymn come to mind in response to all we've learned today. Meditate on these words and even sing this wonderful hymn as your response to your Lord who loves you.

> My Jesus, I love Thee, I know Thou art mine;
> For Thee all the follies of sin I resign;
> My gracious Redeemer, my Savior art Thou:
> If ever I loved Thee, my Jesus 'tis now.
>
> I love Thee because Thou hast first loved me,
> And purchased my pardon on Calvary's tree;
> I love Thee for wearing the thorns on Thy brow:
> If ever I loved Thee, my Jesus 'tis now.
>
> I'll love Thee in life, I will love Thee in death,
> And praise Thee as long as Thou lendest me breath;
> And say when the death dew lies cold on my brow:
> If ever I loved Thee, my Jesus 'tis now.
>
> In mansions of glory and endless delight,
> I'll ever adore Thee in heaven so bright;
> I'll sing with the glittering crown on my brow:
> If ever I loved Thee, my Jesus 'tis now.

REST IN HIS LOVE

"Christ also loved the church and gave Himself up for her, so that He might sanctify her, having cleansed her by the washing of water with the word, that He might present to Himself the church in all her glory, having no spot or wrinkle or any such thing; but that she would be holy and blameless" (Ephesians 5:25-27).

ONLY JESUS

No one comes to the Father but through Me. John 14:6
Cathedral Rock, Sedona, Arizona, USA
Nikon D7000, ISO 100, f11, AEB, Adobe Photoshop, Nik Silver Efex Pro
MYPHOTOWALK.COM—CATHERINEMARTIN.SMUGMUG.COM

SERVING THE LORD

So the sons of Israel did all the work according to all that the Lord had commanded. And Moses examined all the work, and behold, they had done it, just as the Lord had commanded, this they had done. So Moses blessed them.

EXODUS 39:42-43

PREPARE YOUR HEART

Oh what a journey we have had in Exodus this week as we have been given a glimpse into God's heart. What a privilege to be able to go with Moses to Mount Sinai and hear some of his most intimate conversations with God. Today in our day of study we are going to come down from Mount Sinai and see what happened when the people of Israel received the plans for the tabernacle. As you begin your quiet time today, ask God to feed you with His Word and give you a heart to serve Him.

READ AND STUDY GOD'S WORD

1. Once Moses came down from Mount Sinai, the work of the tabernacle began in earnest. How did the people of Israel respond after all they had been through and what was the result? Read Exodus 39:42-43 and write out your most significant insights. (Optional: Depending on your time, you can read all the details in Exodus 35-39.)

2. The people of God served Him in obedience and did all the work according to God's commands. And what was the result—the blessing of the Lord. Now, God's plans and purposes could be experienced and God could dwell with His people, setting them apart from all other nations. Read Exodus 40:33-38 and write out all that happened as a result of their faithful work in obedience to God.

3. Notice how the people served according to "all that the Lord commanded" (Exodus 39:42) and Moses "finished the work" (Exodus 40:33). How does this help you in understanding how to serve the Lord?

4. So many in the church today have an agenda that is worldly and have not sought God to serve in His work, in His way, with His strength. Read the following verses and write out what you learn.

1 Corinthians 15:58

2 Corinthians 2:14-17

2 Corinthians 9:8

Philippians 4:13

Colossians 3:23-24

1 Thessalonians 5:24

2 Timothy 1:9

1 Peter 4:10-11

ADORE GOD IN PRAYER

Pray the words of F.B. Meyer today: "O Holy Savior, make my life deeper, stronger, richer, gentler, more Christlike, more full of the spirit of heaven, more devoted to your service and glory, so that I may ever bless and praise you, and magnify your name and adorn your Gospel in all things."

YIELD YOURSELF TO GOD

God is not looking for people to work for Him but people who let Him work mightily in and through them: "The eyes of the Lord run to and fro throughout the whole earth, to give strong support to those whose heart is blameless toward him" (2 Chron. 16:9). God is not a scout looking for the first draft choices to help His team win. He is an unstoppable fullback ready to take the ball and run touchdowns for anyone who trusts Him to win the game…[16]

JOHN PIPER IN BROTHERS, WE ARE NOT PROFESSIONALS

ENJOY HIS PRESENCE

Lilias Trotter wrote in one of her journals some beautiful words next to one of her watercolors of purple desert wildflowers[17]:

Long is the time to learn
Short is the time to do,
Yet it is worth it all
If the work in the end be true.

LILIAS TROTTER IN A BLOSSOM IN THE DESERT

Today in your quiet time you saw the profound result of the dedicated service of the people of Israel in performing all that the Lord commanded. When we serve in His power, according to His calling, His purpose, and His plan, we will see the results He had in mind. Just think, the people of Israel were able to have God in their midst as they carried the tabernacle that they built from place to place. They were witnesses of redemption in their day as we are in ours. What does the Lord have in mind for you? What is on your heart as you think about serving the Lord? Write your thoughts and a prayer in your Journal as you close your quiet time today.

REST IN HIS LOVE

"So, my dear brothers and sisters, be strong and immovable. Always work enthusiastically for the Lord, for you know that nothing you do for the Lord is ever useless" (1 Corinthians 15:58 NLT).

BURNING HEARTS

Were not our hearts burning within us. Luke 24:32
Upper Red Rock Loop, Sedona, Arizona, USA
Nikon D7000, ISO 125, f11, AEB, Adobe Photoshop, Nik Silver Efex Pro
MYPHOTOWALK.COM—CATHERINEMARTIN.SMUGMUG.COM

DEVOTIONAL READING
BY ANDREW MURRAY

DEAR FRIEND,

This week you had the opportunity to journey with Moses and the Israelites to the very heart of God Himself. Look over your quiet times from Week Seven. What was the most profound truth you learned about God?

What were your most meaningful discoveries this week as you spent time with the Lord?

Most meaningful insight:

Most meaningful devotional reading:

Most meaningful verse:

As you think about all that you have learned this week, meditate on these words by Andrew Murray: "Man needs to be alone with God. Without this, God cannot have the opportunity to shine into his heart, to transform his nature by His divine working, to take possession of him, and to fill him with His fullness. Man needs to be alone with God, to yield to the presence and power of His holiness, of His life, and of His love…Alone with God—that is the secret of true prayer, of true power in prayer, of real living, of face-to-face fellowship with God, and of power for service. There is no true, deep conversion; no true deep holiness; no clothing with the Holy Spirit and with power; no abiding peace or joy, without being daily alone with God. As someone has said, "There is no path to holiness, but in being much and long alone with God." The institution of daily, secret prayer is an inestimable privilege. Let it be the one thing our hearts are set on: seeking, finding, and meeting God. Take time to be alone with God.[18]

ANDREW MURRAY IN GOD'S BEST SECRETS

Viewer Guide
❧ WEEK SEVEN ☙

Let Me Know Your Ways

In Week Seven of *One Holy Passion*, we studied Exodus 32-39 and took a sacred journey in Exodus deeper into the heart of God. Today we are going to look at the intimate relationship between Moses and God. So grab your Bible, these notes, and let's dig in to the amazing Word of God and learn more about the ways of God so that we may know Him more.

"Now therefore, I pray You, if I have found favor in Your sight, let me know Your ways that I may know You, so that I may find favor in Your sight" (Exodus 33:13.

What happens when we spend intimate quiet time alone with God?

1. We are going to be filled with a desire to _____God and His ways. Exodus 33:13

2. We are going to see His _____. Exodus 33:14

3. We become aware that God knows us and _____us. Exodus 33:17

4. He will move us to great _____. Exodus 33:18

5. He will _____Himself to us in new and deeper ways and we will experience His _____. Exodus 33:19, 34:6-7

6. He becomes our _____love. Exodus 34:14-15

7. We are led into ministry where we _____Him with our gifts and talents. Exodus 39:42-43

How can you cultivate a vibrant love relationship with the Lord?

1. _____ with the Lord.

2. Go on a _____ with the Lord.

3. _____ together with a friend.

4. Find ways to _____ the Lord.

5. Read a powerful _____ of someone who knew and loved God.

6. Write love _____ to the Lord.

≋ *Video messages are available on DVDs or as Digital M4V Video. Audio messages are available as Digital MP3 Audio. Visit the Quiet Time Ministries Online Store at www.quiettime.org.*

INTO THE PROMISED LAND

Old and New Testaments

The Canaan of the Old Testament corresponds to the land of full blessing which awaits us all here and now in Jesus Christ our Lord. It is the purpose of God's redemption: He has brought us out that He might bring us in.[1]

ALAN REDPATH

THE JOURNEY OF MOSES

Now Moses went up from the plains of Moab to Mount Nebo, to the top of
Pisgah, which is opposite Jericho. And the LORD showed him all the land…

Deuteronomy 34:1

PREPARE YOUR HEART

Oh what a journey we have had in Exodus—we have seen the love of God for His people as He rescued them from the Egyptians and brought them to Himself. He established a covenant with His people and led them in the wilderness for forty years. He called Moses to lead the people. We left Exodus with God leading His people gloriously in the tabernacle in the sight of Israel. So what is the rest of the story? There is throughout Scripture, both the Old and the New Testaments, a sense of the now and the not yet. This is especially true with the promised land—"a good and spacious land, to a land flowing with milk and honey, to the place of the Canaanite and the Hittite and the Amorite and the Perizzite and the Hivite and the Jebusite" (Exodus 3:8). What is this promised land? It is a real place and experience that God had for the people of Israel, and it is an experience for us as we live in the world that will give way to the reality of heaven as the place where we will live forever and ever.

And now, Moses, the humble man of God, is going to get a glimpse of the promised land, a view he will never forget. Ask God to speak to your heart as you begin this last week of study in *One Holy Passion*.

READ AND STUDY GOD'S WORD

1. The book of Deuteronomy recounts the history of Israel. And in that history we discover a people who were disobedient at every turn and were constantly rebelling against God. In the book of Numbers, we see the people of God living in unbelief. Following the death of Miriam, the sister of Moses, the people were once again in a place with no water. Read Numbers 20:1-13 and write your insights about the following responses:

The people's response

Moses' and Aaron's response

God's response

2. The people grumbled against Moses and once again blamed him for taking them away from the supposed security of Egypt (Numbers 20:4-5). Their loss of memory and ability to create a story in their own minds is astounding when you think about it. Imagine the disappointment in Moses, our hero of the faith. Moses went to God and was instructed to take his staff and speak to the rock. And now we see that all men, even heroes of the faith, have great feet of clay. Moses struck the rock instead of speaking to the rock, as God had commanded. The water came forth abundantly. However, God held Moses accountable for his disobedience as a leader of God. God called it what it was—unbelief and lack of trust. And Moses represented God before the people. It was a holy stewardship and one that could not be taken lightly. God said that Moses would not be the one to bring the people into the promised land. Keep in mind, taking into account the whole counsel of God's Word, that Moses is a hero of the faith, and is held in high esteem. What does the example of Moses teach us about the importance of obedience, belief, and trust in our lives, especially if we are leaders?

3. With Moses, we see the promised land in terms of the "now" and "not yet." Read Deuteronomy 34:1-6 and Matthew 17:1-3 and write what you learn about Moses and his firsthand experience in the Promised Land.

4. Oh to have a heart like Moses. Moses wrote a psalm that gives you insight in his passion for the Lord. Read Psalm 90 and write your most significant insight.

ADORE GOD IN PRAYER

Pray the words of this hymn today as you talk with the Lord: "All to Jesus I surrender. Make me, Saviour, wholly Thine: Let me feel the Holy Spirit, Truly know that Thou art mine. All to Jesus I surrender; Lord I give myself to Thee. Fill me with Thy love and power; Let Thy blessing fall on me. I surrender all. I surrender all. All to Jesus I surrender, I surrender all."

YIELD YOURSELF TO GOD

What glimpses we get of the inner life of this noble man! All that he wrought on earth was the outcome of the secret abiding of his soul in God.. He was nothing; God was all. And all that he accomplished on the earth was due to that Mighty One indwelling, fulfilling, and working out through him, as His organ and instrument, His own consummate plans. Thus Moses drew his life's work to a close. Behind him a long and glorious life, before, the ministry and worship of the heavenly sanctuary. Here, the shekinah; there, the unveiled face. Here, the tent and pilgrim march; there, the everlasting rest. Here, the Promised Land, beheld from afar, but not entered; there, the goodly land beyond Jordan entered and possessed...We are permitted from Pisgah's height to scan the fair land we long for, and are then removed to a better land. We have the answer given to us later, as Moses, who had his prayer gloriously fulfilled when he stood with Christ on the Transfiguration Mount.[2]

F.B. MEYER IN GREAT MEN OF THE BIBLE

We are in the same company as Abraham and Sarah, Isaac and Jacob, Deborah and Ruth, Moses and David, Peter and Paul, Mary and Martha. The One in whom they lived and moved is the One in whom we abide. If He sustained them, will He not also you? He has no thought of retiring from being God—from everlasting to everlasting He can be counted upon.[3]

GEORGE O. WOOD IN A PSALM IN YOUR HEART

ENJOY HIS PRESENCE

Through Moses on this sacred journey in Exodus, we have been taken into the very presence of God and experienced His heart. We have caught glimpses of His glory that would not have been possible had we not stood with Moses when he prayed, "Show me Your glory." What boldness and courage Moses had when he walked on earth. As you think through all you have learned about Moses, how have you seen God's passion for His people and how have you seen Moses' passion for God? How has his relationship with the Lord encouraged you? Write your insights, then close by writing a prayer to the Lord expressing all that is on your heart today.

REST IN HIS LOVE

"Lord, through all the generations You have been our home!" (Psalm 90:1).

THE WATER OF LIFE

Then He showed me a river of the water of life. Revelation 22:1
Sedona, Arizona, USA
Nikon D7000, ISO 110, f36, 1/10sec, Adobe Photoshop, Nik Silver Efex Pro
MYPHOTOWALK.COM—CATHERINEMARTIN.SMUGMUG.COM

THE JOURNEY OF JOSHUA AND ISRAEL

Be strong and courageous, for you shall give this people possession
of the land which I swore to their fathers to give them.

JOSHUA 1:9

PREPARE YOUR HEART

There is a certain quiet sadness when we near the end of a study and in our case, we feel a loss deeply with Moses going home to the Lord. He has been our leader, teacher, and great example throughout Exodus. You can just imagine how the people of God felt. But there had been one who was with Moses the whole time out there in the wilderness. His name was Joshua, Moses' servant. There is always a ripple effect in the lives of great men and women of God. Their lives are powerful influences that touch others throughout the world.

Henrietta Mears is such a wonderful example of the ripple effect of a life. She was the Director of Christian Education at First Presbyterian Church in Hollywood, California. She loved God's Word and even wrote a book, *What The Bible Is All About*. She founded Gospel Light, a publishing company, and Forest Home, a Christian conference center. Through her life and ministry, many were influenced for Christ and served in Christian work including Richard Halverson, Vonette and Bill Bright, and Billy Graham. Her life is an inspiration to remember and carry out the words of C.T. Studd: "Only one life will soon be past. Only what's done for Christ will last." Her passion for Christ was contagious.

As you begin your quiet time today, ask God to give you a contagious passion for the Lord.

READ AND STUDY GOD'S WORD

1. Moses' passion for Yahweh was evident to everyone, especially to Joshua, his servant. Read Exodus 33:11 and note what you learn about Joshua and his nearness to Yahweh.

2. God chose his next leader for His people and gave him a very important calling and set of instructions. So we see that even though Exodus ends with God leading His people in the desert, the history of God's people continues. Now it was time to go into the promised land. Of all the people of Israel who had originally been delivered from Egypt, only Joshua and Caleb remained after forty years. It was a new generation with a new leader. Read Joshua 1:1-9 and write your insights about what God was asking of Joshua.

3. What a potentially intimidating role for Joshua. Yet God had prepared him for it all along. Read the following verses and write about how God worked on behalf of Joshua as a leader and how the people responded to Joshua's leadership.

Joshua 1:16-18

Joshua 3:7

Joshua 4:14

4. Read Deuteronomy 11:8-12 and write out what you learn about the land that God promised His people.

5. Joshua was the one God chose to take the people into the promised land. But it was not going to be a simple task, for the promised land was occupied by other people. But God promised that the land was theirs. All they had to do was take possession. God even promised that they did not need to be afraid, because He had given the kings, peoples, cities and lands into their hands (see Joshua 8:1). Joshua even sent spies into the land and they brought back the report: "Surely the LORD has given all the land into our hands; moreover, all the inhabitants of the land have melted away before us" (Joshua 2:24). As Joshua led the people of Israel into the promised land, they camped at Gilgal, and from there, fought and won many battles, including the battle of Jericho (Joshua 6). There were many victories but also challenges for the people of Israel.

When Joshua came to the end of his life, he summed up what God had done. Read Joshua 21:43-45 and 23:14 and write his summary of what God did. Note how important God's promises in His Word were for Joshua. God had called him to meditate on the Word of God day and night (Joshua 1:8). It is clear that Joshua did as God had asked and held God's Word close to his heart.

6. Joshua, as the faithful leader of God's people, reminded them of what was most important. Read Joshua 23:6-11 and summarize the main encouragements, personalizing them for your own relationship with the Lord i.e. I need to be strong, I need to be careful to obey what is written in God's Word, I need to hold fast to the Lord. These are good words for us to remember in this last week of study in *One Holy Passion*.

7. Joshua expressed the renewal of God's covenant with the people of Israel. In his words, you see all that God did for the people. Read Joshua 24:1-15 as a reminder of all you have studied in Exodus. Then, write out what means the most to you. Think especially about these words from the Lord in Joshua 24:5 NLT — "I brought you out as a free people."

8. The book of Joshua is thought be a picture for us of the Christian life—the experience of beautiful freedom in Christ, an intimate relationship with Christ, and a victorious Christian life. Read Ephesians 4:17-24 and write out your most significant insights about how we are to live.

ADORE GOD IN PRAYER

Pray through the words of Corrie ten Boom: "Thank You, Lord Jesus, that you have freed us from sin and unlocked a treasure chest of grace for our use. Our riches are greater than all the earth's gold and silver combined."[4]

YIELD YOURSELF TO GOD

We were redeemed that we might be His purchased possession; justified that we might be sanctified and glorified. We were brought out that we might be brought in. Yet is it not true that the majority of Christians come far short, and are content with a wilderness experience—justified, but not enjoying the possession of all their inheritance in Christ—Are you in the wilderness of defeat, or in the land of victory? Is your life a constant struggle against the powers of darkness, with a constant defeat, or is it a victorious war waged in the power of the Risen Lord... blessing is bestowed on all who, in the absence of all merit and effort, receive it with open and empty hands of faith. The Christian does not work up toward victory, he works down from it. We do not struggle toward it, but we stand in it because of the Cross and an empty tomb.[5]

ALAN REDPATH IN VICTORIOUS CHRISTIAN LIVING

Christians—and only Christians—have the capacity to transcend the old and put on the new. That is the testimony of Scripture. When we believe in Jesus Christ and receive him as Lord, we are renewed in the depth of our spirit. Christ is our life now, and a radical transformation has taken place. The new self is in the likeness of God, the image of Jesus. You are now identified with Him. If you are a Christian, the life of Christ lives in you. The new urges that come with the new self are urges to love, to understand, to forgive, to accept difficult people, to endure difficult situations, to gently correct those who need correction, to be faithful at all times. The new self is real and genuine. It is love unfeigned. It is not something put on for a moment, not a painted-on smile masking a hostile heart. It is righteous. It is true. It is holy.[6]

RAY C. STEDMAN IN OUR RICHES IN CHRIST

ENJOY HIS PRESENCE

David, the man after God's own heart, prays some wonderful words that summarize what God did for His people: "How great you are, Sovereign LORD! There is no one like you, and there is no God but you, as we have heard with our own ears. And who is like your people Israel—the one nation on earth that God went out to redeem as a people for himself, and to make a name for himself, and to perform great and awesome wonders by driving out nations and their gods from before your people, whom you redeemed from Egypt? You have established your people Israel as your very own forever, and you, LORD, have become their God" (2 Samuel 7:22-24 NIV). In these words, we see the great themes of Exodus—how we are meant for God, gracious freedom, extravagant love, hopeful purpose, and immeasurable abundance. Oh how great is our God with unfailing love and merciful grace!

What did you learn from Joshua, the people of Israel, the words of David, and Ephesians that will help you live intimately with your Lord and walk in victory and freedom, moment by moment? Have you learned the lesson of Joshua, holding God's Word close to your heart, and meditating on it day and night? How will living in God's Word help you have a contagious passion for your Lord?

REST IN HIS LOVE

"In reference to your former manner of life, you lay aside the old self, which is being corrupted in accordance with the lusts of deceit, and that you be renewed in the spirit of your mind, and put on the new self, which in the likeness of God has been created in righteousness and holiness of the truth" (Ephesians 4:22-24).

THE BLESSED HOPE

We wait for the blessed hope. Titus 2:13 NIV
Sedona, Arizona, USA
Nikon D7000, ISO 100, f11, AEB, Adobe Photoshop, Nik Silver Efex Pro
MYPHOTOWALK.COM—CATHERINEMARTIN.SMUGMUG.COM

THE JOURNEY OF JESUS

"If anyone really loves me, he will observe my teaching, and my Father will love him, and both of us will come in face-to-face fellowship with him; yes, we will make our special dwelling place with him.

JOHN 14:23 WMS

PREPARE YOUR HEART

Jonathan Goforth, born in 1859, became a Christian at the age of eighteen. He immediately sensed a call from God to go into the ministry and specifically to be a missionary. He would get up two hours early every morning for Bible study and his Bible was his most precious possession. He read it through again and again.

He went to college and was shocked to discover that not everyone wanted to share the gospel the way he did and even laughed at him when he would tell them stories of sharing the gospel with others. He began a jail ministry his very first Sunday in college. He was quite radical for his day, often going from house to house just to tell others about how they could know the Lord.

Ultimately, Jonathan felt the Lord was calling him to go to an unreached province in China and decided to go via China Inland Mission. Hudson Taylor himself wrote and said that if he wanted to go there he would need to "go forward on his knees."

And so Jonathan and his wife, Rosalind, went "praying all the way." He studied the Chinese language for months but found it very difficult. He made little progress and the Chinese people complained that they could not understand him when he preached.

Suddenly one day while he was trying to preach, words, phrases, and idioms began to flood his mind and he was understood. He found out later that a group of students at Knox College had been praying just for him. From that time on, he was very fluent in the Chinese language.

How can a person who finds languages very difficult, suddenly become fluent in that language? How is it that someone like Jonathan Goforth could preach for 8 hours a day over a period of 5 months to more than 25,000 men and women and see as many as 10-20 saved each time?

Because God takes ordinary men and women like you and me and lives in them through the Holy Spirit, sets their hearts on fire, and accomplishes extraordinary, remarkable things—things that only He can do. Ask God now to speak to your heart as you look at the journey of Jesus and what it means for you.

READ AND STUDY GOD'S WORD

1. It was the time of Passover and Jesus was in the upper room with His disciples. He had just given them some news that shook them to the core of their being. He had told them that one of His disciples would betray Him and that He was going where they could not go (John 13:21, 33-34). They were troubled and Jesus knew it. They did not realize that things were far from over. No, real life was just beginning. You might think of Jesus' next words as good news on a sad day. Read John 14:16-23 and write out your most significant insights about the new kind of relationship that they would experience with Him.

2. Jesus was teaching that the Holy Spirit would make it possible for Christ not to just be "with" them, but "in" them. This teaching from Jesus is seen throughout the gospels. It is a promise that is seen in the New Covenant described in Jeremiah 31. The New Testament is clear that the promises made to Abraham apply not just to his physical descendants, but his spiritual descendants, and that includes believers in Christ (Romans 9:4-9, Hebrews 6:15). As we think about the promised land in the Old Testament, it's important to realize how we can, in a way, spiritually experience a land of promise even now. According to scholar John P. Davis, land, in the theological sense of the word, is the place where God dwells, reveals Himself, and is active in His kingdom work.[7] So what Jesus is teaching is that the Holy Spirit is going to make it possible for *us* to be the place where He dwells, reveals Himself, and is at work. And the Holy Spirit is the guarantee of our eternal inheritance (Ephesians 1:13-18). Land, for us in this world is the experience of a Person, Jesus Christ, as He lives in and through us. He is literally going to tabernacle in us, since we are now temples of the Holy Spirit (1 Corinthians 6:19-20). Read the following verses and write what you learn from Jeremiah and the promise of the New Covenant and then, what you learn from Jesus.

Jeremiah 31:31-34

John 7:37-39

John 15:5

3. Jesus was crucified, then buried. But on the third day something happened that He had promised. Read Matthew 28:5-7 and the words of Paul in 1 Corinthians 15:3-8 and describe what happened.

4. Now, dear friend, comes the powerful truth that we will explore more in our next day of study. But it's time to think about this truth. In Romans 6 Paul teaches that we are united with Christ in every way. We died with Him. We were buried with Him. And we were raised to new life with Him. How is it that we are united with Him? Through the Holy Spirit (See John 16:7). Read Romans 6:3-14 and write your most significant insight from these verses.

5. Finally, meditate on the words of these verses and underline those words and phrases that mean the most to you.

> "I have been crucified with Christ; and it is no longer I who live, but Christ lives in me; and the life which I now live in the flesh I live by faith in the Son of God, who loved me and gave Himself up for me." (Galatians 2:20).

> "For He rescued us from the domain of darkness, and transferred us to the kingdom of His beloved Son" (Colossians 1:13).

> "…Christ in you, the hope of glory" (Colossians 1:27).

ADORE GOD IN PRAYER

Pray the words of this prayer by Andrew Murray as you think about new life in Jesus Christ: "Heavenly Father, how can I thank You for the unspeakable gift of Your Son on the cross? How can I thank You for our eternal salvation, worked out by that death on the cross? He died for me so that I might live eternally. Through His death on the cross, I am dead to sin and live in the power of His life. Father in heaven, teach me what it means that I am dead with Christ and can live my life in Him. Teach me to realize that my sinful flesh is wholly corrupt and nailed to the cross to be destroyed, so that the life of Christ may be manifest in me. Teach me, above all, to believe that I cannot either understand or experience this except through the continual working of the Holy Spirit dwelling within me. Father, for Christ's sake, I ask it. Amen."[8]

YIELD YOURSELF TO GOD

Land in the Old Testament is both a physical reality and a theological symbol. The 2,504 uses of 'land' in the Old Testament speak of its importance to theology. Though God promised to Abraham a specific piece of geography, Abraham apparently understood it as more than geography (Heb. 11:16, 39–40). Theologically, land is the gift of God. Land is the place of blessing. Land is the fulfilment of promise. Land is that sphere of life where one lives out one's allegiance to Yahweh. Land is that place where Yahweh uniquely chooses to dwell and to reveal himself. Land is the sphere of God's kingdom activity. This land promise retains a fulfilled, yet not consummated aspect…To New Testament believers, this 'landedness' presently finds expression in their current experience with Jesus Christ (Col. 1:13) as the fulfilment of the theological symbol, accompanied by an expectation, as seen in the eschatology of the Old Testament prophets and of the New Testament, that the physical reality involves an expansion of the territorial borders to include the entire earth and ultimately the New Creation.[9]

JOHN P. DAVIS

The death of Christ simply means for me that when He died I died, and in God's view I am now as if I had been executed for my own sin and was now recognized as another person who has risen with Christ and is justified from his former sins because he had been executed for them, "…because anyone who has died has been freed from sin" (Romans 6:7). Not only so it is the secret of my sanctification, for on that cross of Calvary I, the sinful self, was put to death; and when I lay myself over with Him upon that cross and reckon myself dead, Christ's risen life passes into me and it is no longer my struggling, my goodness or my badness, but my Lord who lives in me. Therefore, while I abide in Him I am counted even as He, and enabled to walk even as He walked…here it is union with the Person of the Lord Jesus that constitutes the source of spiritual life. The secret, therefore, which Paul had found, "Christ in you the hope of glory" (Colossians 1:27).[10]

A.B. SIMPSON IN CHRIST IN YOU

I was upstairs sitting at my desk reading the Word and praying, and I said, "Lord, open my eyes!" And then in a flash I saw it. I saw my oneness with Christ. I saw that I was in him, and that when he died I died. I saw that the question of my death was a matter of the past and not of the future, and that I was just as truly dead as he was because I was in him when he died. The whole things had dawned upon me. I was carried away with such joy at this great discovery that I jumped from my chair and cried, "Praise the Lord, I am dead"…We need to have our eyes opened to the fact of our union with Christ.[11]

WATCHMAN NEE IN THE NORMAL CHRISTIAN LIFE

I bear witness that never servant had such a master as I have; never brother such a kinsman as he has been to me; never spouse such a husband as Christ has been to my soul; never sinner a better Saviour; never mourner a better comforter than Christ hath been to my spirit. I want none beside him. In life he is my life, and in death he shall be the death of death; in poverty Christ is my riches; in sickness he makes my bed; in darkness he is my star, and in brightness he is my sun; he is the manna of the camp in the wilderness, and he shall be the new corn of the host when they come to Canaan. Jesus is to me all grace and no wrath, all truth and no falsehood: and of truth and grace he is full, infinitely full.

CHARLES SPURGEON IN MORNING AND EVENING

ENJOY HIS PRESENCE

Have you discovered the exciting life of Christ in you, the hope of glory? Do you realize that you have been set free and are now raised with Christ to newness of life? Just as the people of Israel were set free from Egypt, died to that old life, and now had a new life as God's people, so you have died in Christ, are set free from sin (Romans 6:7), and now experience new life in Christ. What is the most important truth you have learned today and how will you apply it to your life?

REST IN HIS LOVE

"For if we have become united with Him in the likeness of His death, certainly we shall also be in the likeness of His resurrection" (Romans 6:5).

CHRIST OUR HOME

Christ will make His home in you as you trust in Him. Ephesians 3:17 NLT
Slide Rock State Park, Sedona, Arizona, USA
Nikon D7000, ISO 160, f11, AEB, Adobe Photoshop, Nik Silver Efex Pro
MYPHOTOWALK.COM—CATHERINEMARTIN.SMUGMUG.COM

YOUR JOURNEY

Blessed be the God and Father of our Lord Jesus Christ, who has blessed us with every spiritual blessing in the heavenly places in Christ."

EPHESIANS 1:3

PREPARE YOUR HEART

Have you ever stood outside a large estate that is surrounded by high fences and gates complete with a gate guard? You know that there is no way you are getting through to enjoy the beauty of the grounds or experience the security of the home. And perhaps you thought that you were poor and life like that is only for a select few. Well, dear friend, today you are going to see just how wealthy you really are. Only your true wealth is not found in the wilderness of this temporal world. You have a treasure that lasts forever that no one can ever take from you. We are going to look at life from the eternal perspective today. Paul says in 2 Corinthians 4:18 that "we look not at the things which are seen, but at the things which are not seen; for the things which are seen are temporal, but the things which are not seen are eternal." The eternal perspective is the ability to see everything from God's point of view and to have what we see affect how we live in the present.

So today, draw near to God and ask Him to give you the eternal perspective seen in His Word.

READ AND STUDY GOD'S WORD

1. Yesterday we saw that from a theological standpoint, land can be understood as the place where God dwells, reveals Himself, and is active in His kingdom work. We then saw that in this life, once we are born again spiritually and the Lord Jesus resides in us through the power of the Holy Spirit, then He is literally tabernacling in us, living His life in and through us. We are thus given the experience of an amazing land of promise from God while we are living here in this temporal world. So much becomes ours since Christ is living in us. You might think of these truths as the milk and honey flowing from the land that we experience even now with Christ living in us through the Holy Spirit. Read the following verses and write out what is yours because of Christ.

1 Corinthians 1:30

Ephesians 1:3

Ephesians 1:11

Ephesians 1:13-14

Ephesians 2:10

Colossians 1:13-14, Hebrews 12:28

Colossians 2:13

2. How is it that you can appropriate who you are in Christ and live a life filled with the Spirit? By faith, dear friend. Every day you make choices based on what you know is true in God's word, not by what you see in the world. It's almost as though the world is a wilderness experience until we are face to face with the Lord in heaven, our eternal promised land. And yet, we can have the promised land experience with Christ living in us, with His power as our strength, and His person as our very life. Remember back in the wilderness when the people of Israel had no water. Instead of turning to the Lord and crying out to Him for help in the circumstance, they acted as though God was not with them and would not care for them. In the same way, day by day, as we are confronted with easy or difficult circumstances, we walk by faith in Christ as He lives His life in and through us. It's not our life, it's His life (Galatians 2:20). Selah [pause, and calmly

think of that]. Now, read the following verses and underline those words and phrases that help you understand how to live.

"These things I have spoken to you, so that in Me you may have peace. In the world you have tribulation, but take courage; I have overcome the world" (John 16:33).

"And so, dear brothers and sisters, I plead with you to give your bodies to God because of all he has done for you. Let them be a living and holy sacrifice—the kind he will find acceptable. This is truly the way to worship him. Don't copy the behavior and customs of this world, but let God transform you into a new person by changing the way you think. Then you will learn to know God's will for you, which is good and pleasing and perfect" (Romans 12:1-2 NLT).

"For we walk by faith, not by sight" (2 Corinthians 5:7).

"But the fruit of the Spirit is love, joy, peace, forbearance, kindness, goodness, faithfulness, gentleness and self-control. Against such things there is no law. Those who belong to Christ Jesus have crucified the flesh with its passions and desires. Since we live by the Spirit, let us keep in step with the Spirit" (Galatians 5:22-25 NIV).

"So be careful how you live. Don't live like fools, but like those who are wise. Make the most of every opportunity in these evil days. Don't act thoughtlessly, but understand what the Lord wants you to do. Don't be drunk with wine, because that will ruin your life. Instead, be filled with the Holy Spirit, singing psalms and hymns and spiritual songs among yourselves, and making music to the Lord in your hearts. And give thanks for everything to God the Father in the name of our Lord Jesus Christ" (Ephesians 5:15-20 NLT).

"Therefore as you have received Christ Jesus the Lord, so walk in Him, having been firmly rooted and now being built up in Him and established in your faith, just as you were instructed, and overflowing with gratitude" (Colossians 1:6-7).

"Since you have been raised to new life with Christ, set your sights on the realities of heaven, where Christ sits in the place of honor at God's right hand. Think about the things of heaven, not the things of earth. For you died to this life, and your real life is hidden with Christ in God. And when Christ, who is your life, is revealed to the whole world, you will share in all his glory. So put to death the sinful, earthly things lurking within you. Have nothing to do with sexual immorality, impurity, lust, and evil desires. Don't be greedy, for a greedy person is an idolater, worshiping the things of this world. Because of these sins, the anger of God is coming. You used to do these things when your life was still part of this world. But now is the time to get rid of anger, rage, malicious behavior, slander, and dirty language. Don't lie to each other, for you have stripped off your old sinful nature and all its wicked deeds. Put on your new nature, and be renewed as you learn to know your Creator and become like him" (Colossians 3:1-10 NLT).

And by that will, we have been made holy through the sacrifice of the body of Jesus Christ once for all… For by one sacrifice he has made perfect forever those who are being made holy (Hebrews 10:10, 14 NIV).

"Therefore, since we have so great a cloud of witnesses surrounding us, let us also lay aside every encumbrance and the sin which so easily entangles us, and let us run with endurance the race that is set before us, fixing our eyes on Jesus, the author and perfecter of faith, who for the joy set before Him endured the cross, despising the shame, and has sat down at the right hand of the throne of God. For consider Him who has endured such hostility by sinners against Himself, so that you will not grow weary and lose heart" (Hebrews 12:1-3).

ADORE GOD IN PRAYER

Talk with God about everything you have learned from Him today in His Word.

YIELD YOURSELF TO GOD

It is for you to BE—it is for Him to DO! Restfully available to the Saving Life of Christ, enjoying "the richest measure of the divine Presence, a body wholly filled and flooded with God Himself," instantly obedient to the heavenly impulse—this is your vocation, and this is your victory![12]

MAJOR W. IAN THOMAS IN THE SAVING LIFE OF CHRIST

ENJOY HIS PRESENCE

The whole theme of our study has been the passion God has for you, the one holy passion—His extravagant, unconditional, amazing love, and the passion you have for Him that grows as you mature in your faith. Can you see the provision that God has made for you as you live in this world? Just as He provided for the people of Israel, so He provides for you (Philippians 4:19). You are in the world, but certainly not of the world. For if you have been born again (see John 3), now Christ lives in you. You are a member of His kingdom, forgiven of your sins, and are the heir of eternal life. You are completely secure knowing that "there is now no condemnation for those who are in Christ Jesus" (Romans 8:1). Oh, you have so much more than anyone who only lives in the world has. The kingdom you belong to is eternal and cannot be shaken. You walk every day in the light of God's great love for you. You are holy and have been made perfect forever according to the writer of Hebrews. And then, you see in those same verses that you are in a process of being "made holy" (Hebrews 10:14). This process of sanctification and consecration occurs in the context of life in the world where you encounter Red Sea places and wilderness times where God is at work in you, drawing you closer to Himself and reviving you in His Word through the power of the Holy Spirit. Surrender to God at every turn matures you, deepens your faith in God, and increases your passion for the impossible. You may be in the wilderness, but united with Christ, your heart is living in the land of promise with your Lord. Never forget that all you possess in Christ is secure—your forgiveness, eternal life, inheritance, and every spiritual blessing. And God is at work in you, accomplishing His plans and purposes. Oh, how exciting it is to watch Yahweh, the God of the impossible, at work in and through you. There is nothing like it—truly, it is the great adventure of knowing God. You can count on His unfailing love for you and His faithfulness, dear friend, no matter what you face in life. That is one of the great messages we discovered in this sacred journey in Exodus where we have experienced God's rescue and the way out in every circumstance, whether it is the impossibility of a Red Sea place or a lack of water in the wilderness. With these truths in mind, what have you learned today that means the most to you?

Rest in His Love

"But by His doing you are in Christ Jesus, who became to us wisdom from God, and righteousness and sanctification, and redemption" (1 Corinthians 1:30).

Unlimited Blessings In Christ

Every spiritual blessing in the heavenly places in Christ. Ephesians 1:3
Sedona, Arizona, USA
Nikon D7000, ISO 100, f11, AEB, Adobe Photoshop, Nik Silver Efex Pro
myPhotoWalk.com—catherinemartin.smugmug.com

THE HEAVENLY COUNTRY

But as it is, they desire a better country, that is, a heavenly one. Therefore God
is not ashamed to be called their God; for He has prepared a city for them.

HEBREWS 11:16

PREPARE YOUR HEART

Lilias Trotter lived most of her life as a missionary in remote places in the desert of Algiers. It was a desolate place in so many ways and yet her journals show a profound beauty in both her words and her watercolor paintings. She walked with the Lord and had an eye always looking to her heavenly country. When she was on her deathbed, she was surrounded with her dearest friends who had served alongside her. While lying there, she looked out towards the light of the window. Someone asked, "Are you seeing beautiful things?" She replied, "Yes, many, many beautiful things." Not long after that moment, she stepped from earth to heaven, completing her journey in this life and beginning that new experience of the promised land where "no eye has seen, no ear has heard, and no mind has imagined what God has prepared for those who love Him" (1 Corinthians 2:9).

Dear friend, what a journey we have had through Exodus where we have seen the passion of our great God every step of the way. Just think back to how He heard the cries of His people, saw their suffering, and remembered His covenant. He resolved to rescue and redeem them, bear them on eagles' wings, and bring them to Himself. Moses was His man for the hour, a faithful, humble servant of God who carried out His plans. At the Red Sea place where God led His people, they learned a new and deeper trust as they watched Yahweh make a way through the sea. Then, we went into the wilderness and saw how God's passionate love for us leads to provision and power. And then, our passion for Him grows. Now, as we close out our time in this study, we are going to see what God has planned for us in the future. And no doubt, you will once again see His one holy passion for you. And your love for Him will grow deeper and stronger.

On your life journey, there is a tension between the now and not yet. If you have received Christ, you are placed in Him through the indwelling Holy Spirit. Not only are you "in Christ," but Christ lives in you (Galatians 2:20). As you live life united with Christ, you experience the blessings of a Spirit-filled life. You experience the fruit of the Spirit—love, joy, peace, patience, kindness, goodness, faithfulness, gentleness, and self-control (Galatians 5:22-23) and victory in spiritual warfare (Ephesians 6:10-18). The power of Christ is yours for every day living. Because you are still on earth and in the world, you will experience tribulation. You have the advantage of the One living in you who has overcome the world. It's Christ's life for your life, and your life is one of faith.

But one day, dear friend, your faith shall be made sight. And you will step into heaven, face to face with your Lord, in the eternal city of God, and as a member of His kingdom, you will find eternal rest in the promised land of heaven. Until that day, you live by faith in Christ, and find your life in Him. He will manifest through you the sweet aroma of the knowledge of Him in every place.

And dear friend, you are being borne on eagles' wings, so to speak, by the Lord as He brings you through this temporal wilderness of a world to Himself in heaven. Jesus, in His parable about the good and faithful servant had these words for him: "Well done, good and faithful servant… enter into the joy of your master" (Matthew 25:21 ESV). Think about the truth and teaching of those words. In the presence of the Lord there is fullness of joy and everlasting love. Blessings are yours in this promised land of heaven, dear friend. It is Paradise, according to Jesus (Luke 23:43). And you have those blessings because of Christ. And you have so much to look forward to! As you begin this last day of study ask God to speak to your heart about the heavenly country where you will live. Ask Him to open your eyes that you may see His great love for you.

READ AND STUDY GOD'S WORD

1. Abraham and others who lived by faith looked beyond the here and now to an eternal future in a heavenly place. Read Hebrews 11:13-16 and write what you learn about your future home, and how to live with the "now and not yet."

2. Read the following verses and underline those phrases that help you see your promised land (both in the "now" and the "not yet").

"'They shall be Mine,'" says the LORD of hosts, "'On the day that I make them
My jewels. And I will spare them as a man spares his own son who serves him'"
(Malachi 3:17 NKJV).

"No eye has seen, no ear has heard, and no mind has imagined what God has prepared for those who love him. But it was to us that God revealed these things by his Spirit. For his Spirit searches out everything and shows us God's deep secrets" (1 Corinthians 2:9-10 NLT).

"For we know that when this earthly tent we live in is taken down (that is, when we die and leave this earthly body), we will have a house in heaven, an eternal body made for us by God himself and not by human hands. We grow weary in our present bodies, and we long to put on our heavenly bodies like new clothing. For we will put on heavenly bodies; we will not be spirits without bodies. While we live in these earthly bodies, we groan and sigh, but it's not that we want to die and get rid of these bodies that clothe us. Rather, we want to put on our new bodies so that these dying bodies will be swallowed up by life. God himself has prepared us for this, and as a guarantee he has given us his Holy Spirit.   So we are always confident, even though we know that as long as we live in these bodies we are not at home with the Lord. For we live by believing and not by seeing. Yes, we are fully confident, and we would rather be away from these earthly bodies, for then we will be at home with the Lord. So whether we are here in this body or away from this body, our goal is to please him" (2 Corinthians 5:1-9 NLT).

"The Lord will rescue me from every evil attack and will bring me safely to his heavenly kingdom. To him be glory for ever and ever. Amen" (2 Timothy 4:18 NIV).

"Praise be to the God and Father of our Lord Jesus Christ! In his great mercy he has given us new birth into a living hope through the resurrection of Jesus Christ from the dead, and into an inheritance that can never perish, spoil or fade. This inheritance is kept in heaven for you, who through faith are shielded by God's power until the coming of the salvation that is ready to be revealed in the last time. In all this you greatly rejoice, though now for a little while you may have had to suffer grief in all kinds of trials. These have come so that the proven genuineness of your faith—of greater worth than gold, which perishes even though refined by fire—may result in praise, glory and honor when Jesus Christ is revealed. Though you have not seen him, you love him; and even though you do not see him now, you believe in him and are filled with an inexpressible and glorious joy, for you are receiving the end result of your faith, the salvation of your souls" (1 Peter 1:3-9 NIV).

"And when the Chief Shepherd appears, you will receive the unfading crown of glory" (1 Peter 5:4).

"Beloved, now we are children of God, and it has not appeared as yet what we will be. We know that when He appears, we will be like Him, because we will see Him just as He is" (1 John 3:2).

3. What will heaven be like? We know because John was given a view of the rest of the story for us from Jesus Himself. Read Revelation 21-22:5 and write out everything you learn that you have to look forward to in heaven.

4. How does all you have learned about God and your heavenly home show you God's amazing love? And how does it inspire a greater passion in you for your Lord?

ADORE GOD IN PRAYER

Pray these words by F.B. Meyer as a prayer to the Lord: "Gracious Father, I thank you for the Son of your love, for all that he has done for us, and will do; for all that he has been to us, and will be. I thank you that he holds me in his strong, pierced hand, loving me with the love that cannot let me go."

YIELD YOURSELF TO GOD

The main joy of heaven will be the heavenly Father greeting us in a time and place of rejoicing, celebration, joy, and great reunion. It will have the dynamics we see in the parable of the prodigal son, returning home from his fallen journey…That may be the only place in holy Scripture where we see God in a hurry—actually running to meet the returning child. So, for followers of Christ, our home is the place where the Father delights in welcoming us even as He sees us coming a long way off. We can expect expressions of love beyond measure; perhaps the intimacy of a hug from God the Father and our Lord Jesus Christ will be our first joy. Wrapped in His loving embrace, we will sense peace, delight, assurance, abundant love, warm fellowship, total security, and absolute calm. Heaven pulses with such purity and joy that it is impossible for anyone to describe it all…heaven itself will reflect the character of our great God. It will be a place of holiness, righteousness, love, justice, mercy, peace, order, and His sovereign rule.[13]

BILL BRIGHT IN THE JOURNEY HOME

The blind will not be sightless in heaven. The lame will not limp, nor will the elderly tremble. The deaf will hear and the mute will sing God's praises. We will carry none of our deficiencies or infirmities to heaven. There, we will never know an aching brow, a weak knee, or a failing eye. "The inhabitant will not say, 'I am sick' " (Is. 33:24). We will have a body that is incapable of any kind of suffering. No heart failure, no depression, no aching limbs, no lethargic soul will worry us there. We will be perfectly delivered from every evil of that kind. Our bodies will be immortal. Our risen bodies will not be capable of decay, much less death. There are no graves in glory.[14]

CHARLES SPURGEON IN BESIDE STILL WATERS

ENJOY HIS PRESENCE

Just think about all that God has prepared for you. Oh how He loves you. Paul says, "we may hold our heads high in the light of God's love" (Romans 5:11 Phillips.) Spurgeon writes: "This world is, to the believer, like a country inn…You are tarrying here only for one short night, and then you will be up and away to your eternal home." How does what you've learned make you look forward to heaven? Turn back to the Introduction of this study and read the Letter to the Lord that you wrote. How has God responded to the words you wrote to Him? Close by writing a new letter in your Journal, a prayer of thanksgiving to your Lord for how He has shown you His one holy passion for you. Include words of love and adoration expressing your one holy passion for Him.

REST IN HIS LOVE

"No eye has seen, no ear has heard, and no mind has imagined what God has prepared for those who love him." (1 Corinthians 2:9).

PATIENT WAITING

Rest in the LORD and wait patiently for Him. Psalm 37:7
Courthouse Butte, Sedona, Arizona, USA
Nikon D810, ISO 100, f22, AEB, Adobe Photoshop, Nik Silver Efex Pro
MYPHOTOWALK.COM—CATHERINEMARTIN.SMUGMUG.COM

DEVOTIONAL READING BY LILIAS TROTTER

DEAR FRIEND,

In your quiet times this week you studied the Promised Land. What were your most meaningful discoveries this week as you spent time with the Lord?

Most meaningful insight:

Most meaningful devotional reading:

Most meaningful verse:

Look back through the weeks of study and write your thoughts on the following questions. How did *One Holy Passion* help you at your Red Sea place?

What helped you experience God's amazing love the most as you studied *One Holy Passion*?

What was your favorite week of study in *One Holy Passion* and why?

What was the most important truth you learned in *One Holy Passion*?

What will you take with you and always remember from this study?

Turn your eyes upon Jesus. It was a little wood in early morning. The sun was climbing behind a steep cliff in the east, and its light was flooding nearer and nearer and then making pools among the trees. Suddenly from a dark corner of purple brown stems and tawny moss, there shone out a great golden star. It was just a dandelion, and half withered—but it was full face to the sun, and had caught into its heart all the glory it could hold and was shining so radiantly that the dew that lay on it still made a perfect aureole round its head. And it seemed to talk, standing there—to talk about the possibility of making the very best of these lives of ours. For if the Sun of Righteousness has risen upon our hearts, there is an ocean of grace and love and power lying all around us, an ocean to which all earthly light is but a drop, and it is ready to transfigure us, as the sunshine transfigured the dandelion, and on the same condition—that we stand full face to God.[15]

LILIAS TROTTER IN BLOSSOM IN THE DESERT

See that rough diamond on the jeweler's wheel? Carefully it is turned and cut on all sides, and it loses much that seems costly. Do you see it now? A glittering ray flows from the greatly cut diamond. Christian, compare yourself to such a diamond. You are one of God's jewels, and this is the time of cutting. You must endure it, so be of good courage. "Through faith and patience inherit the promises" (Heb. 6:12). " 'They shall be Mine,' says the LORD of hosts, 'on the day that I make them My jewels' " (Mal. 3:17).

CHARLES SPURGEON IN BESIDE STILL WATERS

No longer will there be a curse upon anything. For the throne of God and of the Lamb will be there, and his servants will worship him. And they will see his face, and His name will be written on their foreheads. And there will be no night there—no need for lamps or sun—for the Lord God will shine on them. And they will reign forever and ever.

REVELATION 22:3-5 NLT

Viewer Guide
❧ WEEK EIGHT ❧

Living In The Promised Land

It's hard to believe that we have completed our last week of study in *One Holy Passion*. Today I want to look at what the promised land means for us and how to live in the promised land.

"But as it is, they desire a better country, that is, a heavenly one. Therefore God is not ashamed to be called their God; for He has prepared a city for them" (Hebrews 11:16).

"The promised land is the place where God dwells, reveals Himself, and is active in His kingdom work" — John P. Davis in *The Abrahamic Covenant*

Past, present, and future views of the promised land

1. We can view the promised land in the past in the experience of _____ and the children of Israel.

Numbers 20:2-12, Deuteronomy 34:1-6, Joshua 21:43-45

2. The present view of the promised land is something _____ can experience even now.

Jeremiah 31:1-5 (The New Covenant), John 14:21-24, Galatians 2:20, 1 Corinthians 2:14, Colossians 1:13, 3:1-4, Ephesians 5:18, Galatians 5:22-23

3. There is a sense in which the promised land is future. And those who have died and gone home to be with the Lord are experiencing this now. It is the life we look forward to with great _____. It is our glorious future.

Isaiah 25:6-8, 2 Corinthians 5:1

There is a sense of the "now" and the "not yet" of the promised land.

5 Truths from Hebrews 11:13-16

1. This present life is not all there is. There is more — a heavenly _____.

John 14:2

2. This present place in the world is not our _____.

1 John 2:15-17

3. We live as strangers and exiles in this _____.

John 17:13-18

4. Our heavenly home is a _____ country.

Revelation 21-22

5. God has _____this place for us.

1 Corinthians 2:9-10, 13:12-13

≥✿ *Video messages are available on DVDs or as Digital M4V Video. Audio messages are available as Digital MP3 Audio. Visit the Quiet Time Ministries Online Store at www.quiettime.org.*

NOW THAT YOU HAVE COMPLETED THESE QUIET TIMES

You have spent eight weeks consistently drawing near to God in quiet time with Him. That time alone with Him does not need to come to an end. What is the next step? To continue your pursuit of God, you might consider other books from the A Quiet Time Experience series, including *A Heart that Hopes in God, Run Before the Wind, Trusting in the Names of God, Passionate Prayer,* and *Walk on Water Faith.* The Quiet Times For The Heart series are also books of quiet times with titles such as *Pilgrimage of the Heart, Revive My Heart, A Heart that Dances, A Heart on Fire,* and *A Heart to See Forever.* To learn more about quiet time, read signature books from the A 30-Day Journey series such as *Six Secrets to a Powerful Quiet Time* and *Knowing and Loving the Bible.* DVD and HD Digital Leader's Kits with inspirational messages and Leader's Guides are available for many books. Quiet Time Ministries online has exciting resources like *The Quiet Time Notebooks* to encourage you in your quiet time with God. Find daily encouragement from Cath's Blog at www.quiettime.org and view A Walk In Grace, the devotional photo journal featuring Catherine's myPhotoWalk.com photography. Join hundreds of other women online to study God's Word and grow in God's grace at Ministry For Women—Google Plus Community. Resources may be ordered online from Quiet Time Ministries at www.quiettime.org or by calling Quiet Time Ministries directly. For more information, you may contact:

Quiet Time Ministries
P.O. Box 14007
Palm Desert, California 92255
(800) 925-6458, (760) 772-2357
E-mail: catherine@quiettime.org
Website: www.quiettime.org

ABOUT THE AUTHOR

Catherine Martin is a summa cum laude graduate of Bethel Theological Seminary with a Master of Arts degree in Theological Studies. She is founder and president of Quiet Time Ministries, a director of women's ministries for many years, and an adjunct faculty member of Biola University. She is the author of *Six Secrets to a Powerful Quiet Time, Knowing and Loving the Bible, Walking with the God Who Cares, Set my Heart on Fire, Trusting in the Names of God, Passionate Prayer, Quiet Time Moments for Women,* and *Drawing Strength from the Names of God* published by Harvest House Publishers, and *Pilgrimage of the Heart, Revive My Heart* and *A Heart That Dances,* published by NavPress. She has also written *The Quiet Time Notebooks, A Heart on Fire, A Heart to See Forever, Run Before the Wind, A Heart That Hopes in God,* and *Walk on Water Faith,* published by Quiet Time Ministries Press. She is founder of myPhotoWalk.com dedicated to the art of devotional photography, publishing *myPhotoWalk—Quiet Time Moments* and *Savoring God's Promises of Hope.* As a popular keynote speaker at retreats and conferences, Catherine challenges others to seek God and love Him with all of their heart, soul, mind, and strength. For more information about Catherine, visit www.quiettime.org and www.myphotowalk.com.

ABOUT QUIET TIME MINISTRIES

Quiet Time Ministries is a nonprofit religious organization under Section 501(c)(3) of the Internal Revenue Code. Cash donations are tax deductible as charitable contributions. We count on prayerful donors like you, partners with Quiet Time Ministries pursuing our goals of the furtherance of the Gospel of Jesus Christ and teaching devotion to God and His Word. Visit us online at www.quiettime.org to view special funding opportunities and current ministry projects. Your prayerful donations bring countless project to life!

Quiet Time Ministries | *P.O. Box 14007* | *Palm Desert, California 92255*
1.800.925.6458 | *catherine@quiettime.org* | *www.quiettime.org* | *www.myphotowalk.com*

APPENDIX

❧ DISCUSSION QUESTIONS ❧

Introduction

Begin your class with prayer and then welcome everyone to this new book of quiet times. Have the people in your group share their names and what brought them to the study. Make sure each person in your group has a book. Also, gather contact information for all participants in your group including name, address, phone number, and e-mail. That way you can keep in touch and encourage those in your group.

Familiarize your group with the layout of the book. Each week consists of five days of quiet times, as well as a devotional reading and response for days 6 and 7. Each day follows the PRAYER quiet time plan:

Prepare Your Heart

Read and Study God's Word

Adore God in Prayer

Yield Yourself to God

Enjoy His Presence

Rest in His Love

Journal and prayer pages are included in the back of the book. Note that the quiet times offer devotional reading, Bible study, prayer, and practical application. Some days are longer than others and therefore, they should study at their own pace. Days 6-7 are for catching up, review, etc. This is a concentrated, intentional, sacred journey through Exodus with a special focus on God's passion for His people. As you and your group see God's passion more and more throughout the study, the result is a growing passion for God. Encourage your group to interact with the study, underlining significant insights and writing comments in the margins. Ask your group to read the Introduction sometime in their first day of study. Also point out that the Introduction includes a place where they will write a letter to the Lord. Encourage them to draw near to God each day and ask Him to speak to their hearts.

You can determine how to organize your group sessions, but here's one idea: Discuss the week of quiet times together in the first hour, break for ten minutes, and then watch the video message on the companion DVD or HD Digital M4V. There are nine messages for *One Holy Passion*—one for the introduction and one for each week. You might also share with your group a summary of how to prepare for their quiet time by setting aside a time each day and a place. Consider sharing how time alone with the Lord has made a difference in your own life. Let your class know about

Quiet Time Ministries Online, quiet time resources, and Catherine Martin's A Walk In Grace Photo Journal at www.quiettime.org.

Another option is to divide each week (completing the study in 16 weeks) by discussing days 1–3 one week and days 4–7 another week. This allows your group to journey through each quiet time at a slower pace.

Pray for one another by offering a way to record and exchange prayer requests. Some groups like to pass around a basket with cards that people can use to record prayer requests. Then, people take a request out of the basket and pray for someone during the week. Others like to use three by five cards and then exchange cards on a weekly basis.

Close this introductory class with prayer, take a short break, and then show the companion DVD or HD Digital M4V video message.

Week One: Meant For More

This week, the goal of your discussion is to look at some of the main themes that are seen in Exodus and continued throughout the Word of God. You might even give the example of the value of preparation for a trip. Describe how studying a guidebook helps in understanding the best places to visit and important stops along the way. These important themes in Exodus include our relationship with God, gracious freedom, extravagant love, hopeful purpose, and immeasurable abundance.

DAY 1: Meant For God

1. Open your discussion with prayer. Ask any new members of your group to introduce themselves. Share the goal of these quiet times: to go on a sacred journey in Exodus to God's amazing love.

2. What did you learn from the Introduction about this study? What is our study going to be about? And what does "one holy passion" mean? Also, point out the importance of 1 Corinthians 10:11 and how the things that happened to people of Israel are written for our instruction. Therefore, God is going to teach us biblical principles that are relevant for our life.

3. Day 1 began with the story of Ponnamal. Ask your group to describe the life of Ponnamal and what impressed them the most about how God worked in her life.

4. Describe how the book of Exodus begins. What kind of troubles are the people of Israel facing?

5. What did you learn from the theme verse in Exodus 19:4?

6. What verse about God meant the most to you in your study?

7. What encouraged you the most in Day 1 (from the story of Ponnamal, the devotional reading, or the study in God's Word)?

8. How did this study today help you in beginning to think about where you are in your own journey with God?

DAY 2: Meant For Gracious Freedom

1. In Day 2 we studied the theme of gracious freedom? What kinds of things can hold us captive? And if you'd like to share, what do you struggle with the most?

2. As you studied Exodus 1, what happened to the people of Israel, and why did they need to be set free?

3. What was your favorite verse about freedom?

4. What did you learn about Jesus and how He sets us free?

5. What did you learn from the devotional reading in Yield Yourself To God?

DAY 3: Meant For Extravagant Love

1. On Day 3 we looked at the extravagant, amazing, unconditional love of God. One of the main goals in our study will be to see His passion for us and His great love. What did you learn from Deuteronomy 7:6-10 about the character of God?

2. What was your favorite verse about the love of God in your study today and why?

3. In what ways is God's love extravagant, amazing and unconditional? And how were you impacted by His love for you?

4. What was your favorite quote in the devotional reading?

DAY 4: Meant For Hopeful Purpose

1. In Day 4 you studied God's hopeful purpose. In this you saw that God is not haphazard or capricious, but instead does everything with intention and purpose. He has a plan. How did this encourage you?

2. In Exodus 6:1-8 what did you learn about God's plan and purpose?

3. What did you learn about covenant?

4. You had the opportunity to read verses that spoke of God's plans and purposes. What was your favorite and why? How can these verses encourage us when we are going through a difficult time?

5. How did the devotional reading from Kay Arthur help you understand covenant more?

6. How does knowing that God has a plan and purpose help us see His passion for us?

DAY 5: Meant For Immeasurable Abundance

1. In Day 5 we studied the theme of immeasurable abundance. What did you learn about how God works in the lives of His people?

2. How did Jesus demonstrate a heart that does more than we ask or imagine?

3. How did you see God's work of immeasurable abundance in the verses you read? What was your favorite verse?

4. What was your favorite quote in the devotional reading?

DAYS 6 AND 7: Devotional Reading by A.W. Tozer

1. What was your favorite verse, insight, or quote from your quiet times this week?

2. What did you learn from the excerpt written by A.W. Tozer in Day 6 and 7?

3. What was your favorite photo this week in your quiet times?

4. Close your time together in prayer.

Week Two: When God Remembers His People

This week you read and studied Exodus 1-3 focusing on the life of Moses and the slavery of the people of Israel. But the main focus is on the heart of God and the fact that He "remembers" His people. And when God remembers, things begin to happen. We are going to see that when God remembers, He helps in troubled times, He knows His people, He calls his leader, He reveals His name, and He declares His promise.

DAY 1: God Helps In Troubled Times

1. Open your discussion with prayer. Then share that this week you had the opportunity to look at what it means when God "remembers." Read Exodus 2:24-25 and the point out that you study these verses in Day 2. In Day 1 we studied the events that lead up to God remembering His covenant.

2. Have someone read the quote by Matthew Henry on the Week 2 page (p. 55). Then point out that we are going to see that God is at work even though we may not realize it and that He initiates in our relationship with Him.

3. What did you learn about the book of Exodus in Read and Study God's Word that meant the most to you?

4. What did you learn from the life of Moses? What meant the most to you?

5. What did Moses do by faith and how does this encourage you in your own faith?

6. How did the verses about God at work in our lives encourage you?

7. How have you seen God at work in your own life?

DAY 2: God Knows His People

1. In Day 2 you studied God's response to the cry of His people. How did God respond, according to Exodus 2:23-25?

2. What does it mean when God "remembers"?

3. What was the most significant truth you learned about God? And how does this show you His passion for His people?

4. What meant the most to you from the devotional reading?

5. How do you need God to "remember" you? And how have you seen Him "remember" you?

DAY 3: God Calls His Leader

1. In Day 3 you studied the call of Moses. Read Moody's quote about Moses in Prepare Your Heart.

2. How did Moses' life in Midian differ from his life in Egypt and how do you think that was a good preparation for him as God's leader?

3. Describe what happened on Mount Sinai while Moses was shepherding the flock of Jethro, his father-in-law (Exodus 3).

4. What was your most significant insight about this event?

5. How does this encourage you in your own times in the wilderness? Why is the Word of God so important for us and what will help us turn aside to look so that we can hear from God?

6. What did you learn from the devotional reading?

DAY 4: God Reveals His Name

1. In Day 4 you studied God's name, Yahweh. What did you learn about this name for God?

2. How does Jesus expand on this name, Yahweh? What did you learn?

3. How do you need Yahweh in your life today? How does this name for God encourage you?

4. What was your favorite quote in the devotional reading?

DAY 5: God Declares His Promise

1. In Day 5 you studied the fact that God gave the people of Israel promises and He also gives us promises. Why are the promises of God so important for us?

2. What did God promise in Exodus 3?

3. What did God promise about Himself in Deuteronomy 7:6-9?

4. What did you learn about the promises of God from the verses you read?

5. What was your favorite promise of God in your study in Day 5?

DAYS 6 AND 7: Devotional Reading by Charles Swindoll

1. What was your favorite verse, insight, or quote from your quiet times this week?

2. What did you learn from the excerpt by Charles Swindoll in Days 6-7?

3. How are you beginning to see God's passion for His people and how is it helping you grow in your own passion for the Lord?

4. What was your favorite photo this week in your quiet times?

5. Close your time together in prayer.

Week Three: That All May Know

Week Three is such an important part of our sacred journey in Exodus, covering Exodus 4-12. In this week of study we are given a deeper glimpse into God's heart as we watch Him in action on behalf of His people. It is a powerful moment when He says, "Let My people go that they may serve Me" (Exodus 8:1). This week we saw that God gives us hope, defends us, wants all to know that He is the Lord our God, fights our battles, and redeems us.

DAY 1: He Gives You Hope

1. Open your discussion with prayer. Give a brief review of what they've learned in the last two weeks of study. Then you might begin by sharing that this week we are going to see our God in action on behalf of His people. Point out the importance of 1 Corinthians 10:11 and how these things are written for our instruction, so we are going to learn truths we can apply to our lives.

2. How did Moses respond to God's call of him? And how did God respond to Moses? What did God say to Moses?

3. Isn't it interesting that the people of God had no idea what God was planning? According to Exodus 4:27-31, how did they respond? What was it that gave them so much hope?

4. How do you need hope today and what have you learned that gives you hope?

5. Share your most significant insight from the devotional reading in Day 1.

DAY 2: He Defends You

1. What reasons did God give for wanting Pharaoh and Egypt to let His people go?

2. What did you learn about Pharaoh's response to God?

3. What was your favorite verse about how God defends you and is your deliverer?

4. In Enjoy His Presence, you read about ways we can be enslaved and ways that God delivers and sets free. What did you learn?

5. How do you need a rescue today?

DAY 3: He Is The Lord Your God

1. In Day 3 you saw the repetition of a desire from God. Again and again He expressed the desire that He wanted others to know that He was the Lord. Who all did He want to know this?

2. What did you learn about the kind of relationship God wants according to Exodus 6:7?

3. How did your study today show you God's passion—His extravagant, unconditional love—for His people?

DAY 4: He Fights Your Battle

1. In Day 4 you saw an epic battle between Pharaoh and God. How did God fight this battle on behalf of His people?

2. As you think about God's purpose with the plagues, how did you see His passion and power demonstrated?

3. How has God rescued you and fought your battle according to Romans 5:6-10?

4. How does knowing God fights our battles encourage you today?

DAY 5: He Redeems You

1. Day 5 is all about redemption. What does redemption mean and how did God redeem the people of Israel according to Exodus 12:1-13?

2. What does "Passover" mean?

3. How is Christ our Passover? And what did you learn about Him from the verses you studied?

4. What was most significant to you about the Feast of Unleavened Bread?

5. What was your favorite quote in the prayer and devotional reading?

DAYS 6 AND 7: Devotional Reading by Charles Spurgeon

1. In Days Six and Seven you had the opportunity to read from Charles Spurgeon. What was your favorite truth from his writing?

2. What was your favorite verse, insight, or quote from your study in Week Three?

3. What truth about God helped you the most in seeing His passion for you—His extravagant, unconditional love? And how are you growing in your love for Him?

4. What was your favorite photo this week in your quiet times?

Week Four: The Red Sea Place

The goal for your discussion is to lead your group to a deep understanding of what it means to be at the Red Sea place and how to trust God in that difficult time. It will be a most meaningful time as everyone shares what they have learned and how they have personalized these truths in their own lives.

DAY 1: God Leads The way

1. Open your discussion with prayer. Share briefly about your discussion last week about how God rescued and redeemed His people. Review the fact that Exodus is all about "the way out." And God has led His people out of Egypt. You might want to also review some of the important information from the overview of Exodus found in Week 2, Day 1, the Read and Study God's Word section (p. 58). Begin by asking what their study of the Red Sea place meant to them this week.

2. In Exodus 13:17-22 you learned about how God leads His people. What was most significant to you?

3. Describe the Red Sea place for the people of Israel according Exodus 14:1-12. How did the people respond?

4. Describe our own Red Sea places. What are some examples? Has there been a time when you have experienced a Red Sea place? If so, how did you see God work?

5. What is the value of a Red Sea place and what does God teach us?

6. What was your favorite quote in the devotional reading?

DAY 2: God Answers Your Fear

1. In Day 2 we looked at fear vs. faith. Why do we become afraid at the Red Sea place?

2. What can help us have faith in God?

3. What was the most important truth for you from the verses you studied that will help you not to live in fear?

4. What is your favorite part of Annie Johnson Flint's poem about the Red Sea place?

DAY 3: God Calls You To Trust

1. In Day 3 we studied what it means to trust God. How did the example of Luis Palau in Prepare Your Heart encourage you?

2. How was God asking the people and Moses to trust Him? What were the challenges for them in trusting God?

3. What was your favorite verse that showed you what to trust when you are at your Red Sea place?

4. How does the Red Sea place become an opportunity instead of an obstacle?

5. How does understanding these truths help you live in freedom?

6. What was your favorite quote in the devotional reading today?

DAY 4: You Will See And Believe

1. In Day 4 we saw God accomplish the impossible. Describe what happened in Exodus 14:19-30 as God worked, and Moses and God's people responded to His Word.

2. How did you see the people grow in their faith according to Exodus 14:31?

3. How does trusting God and believing Him set you free to serve and worship Him?

4. How have you seen God work in your own life and how did it fill you with awe?

5. What was your favorite quote in the devotional reading today?

DAY 5: You Will Worship

1. Day 5 was all about worshipping the Lord. What encouraged you from the life of Fanny Crosby in Prepare Your Heart?

2. What did you learn about God in Exodus 15?

3. As you think about all that has happened in the lives of the people of Israel, how is their life and relationship with God already different than when they were living in Egypt?

4. What three words did you think of when asked how knowing Christ has made a difference in your own life?

DAYS 6 AND 7: Devotional Reading by James McConkey

1. In days 6 and 7 you had the opportunity to read from James McConkey. What was your favorite truth from his writing about the foolish and the wise sheep?

2. Did you have a favorite quote, insight, or verse from Week Four?

3. What was your favorite photo this week in your quiet times?

4. Close your time together in prayer.

Week Five: Into The Wilderness

Your goal in your discussion this week is to help those in your group learn from the examples of Moses and the people of Israel about wilderness experiences and all that God teaches us in those times.

DAY 1: To Experience God's Healing

1. Open your discussion with prayer. Share briefly about all you learned last week at the Red Sea place. As you begin your time of discussion today, read the quote by Matthew Henry on the Week Five page.

2. In Prepare Your Heart, we read about the life of Lilias Trotter. Describe her life. How can there be beauty in the wilderness and have you ever experienced a time of blessing in a wilderness experience?

3. Describe what being in the wilderness is like?

4. In Exodus 15:22-27 we read about the people of Israel and their first experience in the wilderness. What happened and what did they learn about their Lord?

5. In Psalm 78:14-24 you learned about how the people acted in the wilderness. What did this teach you about God's perspective of your time in the wilderness and how important your attitude and actions are? What does God expect from you in the wilderness according to 1 Corinthians 10:1-13?

6. What was your favorite quote in the devotional reading?

DAY 2: To See God's Provision

1. Probably one of the most difficult aspects of the wilderness experience is having great needs and no visible means of support or provision. And yet, God promises to provide. How did God provide for His people in the wilderness?

2. What did you learn from Deuteronomy 8:1-10 about what God was teaching His people in their needs and His provision?

3. What did you learn in the event at Rephidim described in Exodus 17:1-7?

4. What are you learning that helps you rely on God's provision in your own life?

5. How are you seeing God's passion for His people and how does His provision grow your own passion for Him?

6. What was your favorite quote in the devotional reading?

DAY 3: To Know God's Power

1. As you began Day 3, you prayed a prayer from The Valley of Vision. What was your favorite part of that prayer?

2. Describe how God's people needed to trust God in the battle with Amalek?

3. What new name of God did they learn?

4. What verse encouraged you the most about God's power and ability to fight your battles?

5. What was your favorite insight from the devotional reading in Day 3?

DAY 4: To Meet With God

1. As you begin today's study, remind your group that Exodus can be thought of in two divisions: 1-18 (God rescues and redeems His people, and delivers them out of Egypt) and 19-40 (God reveals Himself to His people, brings them near to Himself in a covenant relationship, and is intent on getting Egypt out of the people).

2. In Day 4 we see that Moses went up to God and called to him from the mountain. What did God promise His people and how did they respond?

3. How can we meet with God and experience His presence today?

4. What is God using in your life to draw you near to Him? What will help you to step away from the busyness of life and meet alone with God?

DAY 5: To Learn God's Ways

1. In Day 5 we read about how God gave the Ten Commandments. What are the Ten Commandments and why are they important? What do they tell you about your God?

2. Describe the Old Covenant vs. the New Covenant. What are some of the main differences?

DAYS 6 AND 7: Devotional Reading by Jeff Manion

1. What was your favorite verse, insight, or quote from your quiet times this week?

2. What did you learn from the excerpt by Jeff Manion?

3. What was your favorite photo this week in your quiet times?

4. How did you see God's holy passion—His extravagant, unconditional love—in your study this week? And how are you inspired to a greater passion for your Lord?

5. Close your time together in prayer.

Week Six: Experiencing God

In Week Six you are continuing your sacred journey in Exodus at Mount Sinai, the place where we will draw near to God, and experience Him in a deeper and more intimate way. The goal for your discussion is to help your group share what they have learned about God and His desire for them to know Him. In this week of study we saw God ratify and establish His covenant with His people and then give instructions for the sanctuary where He will dwell with His people. Keep in mind that we are focusing on all we learn about God in Exodus 24-31. These chapters include many intricate details about the covenant and the tabernacle. And while every detail in God's Word is important, our goal is to discover more about God and His passion for His people—His extravagant, unconditional, amazing love for us. And we want to love Him more as a result. The truths in this week's study in God's Word are so very powerful.

DAY 1: Through Worship

1. Open your discussion with prayer. Share briefly about your discussion last week about the wilderness and all that can be learned in a wilderness experience. Now, this week, we are going to learn more about how to experience and intimate relationship with God. Begin by reading the first paragraph in Prepare Your Heart in Day 1. Ask your group how this week of studied encouraged them in their relationship with the Lord.

2. What did you learn about worship in the verses you studied today?

3. Describe a time when you experienced intimate worship with God.

4. How does the Word of God help you worship God?

DAY 2: With Covenant

1. In Day 2 we studied how God established the covenant with His people in Exodus 24:4-11. What did you learn about this covenant and what did it mean for the experience of God's people with their God?

2. What did you learn about Jesus and the New Covenant from the verses you studied in Day 2?

3. How did the devotional reading help you understand covenant and its importance?

DAY 3: On Mount Sinai

1. In Day 3 we saw Moses on Mount Sinai with God. What did you learn about God in Exodus 24:12-18?

2. What happened on the Mount of Transfiguration as seen in Matthew 17:1-8?

3. How has this study in Exodus encouraged your own quiet time with the Lord?

DAY 4: In The Sanctuary

1. In Day 4 we learn a powerful truth about God. What did the fact that He wanted His people to build a sanctuary, a tabernacle, mean? Why did God want them to build the sanctuary according to Exodus 25:1-9?

2. Describe the different parts of the tabernacle and how Jesus fulfilled each one.

3. How did Jesus show us that God wants to dwell with His people?

4. How is God dwelling with us now?

5. What will be the ultimate fulfillment of God dwelling with Him people?

6. What impressed you the most as you looked at the diagram of the tabernacle and the organization of the camps around the tabernacle?

7. In all of this study today, how do you see God's passion for you? And how does it move you to a greater love for your Lord?

DAY 5: With Offerings

1. As you read select verses in Exodus 28-30, what impressed you the most about the priests and the offerings?

2. What did you learn about Jesus, your Great High Priest in Hebrews 4 and Hebrews 9?

3. In Exodus 31 what did you learn about the Sabbath? How do we experience a Sabbath Rest even now?

4. According to Romans 12:1, what offering can you make now that becomes your "spiritual service of worship?"

5. Can you share a time when you surrendered yourself to God in a new and deeper way and what it meant for you and your relationship with the Lord?

DAYS 6 AND 7: Devotional Reading by F.B. Meyer

1. What was your favorite verse, insight, or quote from your quiet times this week?

2. What did you learn from the excerpt by F.B. Meyer?

3. What was your favorite photo this week in your quiet times?

4. Close your time together in prayer.

Week Seven: Journey To The Heart Of God'

The goal for your discussion this week is to talk about all that you are learning about God on your sacred journey in Exodus 32-40.

DAY 1: He Is All Grace

1. Open your discussion with prayer. Share briefly about all that we have been learning on this journey in Exodus. Once you have reviewed quickly what we have studied thus far, ask your group how they are being encouraged in their relationship with God in this study. Ask them what has impressed them the most about God and His one holy passion—His extravagant, unconditional, amazing love.

2. In Day 1 of Week Seven we begin on Mount Sinai with Moses and God. And God saw what Moses could not see. In Exodus 32:1-14, how did God describe the people and what they were doing?

3. What happened when Moses came down from the mountain?

4. How would you describe God's grace? How did you see the grace of God in this event in Exodus?

5. What did you learn about the grace of God in the New Testament verses you read?

6. How does knowing that God is a God of grace encourage you today? How does His grace reveal His passion for His people?

7. What was your favorite part of the devotional reading?

DAY 2: He Disciplines His People

1. In Day 2 what encouraged and blessed you about God's heart in all you read in Prepare Your Heart?

2. How did God respond to the sin of His people?

3. How did the people respond and how does this show that they are growing in their relationship with the Lord?

4. What did you learn about the discipline of the Lord in Hebrews 12 and how does it reveal His passion for His people?

5. What was significant to you in the devotional reading?

DAY 3: Face To Face With God

1. In Day 3 you had the opportunity to be with Moses as he talked face to face with God. What were Moses' requests of God and how did God respond?

2. How did you see God's heart in a more intimate and beautiful way in His responses to Moses?

3. What effect did God's presence have on Moses?

4. How are we given the opportunity for a face to face relationship with our Lord now?

5. What was your favorite quote in the devotional reading today?

6. What was your favorite insight from your study today?

DAY 4: No Rival Love

1. In Day 4, you learned His name is "Jealous." What does this mean?

2. What did you learn about God's love for you in the verses you read

3. What meant the most to you in Day 4?

DAY 5: Serving The Lord

1. In Day 5 we saw that the people did all the work that God had given them. In Exodus 40:33-38 what happened as a result of their faithful work?

2. What did you learn about how to serve the Lord from the verses you read?

3. How has God led you in serving the Lord?

DAYS 6 AND 7: Devotional Reading by Andrew Murray

1. What was your favorite verse, insight, or quote from your quiet times this week?

2. What was your favorite insight from the words of Andrew Murray?

3. How did you see God's passion for His people as you studied in Week Seven?

4. What was your favorite photo this week in your quiet times?

5. Close your time together in prayer.

Week Eight: Into The Promised Land

And now we come to this last week of study in *One Holy Passion*. The goal of your discussion today is to help your group share what they've learned about the Promised Land. You want to help them realize the "now and not yet" nature of the Promised Land, And then, you will want to allow time for sharing all that those in your group have learned in *One Holy Passion*.

DAY 1: The Journey Of Moses

1. Open your discussion with prayer. Begin by expressing how much you've enjoyed leading the group and sharing together during this journey in Exodus to God's amazing love. And share how wonderful the discussions have been. As you discuss together for one last time in *One Holy Passion*, ask your group what has been their favorite part of this study.

2. This week we studied many different aspects of the Promised Land, from Moses, Joshua, and the people of Israel to our own journey to the Promised Land.

3. How is the Promised Land described in Exodus?

4. In Day 1 you read about an incident involving Moses and the people in Numbers 20:1-13. What happened and how did this impact Moses and his journey?

5. Why do you think God didn't let Moses lead the people into the Promised Land?

6. Describe what happened with Moses on the mountain in Deuteronomy 34:12 and also Matthew 17:1-3?

7. What has impressed you the most about Moses in this sacred journey in Exodus?

8. What encouraged you in the devotional reading today?

DAY 2: The Journey Of Joshua And Israel

1. In Day 2 we looked at Joshua and the people of Israel and how they experienced the Promised Land. Joshua was the next leader of the people of Israel. Why was he such a good choice?

2. What did you learn from the call of Joshua in Joshua 1:1-9?

3. Describe what you learned about the promised land in Deuteronomy 11:8-12.

4. What was most impressive to you about the battle of Jericho?

5. At the end of his life, how did Joshua describe all that God had done?

6. What was your favorite insight in Ephesians 4:17-24 about how we are to live?

7. What was the most significant truth you learned in Day 2?

DAY 3: The Journey Of Jesus

1. How did the life of Jonathan Goforth encourage you?

2. Why were the words of Jesus in John 14:16-23 good news on a sad day?

3. What did you learn about the "land" theologically that helps you in understanding how we can experienced the Promised Land even now?

4. What did you learn about how the Lord tabernacles in us now?

5. What is true about us as seen in Romans 6 that helps you understand your union with Christ?

6. What was your favorite quote in the devotional reading?

DAY 4: Your Journey

1. This week you have seen that land is the place where God dwells, reveals Himself, and is active in His kingdom work. We saw that we are now united with Christ. In Day 4 we saw what is ours because of Christ. What did you learn?

2. What did you learn from the verses you studied about how to live in the temporal wilderness of this world until you step into heaven?

3. What is the most important truth you learned today?

DAY 5: The Heavenly Country

1. On Day 5 you studied the ultimate fulfillment of the Promised Land? What did you learn about your future home in Hebrews 11:13-16?

2. What were your favorite words and phrases in the verses that are descriptions of your future with your Lord?

3. What did you learn in Revelation 21-22:5 about heaven?

4. How does all you have learned about the heavenly country show you God's passion for you? And how does it cause you to love Him even more?

5. What was your favorite quote from your Day 5 quiet time?

6. How did God answer the prayer that you wrote in your letter to Him at the beginning of the study? Would you like to share anything from the prayer of thanksgiving that you wrote as you closed your Day 5 quiet time?

DAYS 6 AND 7: Devotional Reading by Lilias Trotter

1. What encouraged you from the excerpt by Lilias Trotter?

2. You had an opportunity to take some time and leaf through these eights weeks of quiet times to look at all you have learned. What are some of the most important principles and truths we've learned on our sacred journey through Exodus?

3. What is the most important truth you have learned about God in this book of quiet

times? What will you take with you? (If you have a visual aid such as a whiteboard, you might even write these truths out for your class to see).

4. What was your favorite week in *One Holy Passion* and why?

5. What was your favorite photo in *One Holy Passion*? In what way was the devotional photography meaningful to you in your quiet times?

6. If you didn't answer before, would you like to share how God answered the prayer that you wrote in your letter to Him at the beginning of the study?

7. What will you take with you from *One Holy Passion*? What will you always remember?

8. Close your time together in prayer.

 NOTES

INTRODUCTION

1. PHOTOGRAPHY: *Never Alone*, Psalm 16:8 NLT, Bell Rock—Courthouse Butte, Sedona, Arizona, USA, Nikon D800E, Nikkor 16-35mm, FL 19mm, ISO 100, f/16, AEB, Photomatix Pro, Adobe Camera Raw, Adobe Photoshop, Topaz Adjust, Nik Software. myPhotoWalk.com—Catherine Martin.SmugMug.com.

WEEK 1

1. Dr. Ronald F. Youngblood, *Exodus* (Chicago: Moody Press, 1983), pp. 7-8.

2. J.I. Packer, *Knowing God* (London: InterVarsity Press, 1973), p. 29.

3. A.W. Tozer, *The Pursuit Of God* (Camp Hill: WingSpread, 2006), p. 65.

4. A.W. Tozer and G.B. Smith, *Men Who Met God* (Camp Hill: WingSpread, 1986) pp. 55-56.

5. Corrie ten Boom, *Each New Day* (Grand Rapids: Flaming H. Revell, 1977) p. 135.

6. Bill Bright, *Come Help Change The World*, (Campus Crusade For Christ: New Life Resources, 2011) p. 644-651 Kindle Edition.

7. F.B. Meyer, *Daily Prayers* (Wheaton: Harold Shaw Publishers, 1995) p. 71.

8. Taken from *My Utmost For His Highest* by Oswald Chambers, © 1935 by Dodd Mead & Co., renewed © 1963 by the Oswald Chambers Publications Assn. Ltd. Used by permission of Discovery House, Grand Rapids, MI 49501. All rights reserved. March 7 selection.

9. Elisabeth Elliot, *A Pathway Through Suffering*, (Ann Arbor: Servant Publications, 1990), p. 20.

10. Kay Arthur, *How Can I Live*, (Old Tappan: Fleming H. Revell, 1982), p. 215.

11. Kay Arthur, *How Can I Live*, pp. 254-255.

12. Kay Arthur, *Our Covenant God*, (New York: WaterBrook Press, 1999), pp. 3-4.

13. James McConkey, *The Sure Shepherd*.

14. Richard Baxter, *The Saint's Everlasting Rest*, pp. 44-46.

15. A.W. Tozer, *The Knowledge Of The Holy* (New York: HarperCollins, 1961), p. 156.

WEEK 2

1. Corrie ten Boom, *Amazing Love* (Fort Washington, Christian Literature Crusade, 2001) pp. 8-9.

2. F.B. Meyer, *Great Men of the Bible* (Grand Rapids: Zondervan Publishing House, 1981) pp. 156-157.

3. Dr. Ronald Youngblood, *How It All Began*, (Ventura: Regal Books, 1980) p. 119.

4. Stuart Douglas, *The New American Commentary: Exodus Volume 2* (Nashville: Broadman and Holman Publishers, 2006) p. 104.

5. George O. Wood, *A Psalm In Your Heart* (Springfield: Gospel Publishing House, 2008) p. 559.

6. Dr. Ronald Youngblood, *Exodus* (Chicago: Moody Press, 1983), p. 31.

7. Oswald Chambers, *My Utmost For His Highest*, April 18. Taken from *My Utmost For His Highest* by Oswald Chambers, © 1935 by Dodd Mead & Co., renewed © 1963 by the Oswald Chambers Publications Assn. Ltd. Used by permission of Discovery House, Grand Rapids, MI 49501. All rights reserved, April 18 selection.

8. John G. Butler, *Moses* (Clinton: LBC Publications, 1996) pp. 79-80.

9. Herbert Lockyer, *All The Divine Names and Titles in the Bible* (Grand Rapids: Zondervan Publishing House, 1975) p. 17..

10. Catherine Martin, *Trusting In The Names Of God* (Eugene: Harvest House Publishers, 2008).

11. As quoted by Nelson G. Mink in *Pocket Pearls* (Wheaton: Tyndale House Publishers, Inc., 1987) p. 16.

12. Charles Swindoll, *Moses* (Nashville: Word Publishing, 1999) p. 117.

13. Warren Wiersbe, *Be Delivered* (Colorado Springs: Chariot Victor Publishing, 1998) p. 18.

14. Corrie ten Boom, *Amazing Love*, pp. 17-19.

15. Corrie ten Boom, *Each New Day* (Grand Rapids: Flaming H. Revell, 1977) p. 76.

16. Charles Swindoll, *Moses*, pp. 103-104.

17. Charles Swindoll, *Moses*, pp. 105-106.

WEEK 3

1. A.B. Davidson, *The Theology of the Old Testament*, (New York: Charles Scribner's Sons, 1936), p. 34.

2. Taken from *My Utmost For His Highest* by Oswald Chambers, © 1935 by Dodd Mead & Co., renewed © 1963 by the Oswald Chambers Publications Assn. Ltd. Used by permission of Discovery House, Grand Rapids, MI 49501. All rights reserved. March 7 selection. October 4 selection.

3. Dr. Ronald Youngblood, *Exodus* (Chicago: Moody Press, 1983), p. 38.

4. Quoted in *All The Divine Names and Titles in the Bible*, Herbert Lockyer (Grand Rapids: Zondervan Publishing House, 1975) p. 18.

5. George O. Wood, *A Psalm In Your Heart* (Springfield: Gospel Publishing House, 2008) p. 404.

6. Dr. Ronald Youngblood, *Exodus*, pp. 45-46.

7. John Henry Jowett, *The Eagle Life* (New York: George H. Doran Company, 1922) pp. 63-64.

8. A.W. Tozer, *The Pursuit Of God* (Camp Hill: WingSpread, 2006), p. 31.

9. From *Moses and the Gods of Egypt* by John J. Davis, copyright 1971, 1986 by BMH Books. Reprinted with permission of BMH Books. Pages 127-128, 138.

10. R.C. Sproul, *Before The Face Of God*, (Grand Rapids: Baker Book House 1992) p. 34.

11. Mark Ashton, *Winning At Life: Jesus' Secrets Revealed*, (Grand Rapids: Zondervan Publishing House 2001).

12. Steve Jeffery, Michael Ovey, Andrew Sach, *Pierced For Our Transgressions* (Wheaton: Crossway Books 2007) pp. 41-42.

WEEK 4

1. Mrs. Charles Cowman, *Streams in the Desert* ((The Oriental Missionary Society) Selection by Carrie Montgomery in The Life of Praise.

2. V. Raymond Edman, *They Found the Secret* (Grand Rapids: Zondervan Publishing House, 1984) pp. 81-82.

3. B.H. Pearson, *The Vision Lives* (Fort Washington: Christian Literature Crusade 1972) p. 91.

4. Mrs. Charles Cowman, *Springs in the Valley* (The Oriental Missionary Society) p. 319.

5. Robert Morgan, *The Red Sea Rules*, (Nashville: Thomas Nelson Publishers 2014) pp. 6-10.

6. V. Raymond Edman, *The Disciplines of Life*, (Chicago: Van Kampen Press 1948) p.16.

7. Mrs. Charles Cowman, *Springs in the Valley*, p. 343.

8. Annie Johnson Flint, *Best Loved Poems* (Toronto: Evangelical Publishers), p. 23

9. John Woodbridge ed., *More Than Conquerors*, (Chicago: Moody Press 1992) pp. 182-183.

10. Taken from *My Utmost For His Highest* by Oswald Chambers, © 1935 by Dodd Mead & Co., renewed © 1963 by the Oswald Chambers Publications Assn. Ltd. Used by permission of Discovery House, Grand Rapids, MI 49501. All rights reserved. October 31 selection.

11. Priscilla Shirer, *One In A Million: Journey To Your Promised Land* (B & H Publishing Group 2013) p. 22.

12. Ruth Paxson, Rivers of Living Water (London: Marshall, Morgan & Scott) pp. 90-91.

13. From *Moses and the Gods of Egypt* by John J. Davis, copyright 1971, 1986 by BMH Books. Reprinted with permission of BMH Books. Page 183.

14. Warren Wiersbe, *Be Delivered* (Colorado Springs: Chariot Victor Publishing, 1998) pp. 62-63.

WEEK 5

1. Jeff Manion, *The Land Between* (Grand Rapids: Zondervan Publishing House, 2010) pp. 182-184.

2. Miriam Rockness, *A Passion For The Impossible* (Grand Rapids: Discovery House Publishers 1999, 2003).

3. Prayer taken from *The Valley of Vision* published by The Banner of Truth Trust, copyright Arthur Bennett 1975, used here by permission, p. 166. www.banneroftruth.org.

4. Corrie ten Boom, *Each New Day* (Grand Rapids: Flaming H. Revell, 1977) p. 12.

5. F.B. Meyer, *Great Men of the Bible* (Grand Rapids: Zondervan Publishing House, 1981) pp. 153-154.

6. A.W. Tozer, *The Pursuit of God* (Camp Hill: WingSpread, 2006) pp. 52-56.

7. W. Ross Blackburn, *The God Who Makes Himself Known*, (Downers Grove: InterVarsity Press 2012) p. 89.

8. Dr. Ronald Youngblood, *Exodus* (Chicago: Moody Press, 1983), p. 101.

9. John G. Butler, *Moses, Emancipator of Israel*, (Chicago: LBC Publications 1996), p. 500.

10. Jeff Manion, *The Land Between* pp. 852-855.

11. Anne Graham Lotz, *Wounded By God's People* (Grand Rapids: Zondervan Publishing House 2013) pp. 132-133.

WEEK 6

1. Charles Spurgeon, *Spurgeon's Sermons, Vol. 20* Delivered December 6, 1874 at The Metropolitan Tabernacle.

2. Don Postema, *Space For God—The Study and Practice of Prayer and Spirituality* (Grand Rapids: CRC Publications 1983) pp. 179-180.

3. Dr. Ronald Youngblood, *Exodus* (Chicago: Moody Press, 1983), p. 110.

4. William L. Lane, *Hebrews*, (Peabody: Hendrickson Publishers 1985) pp. 127-128.

5. Sinclair Ferguson, *A Heart For God* (Carlisle: The Banner of Truth Trust 1987) pp. 36-37.

6. Andrew Murray, *God's Best Secrets* (New Kensington: Whitaker House 1998) p. 86.

7. Dr. Ronald Youngblood, *Exodus*, pp. 114-115.

8. From *Moses and the Gods of Egypt* by John J. Davis, copyright 1971, 1986 by BMH Books. Reprinted with permission of BMH Books. Page 278.

9. William L. Lane, *Hebrews*, p. 55.

WEEK 7

1. Amy Carmichael, *Gold By Moonlight*, (Fort Washington: Christian Literature Crusade) p. 73.

2. A.W. Tozer, *The Pursuit of God* (Camp Hill: WingSpread, 2006) pp. 13-14.

3. Joseph Cook, *Celebration of Grace*, (Milton-Freewater: Outwest Printing 1991) p. 13.

4. Catherine Martin, *A Woman's Walk In Grace* (Eugene: Harvest House Publishers 2010) p. 25.

5. A.W. Tozer, *The Pursuit of God* pp. 9-10.

6. Brennan Manning, *The Ragamuffin Gospel*, (Colorado Springs: Multnomah Books 2005).

7. Ken Gire, *Between Heaven and Earth* (San Francisco: HarperCollins 1997), p. v.

8. Tim Stafford, *Knowing The Face Of God* (Grand Rapids: Zondervan Publishing House, 1986) p. 41.

9. Miriam Rockness, *Blossom in the Desert*, (Grand Rapids: Discovery House Publishers 2007) p. 181.

10. James McConkey, *Prevailing Prayer* (Harrisburg: Fred. Kelker 1905) pp. 129-130.

11. J. Steven Babbit, *The Presence of God* (New York: IUniverse Inc.) pp. 20-21.

12. Sinclair B. Ferguson, *A Heart For God* (Carlisle: The Banner of Truth Trust 1987) p. 59.

13. Dr. Ronald Youngblood, *Exodus* (Chicago: Moody Press, 1983), p. 141.

14. N.D. Osborn and H.A. Hatton, *A Handbook On Exodus* (New York: United Bible Societies 1999) p. 808.

15. Dwight Hervey Small, *No Rival Love* (Fort Washington: Christian Literature Crusade 1983) pp. 196-197.

16. John Piper, *Brothers, We Are Not Professionals: A Plea To Pastors for Radical Ministry* (Nashville: B & H Publishing Group 2013) 1307-1310 Kindle Edition.

17. Miriam Rockness, *Blossom in the Desert*, p. 224

18. Andrew Murray, *God's Best Secrets* (New Kensington: Whitaker House 1998) p. 90.

WEEK 8

1. Alan Redpath, *Victorious Christian Living*, (Grand Rapids: Fleming H. Revell Company 1955) pp. 37-38.

2. Meyer, *Great Men of the Bible* (Grand Rapids: Zondervan Publishing House, 1981) pp. 211, 213.

3. George O. Wood, *A Psalm In Your Heart* (Springfield: Gospel Publishing House 2008) p. 364.

4. Corrie ten Boom, *Each New Day* (Grand Rapids: Flaming H. Revell, 1977) p. 131.

5. Alan Redpath, *Victorious Christian Living* pp. 20-22.

6. Ray Stedman, *Our Riches In Christ* (Grand Rapids: Discovery House Publishers 1998) p. 248.

7. John P. Davis, "The Abrahamic Covenant" (Evangelical Review of Theology: 29 2005) p. 13.

8. Andrew Murray, *God's Best Secrets* (New Kensington: Whitaker House 1998) p. 189.

9. John P. Davis, "The Abrahamic Covenant" p. 13.

10. A.B. Simpson, *Christ In You*, (Camp Hill: Christian Publications 1997) pp. 8-9, 12.

11. Watchman Nee, The Normal Christian Life (Fort Washington: Christian Literature Crusade 1957) pp. 64-65.

12. Major W. Ian Thomas, *The Saving Life of Christ*, (Grand Rapids: Zondervan Publishing House 1961) p. 143.

13. Bill Bright, *The Journey Home* (Nashville: Thomas Nelson Publishers 2003) pp. 146-147.

14. Charles Spurgeon, *Beside Still Waters*.

15. Miriam Rockness, *Blossom in the Desert*, (Grand Rapids: Discovery House Publishers 2007) p. 35.

ACKNOWLEDGMENTS

How does a book like *One Holy Passion* come to life? It takes years of God etching these principles from the Word of God on the heart in such a way that it is lived out in life. In this case, the Lord took me through a dark night of the soul and led me into the book of Exodus. He taught me so much that I couldn't wait to write the words that became *One Holy Passion*. This is the sixth in the A Quiet Time Experience series—quiet times for the busy person to use in their quiet time to go deep with God and grow in their intimate relationship with Him.

Thank you to my precious family; David, Mother and Dad (both now with the Lord), Robert, Kayla, Linda, Christopher, Andy, Keegan, and James. Thank you especially for your unconditional love and encouragement as I write books and share the message that God has laid on my heart in my quiet times alone with Him.

I want to especially thank my husband, David, for your love, wisdom, and brilliance as together we run this race set before us and serve in Quiet Time Ministries. And thank you for the beautiful cover design of *One Holy Passion*.

I am so very thankful over these many years for the Quiet Time Ministries team for serving the Lord together with me—Kayla Branscum, Shirley Peters, Conni Hudson, Cindy Clark, Sandy Fallon, Paula Zillmer, Karen Darras Hawley, and Kelly Wysard.

And then, thank you for dear friends who have offered such words of truth, encouragement, and hope that I have needed all along the way: Beverly Trupp, Conni Hudson, Cindy, Clark, Andy Kotner Graybill, Julie Airis, Stefanie Kelly, Joe and Judy Patti, Betty Mann, Kelly Wysard, Jan Lupia, Barbara Waddell, and Vonette Bright.

Thank you to the Board of Directors of Quiet Time Ministries: David Martin, Conni Hudson, Andy Kotner Graybill, and Jane Lyons, for your faithfulness in this ministry. And thank you to all who have partnered with me both financially and prayerfully in Quiet Time Ministries. You have helped make possible this idea the Lord gave me so many years ago called Quiet Time Ministries and have allowed us to continue to spread God's Word to men and women throughout the world. I also want to thank those who have partnered financially with Quiet Time Ministries to sponsor myPhotoWalk photo shoots and purchase photographic equipment including my Nikon cameras, lenses, tripods, and filters.

Thank you to my Bethel Seminary professors who gave me such a love for God's Word and helped me learn to study with excellence, especially Dr. Ronald Youngblood, Dr. Walt Wessel, Dr. James Smith, and Dr. Al Glenn.

Thank you to those who have been such a huge help to me in the writing and publishing of books: Jim Smoke whose advice and help have, by God's grace, completely altered the course of my life and Greg Johnson, my agent, who has come alongside me and Quiet Time Ministries to help in the goals that the Lord has laid on my heart.

Thank you to those who have encouraged me in devotional photography through workshops, conferences, books, videos, examples, portfolios, and personal training — I am so very thankful for you — Bill Fortney, Dr. Charles Stanley, Laurie Rubin, Kevin Toohey, Kathleen Reeder, Kathleen Clemons, Trey Ratcliff, Scott Kelby, Matt Kloskowski, Sebastian Michaels, R.C. Concepcion, Karen Hutton, His Light Friends, Ben Long, Harold Davis, Art Wolfe, Tom Mangelsen, Chris Orwig, David DuChemin, Bryan Peterson, April Milani, and Diane Varner.

A special thanks to all those leaders who answer God's call to lead others and challenge them to draw near to God, study His Word, and live for His glory. Thank you to all the women I've been privileged to serve with in leadership over the years. Thank you to the Women's Ministries Directors and leaders in churches who encourage their amazing women to live in God's Word and love Him with all their hearts. And a special thanks to all the groups worldwide who are drawing near to God in quiet time using the different quiet time studies from Quiet Time Ministries.

I am so very grateful to those women of God who love His Word and teach it every day of their lives, especially Anne Graham Lotz and Kay Arthur.

Finally, thank you to all those saints who have lived our their life with a passion for God and have encouraged me to love the Lord with all my heart and spend daily quiet time with Him: especially Corrie ten Boom, Charles Haddon Spurgeon, Oswald Chambers, F.B. Meyer, Octavius Winslow, Amy Carmichael, Lilias Trotter, Annie Johnson Flint, A.W. Tozer, Andrew Murray, and Mrs. Charles Cowman.

Thank You, Lord, for Your one holy passion—the wonder of Your extravagant, immeasurable, unconditional, amazing love, the encouragement of Your Word, and the glory of Your creation.

JOURNAL

"Pour out your heart like water in the
presence of the Lord" — Lamentations 2:19 NIV

SIX SECRETS TO A POWERFUL QUIET TIME ©2005

JOURNAL

"Pour out your heart like water in the
presence of the Lord" — Lamentations 2:19 NIV

JOURNAL

"Pour out your heart like water in the
presence of the Lord" — Lamentations 2:19 NIV

SIX SECRETS TO A POWERFUL QUIET TIME ©2005

JOURNAL

"Pour out your heart like water in the
presence of the Lord" — Lamentations 2:19 NIV

JOURNAL

"Pour out your heart like water in the
presence of the Lord" — Lamentations 2:19 NIV

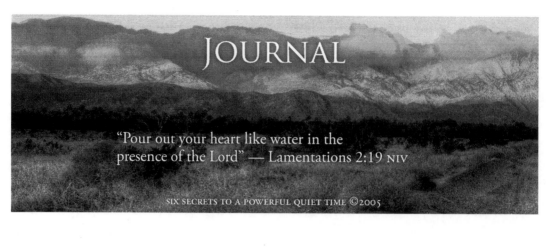

JOURNAL

"Pour out your heart like water in the
presence of the Lord" — Lamentations 2:19 NIV

SIX SECRETS TO A POWERFUL QUIET TIME ©2005

ADORE GOD IN PRAYER

"Don't worry about anything;
instead, pray about everything" — Philippians 4:6 NIV

SIX SECRETS TO A POWERFUL QUIET TIME ©2005

*Prayer for*_____

Date: Topic:
Scripture:
Request:

Answer:

Date: Topic:
Scripture:
Request:

Answer:

Date: Topic:
Scripture:
Request:

Answer:

Date: Topic:
Scripture:
Request:

Answer:

Date: Topic:
Scripture:
Request:

Answer:

ADORE GOD IN PRAYER

"Don't worry about anything;
instead, pray about everything" — Philippians 4:6 NIV

SIX SECRETS TO A POWERFUL QUIET TIME ©2005

*Prayer for*_____

Date: Topic:
Scripture:
Request:

Answer:

Date: Topic:
Scripture:
Request:

Answer:

Date: Topic:
Scripture:
Request:

Answer:

Date: Topic:
Scripture:
Request:

Answer:

Date: Topic:
Scripture:
Request:

Answer:

ADORE GOD IN PRAYER

"Don't worry about anything;
instead, pray about everything" — Philippians 4:6 NIV

SIX SECRETS TO A POWERFUL QUIET TIME © 2005

*Prayer for*_____

Date: Topic:

Scripture:

Request:

Answer:

_____

Date: Topic:

Scripture:

Request:

Answer:

_____

Date: Topic:

Scripture:

Request:

Answer:

_____

Date: Topic:

Scripture:

Request:

Answer:

_____

Date: Topic:

Scripture:

Request:

Answer:

_____

ADORE GOD IN PRAYER

*"Don't worry about anything;
instead, pray about everything"* — Philippians 4:6 NIV

SIX SECRETS TO A POWERFUL QUIET TIME © 2005

*Prayer for*_____

Date: Topic:

Scripture:

Request:

Answer:

_____

Date: Topic:

Scripture:

Request:

Answer:

_____

Date: Topic:

Scripture:

Request:

Answer:

_____

Date: Topic:

Scripture:

Request:

Answer:

_____

Date: Topic:

Scripture:

Request:

Answer:

_____

ADORE GOD IN PRAYER

*"Don't worry about anything;
instead, pray about everything"* — Philippians 4:6 NIV

*Prayer for*_____

Date: Topic:

Scripture:

Request:

Answer:

_____

Date: Topic:

Scripture:

Request:

Answer:

_____

Date: Topic:

Scripture:

Request:

Answer:

_____

Date: Topic:

Scripture:

Request:

Answer:

_____

Date: Topic:

Scripture:

Request:

Answer:

_____

ADORE GOD IN PRAYER

"Don't worry about anything;
instead, pray about everything" — Philippians 4:6 NIV

Prayer for_____

Date: Topic:
Scripture:
Request:

Answer:

Date: Topic:
Scripture:
Request:

Answer:

Date: Topic:
Scripture:
Request:

Answer:

Date: Topic:
Scripture:
Request:

Answer:

Date: Topic:
Scripture:
Request:

Answer:

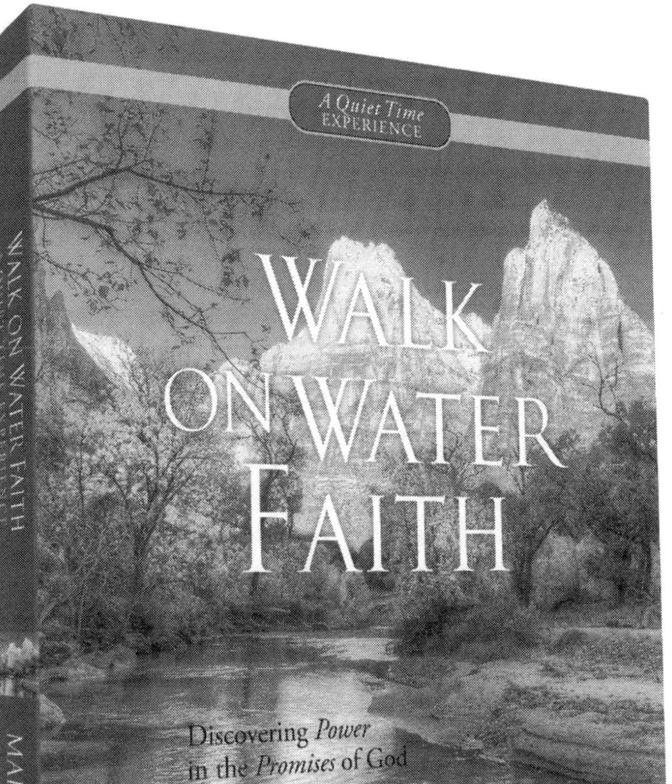
A Quiet Time
EXPERIENCE
WALK
ON WATER
FAITH
Discovering Power
in the Promises of God
CATHERINE MARTIN
Author of Run Before the Wind
WALK ON WATER FAITH
MARTIN

A Quiet Time
EXPERIENCE

TRUSTING IN THE NAMES OF GOD

EIGHT WEEKS OF GUIDED DEVOTIONS

- Inspirational Readings
- Prayer Starters and Journal Ideas
- Questions for Reflection

CATHERINE MARTIN

Author of *Knowing and Loving the Bible*

MYPHOTOWALK
QUIET TIME MOMENTS
Devotional Photography to Refresh Your Heart
CATHERINE MARTIN
MYPHOTOWALK – QUIET TIME MOMENTS
MARTIN

MYPHOTOWALK
DEVOTIONAL PHOTOGRAPHY

SAVORING
GOD'S PROMISES
OF HOPE

Discovering the Power of God
Who Makes Things Happen

CATHERINE MARTIN

Author of *myPhotoWalk—Quiet Time Moments*

Made in the USA
Columbia, SC
24 May 2018